Immigration and Metropolitan Revitalization in the United States

THE CITY IN THE TWENTY-FIRST CENTURY

Eugenie L. Birch and Susan M. Wachter, *Series Editors*

A complete list of books in the series
is available from the publisher.

IMMIGRATION AND METROPOLITAN REVITALIZATION IN THE UNITED STATES

Edited by
Domenic Vitiello and Thomas J. Sugrue

PENN

UNIVERSITY OF PENNSYLVANIA PRESS

PHILADELPHIA

Published by
University of Pennsylvania Press
Philadelphia, Pennsylvania 19104-4112
www.upenn.edu/pennpress

Printed in the United States of America on acid-free paper
10 9 8 7 6 5 4 3 2 1

Library of Congress Cataloging-in-Publication Data
ISBN 978-0-8122-4912-5

CONTENTS

Immigration and the New American Metropolis

Domenic Vitiello and Thomas J. Sugrue

From Urban Crisis to Immigrant-Led Revitalization

In less than a generation, the dominant image of American cities has transformed from urban crisis to revitalization. Poverty, violence, job losses, and distressed schools still make headlines. But large parts of central cities and older suburbs are attracting new residents and substantial capital investment. The U.S. Census Bureau's American Community Survey found that after decades of population loss, most of America's large old industrial cities, from Philadelphia to Milwaukee, grew between 2010 and 2014, as did forty-nine of the fifty-one largest cities in the nation overall. Even the two that lost population, Detroit and Cleveland, have been the focus of intense planning and investments in revitalization and have seen some neighborhoods grow.

Some of the most visible changes in American cities include high-profile downtown redevelopment projects and gentrified neighborhoods. News and social media increasingly obsess over pop-up parks, rooftop beer gardens, and gourmet food trucks that represent a new "urban imaginary"—not only in New York, Chicago, and San Francisco but also in Providence, Cincinnati, and Kansas City.[1] Central cities once written off as hopeless, from Baltimore to Oakland, have begun to gentrify. While places such as Buffalo and St. Louis remain stark examples of disinvestment and decline, even these most distressed cities have attracted new residents and investors with grand visions of downtown and neighborhood renewal. Housing markets, commercial districts, and town centers have revived in many older suburbs, too.

Immigration and immigrants belong at the center of this story of metropolitan revitalization in the United States. However, in most accounts of urban and suburban revitalization, native-born empty nesters, their millennial children, and other well-educated professionals of the "creative class" are the agents of change. They "bring the city back" by attracting outside investors, patronizing galleries, restaurants, and high-end shops; rehabilitating historic properties; and developing new houses on vacant lots.[2] Yet in the past decade, policy makers and scholars across the United States have come to understand that immigrants are driving metropolitan revitalization at least as much as these actors. This volume is the first collection of leading social scientists' research on the relationship of immigration to metropolitan revitalization assembling the work of scholars in criminology, demography, economics, geography, history, sociology, and urban planning.

Urban scholars and policy makers have only recently begun considering the role of immigration in the recent transformations of metropolitan America, including population shifts, economic reinvestment and growth, and housing markets. In a survey of urban scholars taken in 1999, immigration did not make the list of top ten forces that had shaped U.S. cities in the twentieth century. Segregation and discrimination, white flight, suburban sprawl, and other causes of urban crisis dominated the discussion. Nor did immigration make their list of forces likely to influence cities most profoundly in the twenty-first century, though they did cite integration and diversity of urban neighborhoods.[3]

Yet, as demographer Dowell Myers argued in response, immigration has been a "fundamental force" determining the fortunes of American cities in the past, present, and future. Not only did mass immigration fuel the birth of metropolitan America in the late nineteenth and early twentieth centuries, but the closing of U.S. borders between the 1920s and 1960s deprived cities of replacement population for the masses who moved out. Immigration's absence thus played a critical, if silent and invisible, part in the urban crisis. It was no accident that cities began to revive in the late twentieth century, after the Immigration and Naturalization Act of 1965 reopened the borders, asserted Myers. And as the baby boom generation ages and Americans have fewer children, arguably no force will define the future of U.S. cities and suburbs more than immigration.[4]

Over the past decade, a growing chorus of social scientists has asserted the primacy of immigration in reviving American cities and regions. In an article in 2005, historian Robert Fishman proclaimed that a "Fifth Migration" was under way, as immigration to central cities was helping to counter the long-dominant "Fourth Migration," a term coined by Lewis Mumford in 1925 to describe city residents' departure for the suburbs.[5] In 2006, the *New York Times* published sociologist Robert Sampson's finding that increased immigration was a major factor in the dramatic drop in crime that U.S. cities experienced in recent decades.[6] The following year, the Census Bureau announced that without immigration, the New York metro area would have lost almost 600,000 in total population from 2000 to 2006, while metropolitan Los Angeles would have declined by more than 200,000, San Francisco by 188,000, and Boston by 101,000. The census also showed that population growth in smaller cities and metro areas—such as Battle Creek, Michigan, Ames, Iowa, and other new gateways—likewise depended on immigration.[7]

Immigration has gained prominence not only in our understanding of how metropolitan revitalization has happened but also in cities' pursuit of growth. City halls and economic development boosters in big and small cities from Philadelphia to Dayton, Ohio, and Utica, New York, have turned to immigrant and refugee recruitment and integration as strategies for repopulation and economic development.[8] They have recruited foreign companies and high-skilled workers, implemented language access and multicultural programs, and targeted support to immigrant small business owners and ethnic community development organizations. Some suburbs, too, have supported immigrant merchants and welcoming practices in schools, libraries, and law enforcement. More and more U.S. cities have joined national and international networks promoting immigrant integration as a path to growth, notably Welcoming America and Cities of Migration.[9] Public authorities and private and nonprofit developers across the nation have recruited investor immigrants to fund the construction of condominiums, malls, and even public transit and highways. Property development and infrastructure upgrades in metropolitan America increasingly depend on this source of capital.[10]

Local revitalization is a central concern in the explosive politics of immigration of recent years, even if this is not always explicit in policies and debates. The "sanctuary" policies and illegal immigration relief acts passed by cities and towns to alternately protect or expel unauthorized immigrants are motivated in large part by local leaders' and their constituents' concerns about revitalization. Sanctuary policies that limit local police involvement in deportation or recognize unauthorized immigrants' identification cards in cities and suburbs from Los Angeles to Pontiac, Michigan, largely promote public safety, an essential condition for revitalization. These laws also draw inspiration from local officials' desire to sustain the growth of immigrant communities and their investment in local housing and commerce. Alternately, the exclusionary laws passed by suburbs and smaller cities, such as Hazleton, Pennsylvania, have stemmed partly from concerns that the presence of undocumented immigrants will forestall the revitalization that their leaders envision. Ironically, these acts have led to shuttered storefronts and reversed housing market revivals in some of these towns, though in Hazleton continued Latino immigration offset white population decline in the decade since its pioneering illegal immigration relief act.[11]

The divergent responses to immigration by different municipalities reflect an increasingly contested set of hopes and fears about the local benefits and costs of immigration. They also reveal diverse visions of what is to be revitalized as well as how and for whom. Generally, social scientists agree that the fiscal costs and benefits of immigration are unevenly distributed between and within metropolitan regions and that costs and benefits fluctuate over time, but at the national level and over the long-term immigration produces net economic gains.[12] In the short-term, and in particular cities and neighborhoods, this means widely varied experiences of immigration and revitalization.

The Diversity of Immigrant and Receiving Communities

Diversity is a defining feature of immigration and of the new American metropolis. Immigrants since 1965 come from a wider range of nations, ethnic and racial groups, and education and class backgrounds than the overwhelmingly working-class European newcomers in the era of mass immigration a century ago.[13] Accelerating in the 1990s, immigrant settlement spread to regions beyond the long-standing gateways of New York, Chicago, Miami, California, and the Southwest.[14] Within metro regions, the majority of immigrants now settle first in the suburbs, helping to drive edge city growth and repopulation of working- and middle-class suburbs that millennials and their parents are leaving.[15] As residents, workers, business owners, and consumers, immigrants and refugees play a wide variety of roles in the revitalization of different downtowns and city and suburban neighborhoods. Yet these roles—and newcomers' experiences more broadly—also reflect another of metropolitan America's defining characteristics: social inequality.

Within the opportunity structure of metropolitan America, its labor and housing markets and also its immigration system, the economic diversity of

immigrants really means bifurcation. Mirroring the U.S. population overall, immigrants typically work either in high-paid, high-skilled service- and
knowledge-sector jobs that require higher education or in low-paid jobs with
few benefits in sectors such as domestic service and food service. Fewer and
fewer family-sustaining, middle-income jobs exist today in America's postindustrial economy for either the native or foreign born.[16]

Immigration policy has reinforced this pattern of socioeconomic bifurcation. While family reunification still accounts for most immigration to the
United States, the federal government has sought to manage the labor market and foreign investment through visas for two distinct groups: those with
high status, including high-wage, high-skilled workers and affluent investor
immigrants, and those with low status, namely temporary workers in agriculture and other low-wage sectors. President Barack Obama's executive
orders regarding deferred action for childhood arrivals and parents of American citizens or lawful permanent residents aimed to incorporate millions
of low-wage service and agricultural workers into formal labor market and
educational institutions "to grow our economy and create jobs."[17] Still, the
bifurcation of favored immigration status versus unlawful or otherwise ten-
uous status fundamentally shapes economic inequality among immigrants.

Following from this, the housing and neighborhood experiences of newcomer and receiving communities are bifurcated, too. In places such as central
New Jersey, South and East Asian professionals buy suburban McMansions.
Immigrant high-tech workers in California's Bay Area invest in downtown
condos, while working-class Latin Americans and black immigrants in metropolitan New York rent walk-up apartments or row houses in inner cities
and old industrial suburbs.[18] In urban America's "global neighborhoods,"
immigrant settlement and turnover of old residents have increased ethnic
diversity but also reinforced divisions of class and black-white segregation.[19]

Immigration thus inevitably intersects with America's metropolitics,
reinforcing patterns of inequality between different cities and towns in the
same region. Metro regions' bifurcated labor and housing markets produce
large fiscal inequities between different municipalities and school districts.
Suburban office centers reap business, sales, and wage taxes from immigrant
and native workers in pharmaceutical labs, housekeeping, and food service,
while other less affluent towns often pay for the public schools, libraries,
health clinics, and other services for working-class immigrants and their
families. This dynamic owes little to immigration per se, yet the settlement
of high- and low-wealth immigrants in affluent and poor city and suburban

neighborhoods reinforces metropolitan inequality.[20] These economic, social, spatial, and fiscal patterns all help make city and suburban revitalization about as diverse, complex, and contested as immigration is.

Revitalization: Diverse and Contested

In both rhetoric and practice, revitalization means different things in different contexts, shaped by different populations and processes. Some city leaders cast the attraction of global capital, largely in the form of high-skilled, high-wage immigrant workers, as *the* way to deploy immigration for urban economic growth. Their strategies include trade missions by corporate and political leadership, airport expansion to lure new direct flights to global economic centers, and marketing campaigns aimed at foreign investors and visitors. Other city governments emphasize the contributions of working-class immigrants to smaller-scale revitalization of neighborhood commercial corridors, housing markets, and labor markets ranging from construction to restaurants. Community organizations led by immigrants and natives often promote local revitalization efforts, from housing and workforce development programs to merchant associations and community policing.

Urban scholars, too, employ different definitions and ask different questions about revitalization. The contributors to this book employ diverse methods, study distinct places and groups of immigrants, and examine different manifestations of revitalization. Their measures include population and economic growth, housing demand and commercial occupancy, declines in violence, community mobilization, and even public perceptions of business districts or real estate markets. Some appraise revitalization as an outcome, while others evaluate it as a process. Some authors explore visions, debates, identity, and power dynamics among old and new residents. Still others examine the interventions of municipalities or community and economic development institutions. Many highlight working-class immigrants' contributions to economic growth and neighborhood vitality, a subject little explored by scholars of urban revitalization. Grasping this range of perspectives is critical for comprehending the diversity and complexity of immigration and revitalization.

Understanding immigration's relationship with revitalization in metropolitan America also requires attention to different regions and to various scales, from neighborhood to regional and transnational. The chapters in this book parse immigration's impacts and meanings for revitalization in diverse places and communities, across multiple decades and generations. Some examine the relationships between immigration and revitalization at the national and metropolitan scales, analyzing large sets of quantitative data. Others explore the history, politics, processes, and sometimes limits of revitalization in particular immigrant, receiving, and also sending communities, at the municipal and interregional and transnational scales. Together, they demonstrate the many different ways that immigration is tied to—and largely responsible for—revitalization in an increasingly diverse and dispersed geography of cities and suburbs across the United States and in places around the world to which migration connects them.

The chapters in the first two sections of this volume present clear, measured evidence that immigration is responsible for much of the urban revitalization in the United States over the last few decades. In section one, the chapters by Robert Sampson, Jacob Vigdor, and Gary Painter examine large data sets at the national and big-city scale to enumerate the broad impacts of immigration on crime, economies, population, housing, and related dimensions of urban America's return from its urban crises of the 1960s, 1970s, and 1980s. The chapters in section two, by Marilynn Johnson and by Michael Katz and Kenneth Ginsburg, highlight the diversity and limits of revitalization in different settings in the Northeast, from the suburbs of Boston to old mill towns in New Jersey. They challenge traditional notions of revitalization and question the growing assumption that immigration necessarily leads to prosperity for all sorts of newcomer and receiving communities. Chapters in both sections show how the dynamics of immigrant integration and intergenerational mobility profoundly influence the fortunes of places and their residents. They also demonstrate the importance of measuring immigration's relationship to revitalization using diverse variables and in different settings.

The third and fourth sections of this volume examine immigrant and receiving communities' relationships with one another and with revitalization. This bottom-up scholarship places people and their experiences squarely at the center of the story. Jamie Winders and Gerardo Sandoval explore struggles over the meanings and forms of revitalization in Nashville and Los Angeles in section three. In section four, chapters by A. K. Sandoval-Strausz and by Domenic Vitiello and Rachel Van Tosh examine immigrant community-led revitalization at the transnational scale. They show how community and economic development in Chicago and Philadelphia—and in Atlanta, Baltimore, Dallas, Minneapolis, and most other immigrant gateways—are tied to revitalization pursuits in Africa, Latin America, and other migrant-sending regions. These four chapters challenge widespread assumptions, in popular and social science circles, about which sorts of immigrants and what sorts of capital are responsible for revitalization. They also explore the difficult question of whether revitalization can occur without gentrification and the sacrifice of receiving communities' ways of life.

An inherent, but healthy and even necessary, tension exists between the different perspectives on revitalization within the chapters in this volume, reflecting a broader reality in social science and urban development. The authors of chapters in section one measure revitalization largely in terms of population and economic growth, as do most social scientists and policy makers. The authors of subsequent chapters frequently take issue with dominant understandings of what revitalization is and which sorts of immigrants are responsible for it. They align with scholars who have critiqued urban research and policy for essentially equating revitalization with gentrification.[21] With immigrants in mind or not, urban revitalization policies and projects remain focused on what Michael Katz called the "growth model," characterized by downtown real estate development, business improvement districts, and amenities for the creative class to consume.[22] He and other authors in this volume highlight revitalization in and by working-class and poor communities, where they argue that different evidence and even that different objectives of revitalization necessarily apply. Katz and Ginsburg, Sandoval, Sandoval-Strausz, and Vitiello and Van Tosh see signs of revitalization in bodegas, community engagement and stabilization, and transnational investments in hometowns. This diversity of perspectives, and the substantial emphasis on working-class as well as high-wealth immigrants, represent key contributions of this volume to the scholarship and debates about revitalization in U.S. cities and suburbs.

As immigration continues to hold a prominent place in debates about the fortunes of cities, regions, and nations, this volume offers the most complete account to date of the complex relationships between immigration and metropolitan revitalization. The chapters in this collection inject findings from diverse sorts of rigorous research into popular and policy debates that too often suffer from a lack of solid empirical evidence. Good social science, we assert, is one of the necessary foundations of good public policy.

PART I

Immigration and
Urban Transformations

CHAPTER 1

Immigration and the New Social Transformation of the American City

Robert J. Sampson

A mysterious thing happened on the way to the widely projected meltdown of American cities in the last quarter of the twentieth century. Instead of collapse, many of our largest and hardest-hit cities embarked on a 180-degree turn, confounding critics and social scientists alike. Why did these cities grow and rebound, witnessing renaissance rather than ruin? Or, to paraphrase University of Pennsylvania historian Michael Katz, why didn't American cities burn?[1] More broadly, what accounts for the remarkable crime declines of recent years in the United States and the return of urban vibrancy?

In this chapter, I make the case for immigration as one answer. Although immigration is certainly not the only factor, I argue that the evidence merits including immigration alongside other more dominant hypotheses for the nation's crime decline and its urban revitalization. I do so by reviewing the logic for why immigration is a compelling hypothesis, explicating social mechanisms to account for the changes we have observed, and considering new empirical evidence. It is important to begin, however, not with the present but instead with the urban trajectory of the last quarter century as it unfolded.

The City Roller Coaster

By the mid-1970s, pundits of all stripes were captivated by the undeniable crises of our central cities. Whether because of the scars of 1960s rioting, population out-migration, job losses, high crime, fiscal collapse, racial inequality, or widespread housing vacancies, cities were thought to be dying—especially older cities in the East and the Midwest Rust Belt. Although the origins of the urban crisis had deep roots stretching back decades,[2] things seemed to come to a symbolic head when President Gerald Ford allegedly told New York City to "drop dead" rather than expect a federal bailout, according to the famous headline in the New York *Daily News* in 1975.[3]

The tailspin of decline continued into the 1980s. James Q. Wilson and George Kelling captured the zeitgeist of angst with their treatise on urban disorder and "broken windows,"[4] while William Julius Wilson's *The Truly Disadvantaged* brought the social transformation and unraveling of the "inner city" to public attention.[5] Although the debate was largely about eastern and midwestern industrial cities, the South and the West were not immune either. Miami suffered one of the nation's worst race riots since the civil rights era at the beginning of the 1980s, and Los Angeles, which by the mid-1980s had become the nation's second-largest city, was the site of racial tension and the subject of apocalyptic predictions before the eruption of the Rodney King riots.[6]

At the end of the 1980s, the crack cocaine epidemic put what seemed to be the final nail in the city coffin. Violence spiraled again and hit its peak in 1990 in New York City, topping out at over 2,200 murders. Having lived in New York City in the mid-1970s during the "Summer of Sam" and in the early 1980s in the Bernhard Goetz era,[7] and having moved to the University of Chicago in 1991 just when homicides in that city were nearing their own twentieth-century highs,[8] I was one of many who witnessed firsthand the urban decay of the 1970s and 1980s.[9]

But then the world changed. Rather than the predicted or seemingly inevitable collapse, violence suddenly began to plummet, and formerly hemorrhaging cities began to grow. Today, some of the basket cases of the decline are the envy of the suburbs, turning the tables on experts. As with the fall of the Soviet Union and the Great Recession, experts were caught off guard and failed to predict major social change.

The magnitude of the turnaround and the scope of urban renaissance are worth noting. In 2014, for example, New York logged fewer than 330 murders despite a population larger than in 1990—the lowest count since comparable records have been kept.[10] Violence in Los Angeles declined markedly as well, as it did across the country. Thus, rather than the arrival of the violent super-predators that were confidently predicted,[11] the violence trend in the last half century follows an inverted U-shaped pattern (Figure 1.1). We are now back

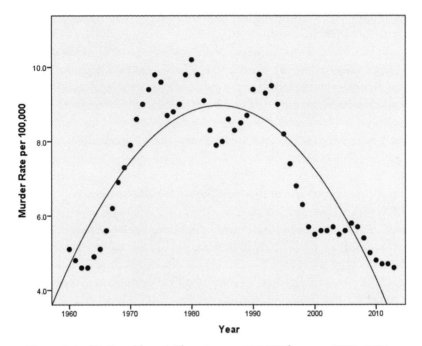

Figure 1.1. National homicide rates per 100,000 by year, 1960–2013.
Quadratic R-squared = .76.

Source: Bureau of Justice Statistics.

to the early 1960s (and, in fact, the tranquil 1950s) in terms of murder, our most reliable indicator of violence.

It was not just crime that pivoted. Today, the Big Apple is thriving and as exciting as ever, as are places such as Los Angeles, Boston, Seattle, and San Francisco. Even Chicago and Miami appear to be back from the brink. These and other central cities are magnets for not only the young but also for empty nesters and families with children, with construction cranes seemingly everywhere in the race to meet demand for city living. Teenage pregnancy is also down, as is mortality—especially among the most disadvantaged groups. For example, from 1990 to 2010, life expectancy increased 7.3 years for black males, compared to 3.8 years for white males. Teen pregnancy declined 56 percent for blacks and 45 percent for whites. Even poverty is no longer a problem confined to cities: poverty increased faster in the suburbs in 2000–2010 than in cities. Indeed, the foreclosure crisis of the recession blanketed many a suburb with vacant houses still dotting the low-rise landscape. Meanwhile, gentrification, population, and housing prices in coastal cities push upward.

To be sure, the urban renaissance did not unfold evenly. While creativity, diversity, lower crime, and bustling streets define cities on the move, inequality is ever present. Detroit is not the only city that still struggles with violence or that has hemorrhaged people and jobs; divergent trajectories of place are the norm. St. Louis and Baltimore continue to struggle, for example, and smaller cities such as Stockton are the face of today's fiscal crisis.

Explaining the New Social Transformation

What explains the trajectory of metropolitan revitalization—both the winners and the losers? There is no one answer, of course, as there is rarely a single cause of any complex social phenomenon, but there is virtue in systematically exploring how far we can take a clear-cut idea. In 2006, I did so by entering what had become a swirling debate about the great decline of American crime.[12] At the time, law enforcement officials, politicians, and social scientists had put forward many explanations for the mysterious large drop in crime rates in America. While each of the suspects—a decline in crack use, aggressive policing, increased prison populations, a relatively strong economy in the late 1990s, aging of the population, increased availability of abortion—had probably played some role, none to my mind had proved to be as dominant a factor as initially suggested. A major publication highlighted the central debate and continuing uncertainty.[13]

One factor was notably absent from the mainstream discussion: immigration.[14] This seemed odd to me, because the transformed vitality of cities was most visible in the places that had seen the greatest increases in immigration. As noted earlier, New York, a leading magnet for immigration had ranked for a decade as one of America's safest cities. Homicide in Los Angeles dropped considerably in the late 1990s (more than 45 percent overall), as it did in other cities with a large Hispanic population such as San Jose, Dallas, and Phoenix. The same can be said for cities along the border, such as El Paso and San Diego, which have ranked as low-crime areas for some time. Moreover, in the 1990s alone, foreign immigration had increased over 50 percent, so we were looking at very large changes and across a broad area. The United States had also become increasingly diverse ethnically not only in our nation's cities but also in suburban and rural areas. Yet overall, crime was down.

Based on these changes, and given a long line of criminological research showing that first-generation immigrants were less crime-prone than their second- and third-generation counterparts, I hypothesized that increased immigration was a factor that deserved attention for its potential link with the lower crime rates of the 1990s and beyond. I naively thought that this was a plausible and largely uncontroversial hypothesis, one that might have been overlooked but was nonetheless rooted in firm logic and prior evidence. The spew of hate mail I received suggested otherwise[15] and included not just the anger and bile that is typical in the online world but also assertions that the idea was crazy—"lunacy," as one respondent put it.

Yet in the ensuing years, the immigration and crime thesis has become increasingly mainstream, and a number of empirical tests have emerged. As acknowledged by the current volume on immigration and metropolitan revitalization, there is also important discussion of the broader impact of immigration on the nation's social fabric. The change in reception is refreshing and is supported on several fronts, to which I now turn.

The Immigration-Crime Nexus

First, immigration is important because of the nature of individuals who elect to immigrate to the United States. Social scientists worry about selection bias because individuals differ in preferences and can, within means, select their environments. Although there are exceptions (and setting aside wartime refugees), it is widely recognized that immigrants, and Mexicans in particular, selectively migrate to the United States based on characteristics that predispose them to low crime, such as motivation to work, ambition, and a desire not to be deported. This scenario is undoubtedly the case and is central to the immigration argument: social selection is a causal mechanism. Namely, to the extent that more people predisposed to lower crime immigrate to the United States (the country's population now includes more than 40 million foreign-born people), they sharply increase the denominator of the crime rate while rarely appearing in the numerator. Selection thus favors the argument that immigration may be causally linked to lower crime.

Second, there is evidence that immigrant composition is directly related to lower crime and a number of other life outcomes. In the "Hispanic paradox" originally identified in the health arena,[16] Latinos do better on various indicators of well-being, such as mortality, than other groups in socioeconomically disadvantaged positions. The pattern in mortality and general health has been consistently documented to the present day in the case of first-generation immigrants.[17]

My original hypothesis at the macrolevel was motivated by a similar pattern for violence at the individual level. In Chicago, my colleagues and I found a significantly lower rate of violence among Mexican Americans compared to blacks and whites.[18] But more than a quarter of all those of Mexican descent were born abroad, and more than half lived in neighborhoods where the majority of residents were also Mexican. In particular, first-generation immigrants (those born outside the United States) were 45 percent less likely to commit violence than third-generation Americans, adjusting for individual, family, and neighborhood background. Second-generation immigrants were 22 percent less likely to commit violence than the third generation. This pattern held true for non-Hispanic whites and blacks as well and took into account poverty and other relevant social characteristics (e.g., income, marital status, and even individual IQ). Moreover, once immigrant status was controlled, Mexican Americans no longer had lower rates of violence than blacks and whites.

Third, we showed that living in a neighborhood of concentrated immigration was directly associated with lower violence (again, after taking into account a host of correlated factors, including poverty and an individual's immigrant status). In this sense, the neighborhood context of immigration appeared protective against violence. The estimated probability that an average male living in a high-risk neighborhood without immigrants will engage in violence is almost 25 percent higher than in the high-risk immigrant neighborhood, a pattern again suggesting the protective rather than crime-generating influence of immigrant concentration.

These findings are broadly consistent with other research in criminology[19] and, when coupled with the magnitude of immigration change, provide a potential explanation of the sweeping crime drop. For example, foreign immigration, especially from Mexico, to the United States rose sharply in the 1990s, as did its concentration in immigrant enclaves in large cities. The foreign-born population increased to over 30 million by 2000; today the foreign population stands at over 40 million. It follows that a significant composition shift in the proportion of first-generation immigrants and immigrant neighborhoods will impact overall crime and well-being.

The pattern of immigration and lower crime nonetheless goes against popular stereotypes and perhaps explains the angry initial reaction. Among the public, policy makers, and many academics, a common expectation is that the concentration of immigrants and the influx of foreigners drive up disorder and crime because of the assumed propensities of these groups to commit crimes and settle in poor, presumably disorganized communities. This belief is so pervasive that, as I have shown elsewhere,[20] the neighborhood concentration of Latinos strongly predicts perceptions of disorder no matter what the actual amount of disorder or the rate of reported crimes. Yet increases in immigration are correlated with *less* crime, and immigrants appear to be less violent than those born in America, particularly when they live in neighborhoods with high numbers of other immigrants.

In brief, we are witnessing a scenario both similar to and different from earlier eras of rapid immigration. In early twentieth-century America, like today, growth in immigration, along with ethnic diversity more generally, was commonly associated with increasing crime and formed a building block for the "social disorganization" theory. The nation's largest cities at the time were virtual poster children for the theory, as they received an influx of European immigrants. Yet even then, some criminologists questioned the immigration link and pointed instead to social change rather than the criminal propensity of first-generation immigrants. And in point of fact, there was evidence that first-generation immigrants in the early twentieth century dispelled then popular stereotypes that linked immigrants to a higher propensity to engage in criminality.[21] Ironically, then, the immigration thesis for lower crime is quintessentially American and thus hardly new, even though today immigration flows are radically different in origin.[22]

Urban Revitalization Writ Large

The immigration thesis becomes more interesting when we move beyond crime proper. Many decaying inner-city areas gained population in the 1990s and became more vital in many ways as a result of immigrant diffusion. As Jacob Vigdor has shown in New York, immigration is linked to population growth, lower vacancy rates, and economic revitalization.[23] This pattern is important, because population loss and high vacancy rates are key elements undermining social order. The pattern is also seen in other cities. One of the most thriving areas of economic activity in the entire Chicago area, for example, is the 26th Street corridor in Little Village, a large immigrant enclave where the streets are teeming with social life.

These kinds of economic and demographic changes are a major social force, and immigrants aren't the only beneficiaries: native-born blacks, whites, and other traditional groups in the United States have been exposed to the gains associated with decreases in segregation, decreases in concentrated poverty and vacancies, and increases in the economic and civic health of central cities. In New York City, for example, the income of blacks in Queens has surpassed that of whites, with the surge in the black middle class driven largely by the successes of black immigrants from the West Indies. From Bushwick in Brooklyn to downtown Miami to large swaths of South Central Los Angeles and the rural South to pockets of the north and south sides of Chicago, immigration is reshaping America. It follows that the spatial externalities associated with immigration are multiple in character and constitute a plausible mechanism to explain broad-based change in the host society.

There are important implications to this line of argument for assessing the crime hypothesis. Simply adjusting for such things as economic revitalization, urban change, and other seemingly confounding explanations is not supported from a causal explanation standpoint, because these factors would instead be mediators or conduits of immigration effects, themselves part of the pathway of explanation. Specifically, to the extent that immigration is causally linked to major social changes such as urban revitalization and processes of spatial diffusion that are in turn part of the explanatory pathway to reduced crime, estimating only direct effects of immigration will give us the wrong answer. This, in fact, is the strategy that much research takes instead of carefully defining the mediating pathways of explanation. Moreover, applying a spatial logic of externalities leads to the hypothesis that the salubrious effects of immigration are magnified in certain regions or spatial regimes of the city, such as formerly segregated ghettos that are being economically rejuvenated through immigration. Working-class white areas that have not recently experienced much ethnic diversity may also benefit from increases in immigration.

Newer Evidence

It bears emphasis that it is hard to show causal links between immigration and crime rate changes or urban revitalization. Much of the data at the macrolevel I have discussed so far is correlational or cross-sectional. Yet there is recent evidence that examines change in a way that better identifies unique effects. In Chicago, for example, I found that increases in immigration and language diversity over the decade of the 1990s predicted decreases in neighborhood homicide rates in the late 1990s and up to 2006, adjusting for a host of internal characteristics.[24] This finding is based on within-neighborhood comparisons that account for alternative explanations rooted in unmeasured factors about the community. In particular, when examining changes in crime associated with changes in immigration, we can adjust for fixed (or stable) effects of the neighborhood.

Going further, in independent work using time-series techniques and annual data for all U.S. metropolitan areas over the 1994–2004 period, Stowell and colleagues examined the impact of changes in immigration on changes in violent crime rates.[25] After adjusting for confounding factors, their research indicated that violent crime rates tended to decrease as metropolitan areas experienced gains in the concentration of immigrants. Their results thus support the hypothesis that the broad reductions in violent crime during recent years are partially attributable to increases in immigration.[26] MacDonald, Hipp, and Gill report that Los Angeles neighborhoods where immigrants were most likely to settle had significant reductions in crime.[27] Vigdor found that in New York City the greatest decreases in crime occurred in police precincts with the most immigration and also found that immigration was related to population growth and a decrease in vacancy rates—immigration disproportionately flowed to those areas hardest hit by the "hollowing out" of the 1960s–1980s.[28]

For an issue on immigration of the *Annals of the American Academy of Political and Social Science*, John MacDonald and I also commissioned some of the most meticulous research to date about the effects of immigration on a cross section of American communities—urban, suburban and rural.[29] The scholars who participated were in agreement: while new immigrants are poorer than the general population and face considerable hardship, there is no evidence that they have reshaped the social fabric in harmful ways. A study appearing after our volume appeared used a quasi experiment of rainfall amounts to estimate the effect of Mexican immigration on U.S. crime rates.[30] The results were null.

Integrating the *ANNALS* volume and independent recent papers, I would thus argue that immigration is either benign with respect to the social fabric or directly linked to crime declines in neighborhoods and cities and at the national level. Combined with my findings in Chicago and research of scholars such as Vigdor and MacDonald, I would also hypothesize that the large influx of first-generation immigrants may reflect a diffusion process with spillover effects or externalities, such as economic renewal in formerly poor areas, reduction in vacancies, population growth, and possibly the diffusion of nonviolent social norms. Not only are recent immigrants (whether white, black, or Latino) less violent, but there also appears to be a protective contextual effect of concentrated immigration. Moreover, increases in immigration at the neighborhood level are linked to decreases in violence, especially in poorer areas and those with histories of racial segregation and exclusion.[31]

The Vacancy Rate Mechanism

A particularly interesting mechanism by which immigration has been posited to trigger revitalization is the reduction of housing vacancies. The hollowing out of the urban core through vacancies is also a key mechanism trumpeted by the "broken windows" thesis explanation of urban disorder and decline.[32] To the extent that immigration leads to population growth and a reduction in vacancies, as appears to be the case in New York City,[33] immigration takes on added significance as a factor in America's urban turnaround. Indeed, vacant or boarded-up housing is one of the key visual indicators of blight that sends a strong message to prospective or current residents about a neighborhood's viability.

I take a step here to assess the vacancy hypothesis at both the national level and in our nation's three largest urban centers—New York, Los Angeles, and Chicago. I gathered census data at the tract level for the periods 1990, 2000, and 2010. The decennial censuses were used for 1990 and 2000, respectively, whereas for 2010 I used the American Community Survey, which averages data from the period 2008–2012. The middle year is thus 2010. I calculated the vacancy rate in each decade and then examined changes from the periods 1990–2000 and 2000–2010. I also examined changes in other major factors linked to housing vacancies, including poverty, racial composition, home ownership, and education. By examining within-tract changes I am able to rule out stable or unobserved characteristics of tracts.

Figure 1.2 shows that increases in immigration from 2000 to 2010 are directly linked to decreases in the vacancy rate across the more than 70,000 neighborhoods, or census tracts, in the United States. Each factor in the graph is expressed in the same units so the coefficients can be directly

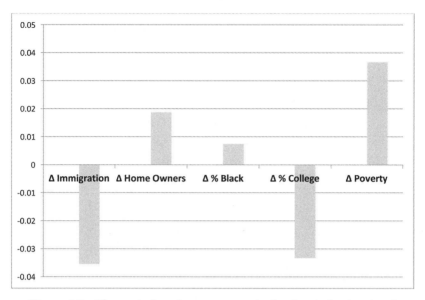

Figure 1.2. Change in housing vacancy rates by change in structural characteristics, U.S. Census Tracts 2000–2010 (N=71,536).

Source: 2000 Census and 2008–2012 American Community Survey, 2010 tract boundaries.

compared. (Because of the large sample size, significance levels are less interesting, although it is worth noting that at the national level, changes in racial composition do not emerge as significant despite the huge number of tracts.) Changes in immigration rival poverty and education changes in terms of magnitude, which is noteworthy because part of the pathway by which immigration is thought to promote revitalization is economic entrepreneurship, new businesses, and, in the long run, economic improvement.

When I repeat the analysis on the nation's three largest areas (New York City, Los Angeles County, and Chicago/Cook County), a similar pattern emerges except that changes in racial composition are much more salient. As shown in Figure 1.3, decreases in vacancy rates are directly associated with increases in immigration, but in this case it is stronger than poverty or educational changes.

Figures 1.2 and 1.3 reflect concurrent changes over the decade, inducing some possibility of reverse causality. Do vacancies serve as an opportunity for immigrants? I thus examined changes across two decades, allowing me to assess the predictive power of immigration trajectories. These results are in

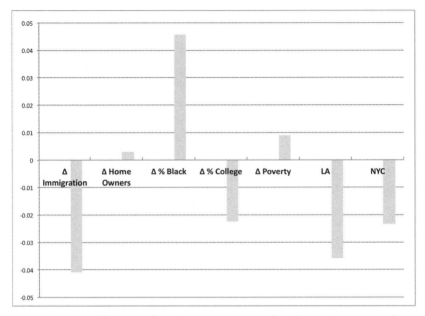

Figure 1.3. Change in housing vacancy rates by change in structural characteristics, New York City, Los Angeles County, and Cook County (Chicago) tracts, 2000–2010 (N=5,176).

Source: 2000 Census and 2008–2012 American Community Survey, 2010 tract boundaries.

Figure 1.4. Surprisingly, perhaps, even though changes over the 2000–2010 period are controlled, tracts on an upward trajectory of immigration in the 1990s saw reductions in vacancies in the next decade, net of both prior and concurrent changes in racial composition, poverty, home ownership and education (a proxy for gentrifiers). Apparently the path dependence of immigration flows portend well for urban revitalization in the form of lower vacancies.

Conclusion

Katz has recently argued that the explosion of immigration in the United States has "irrevocably smashed the black/white frame."[34] This is a provocative assertion that runs up against the enduring legacy of racial inequality, but it is true that the nation has changed in profound ways that have transformed

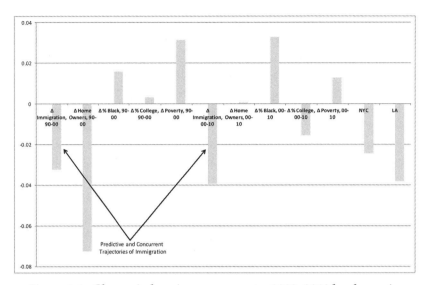

Figure 1.4. Change in housing vacancy rates 2000–2010 by change in structural characteristics, New York City, Los Angeles County, and Cook County (Chicago) tracts, 1990–2000 and 2000–2010 (N=5,176).

Source: 2000 Census and 2008–2012 American Community Survey, 2010 tract boundaries.

the old racial order of the city. If I am right about the evidence, these rapid changes in immigration have had net positive effects on a wide swath of urban social life, with violence reductions as the leading indicator.

But not all of the changes are necessarily positive, and immigration is a work in progress. Residents perceive more disorder when there are more immigrants,[35] and Robert Putnam has provided sobering evidence that neighbors are less trusting the more diverse their neighborhoods.[36] At the international level, changes in welfare provisions tend to decline as societies become more diverse, and we have seen an increase in social division in the Netherlands, France, and other European countries as a result of immigration and diversity. Moreover, there is considerable heterogeneity among immigrant groups—refugees from war-torn countries leave their homeland for very different reasons than economically motivated immigrants. Indeed, the rapid increases in migrant flows from the violence in Syria in 2015 provoked bitter debates, rancorous conflict, and what is seen by many as a refugee migration crisis.[37] These patterns urge caution in drawing strong conclusions about the role of immigration in the revival of American cities.

Substantial population change is also turning cities inside out and call-ing into question traditional urban and criminological models; the city roller coaster continues. For example, unlike the recent past, poverty is increas-ingly concentrated in the suburbs, wealth is concentrated in the center cities, and gentrification is reshaping many formerly working class and poor areas. U.S. cities are in essence becoming more like many European cities, includ-ing Paris. Alan Ehrenhalt has called this process "The Great Inversion."[38] Although demographic "revision" may be more apt than inversion, we do need to revise (or discard) the notion of "inner city" and consider the many implications of changing diversity for crime and urban change.[39]

In sum, cities and neighborhoods are rapidly changing with respect to diversity and immigration. The increasing presence of "global neighbor-hoods"[40] opens up a new set of challenges along with the unsolved problems of race and inequality that have long plagued American cities and criminal justice in America. Still, on balance, the evidence suggests that immigration has yielded a net good and is responsible, at least in part, for the remarkable turnaround of the American metropolis.

CHAPTER 2

Estimating the Impact of Immigration on County-Level Economic Indicators

Jacob L. Vigdor

Does immigration to American communities improve the well-being of long-standing residents? This question is complicated and difficult to answer yet is critical to ongoing immigration policy debates. This chapter uses econometric methods to assess the impact of immigration on three key indicators of local economic vitality: housing prices, the native-born population, and manufacturing employment.[1]

A naive method of assessing the impact would be to compare the experiences of communities that attracted varying numbers of immigrants over time. This method will yield misleading answers whenever immigrants are particularly attracted to more vibrant, thriving communities with expanding economic opportunities. The correlation between community vitality and higher immigration would reflect the former causing the latter, rather than the other way around.

To address this concern about endogenous migration to American communities, this study adopts an econometric strategy used frequently in the study of immigration's effects on a variety of local indicators. While immigrants can be expected to prefer locations with better opportunities, other things being equal, it has also been well-established that immigrants exhibit a tendency to migrate toward destinations where individuals of their own nationality already reside. This tendency enables the use of instrumental variables (IV) analysis, a technique whereby a factor influencing immigration, but otherwise uncorrelated with trends in economic vitality, can reveal the true impact of immigration on vitality.

This study uses three measures of community vitality: the native population, specifically the size of the native population excluding native-born children of immigrants; housing prices; and manufacturing employment. Communities with high or increasing quality of life should attract residents, expanding the population and raising housing prices to the extent that supply in the housing market has trouble keeping up with demand. The analysis of immigration and manufacturing employment addresses a possible rejoinder to the common complaint that immigrants "take" jobs from natives; in an economy where work can be shifted abroad, expanding the workforce may alter business decisions regarding whether to operate domestically or abroad.

The analysis uses the county, or county equivalent, to define communities. Counties are advantageous for purposes of analysis because their boundaries rarely change from decade to decade, eliminating concerns that growth in population or employment could simply reflect annexation. County-level statistics also cover the vast majority of the nation's land area and population, unlike metropolitan statistical areas defined by the Office of Management and Budget.

Results indicate that immigration yields positive impacts on all three outcomes: the exogenous arrival of 1,000 immigrants to a county is predicted to attract 250 additional natives, preserve or create 46 manufacturing jobs, and raise median home values by $116.

The positive impact of immigration on housing prices has important distributional consequences: higher home values are beneficial to owners but may be harmful to renters. Analysis of migration patterns in recent years suggests that immigration has contributed little to the severe housing affordability problems plaguing desirable neighborhoods in coastal metropolitan areas over the past several decades. Instead, immigrants have gravitated to areas that had previously experienced stable or declining home values. The evidence suggests that immigration has contributed significantly to the revitalization of once-declining neighborhoods in many cities.

Conceptual Framework

Contemporary immigration policy debates feature a range of voices, some arguing that immigration harms communities while others claim the opposite. While it is hard to imagine that both points of view can be correct simultaneously, each side can point to a basic economic model to support its beliefs. These economic models are outlined here.

A Case Where Immigration Harms Communities

Economic models presume that the root of all income is the production of goods and services and that goods and services are produced with capital—machinery, land, and other nonhuman factors—and labor. When businesses compete with one another for workers, the wages earned by any employee connect directly to the value that he or she brings to the production process.

Immigration increases the number of potential workers in the labor market; if the number of workers increases while the stock of capital remains the same, standard models predict that wages—which reflect the value that labor brings to production—will decline. In a simple formulation, if a factory has a fixed number of machines to be shared by all its workers and adds more workers, there will be more crowding around the machines, and workers will accomplish less in each hour worked because they will spend more time waiting their turn and less time producing. Employers, noting the reduced worker productivity, will be inclined to reduce wages.

In some cases, businesses are prohibited from reducing wages by contracts or minimum wage laws. In such cases, the expected result is unemployment rather than lower income. In the simple example above, the employer can react to the phenomenon of unproductive employees by firing them or not hiring them in the first place. In such a scenario, any case where immigrants find work must correspond to a case where a preexisting resident has lost his or her job.

When communities have a fixed supply of everything but labor and immigration raises the pool of labor, a second impact will be increased competition in the housing market. More families competing for a fixed number of homes will naturally lead to higher housing prices—a boon to those who already own a home but not to renters. Faced with a combination of lower wages, higher unemployment risk, and higher housing costs, it is easy to imagine how native families might perceive that immigration reduces their quality of life. Some may respond to the reduction in quality of life by leaving for elsewhere. An exodus on the part of native households helps to undo the negative impacts of population growth among those who remain.

Cases Where Immigration Helps Communities

The framework above, where workers can migrate but other factors of production cannot, does not accurately reflect a reality where employers can, and frequently do, move their operations—including machinery and other nonhuman factors of production—across communities and even nations. Indeed, much of American economic history can be read as a story of producers moving their operations in search of less expensive labor: the original industrialization of the Northeast and Midwest beginning in the late nineteenth century, the broad movement of economic activity to the American South in the twentieth century, and, most recently, the rise of imports from lower-wage countries in Asia and Latin America.

Modeling the economy as a set of workers using a common machine to manufacture goods also bears little resemblance to the modern service-driven economy. According to 2012 figures from the Bureau of Labor Statistics, there are more than six jobs in the service sector—incorporating everything from retail trade to health care to state and local government—for every one in traditional goods-producing industries. Demand for services, comprising everything from haircuts to heart bypass surgery, relates directly to the size of the population being served. Even within the goods-producing sector, more than 35 percent of all jobs are in the construction industry—positions that cannot be outsourced and for which population growth is a significant determinant of demand.

In a world of footloose employers and service-driven economies, it is no longer clear that an influx of immigrant workers must deprive natives of employment opportunities. Moreover, the existence of a construction industry introduces the possibility that the impact of immigration on housing prices might be muted, as the housing stock expands to meet rising demand.

A third factor, beyond employer mobility and service-sector employment, supports the view that immigration can boost communities. When communities experience economic decline, the housing stock tends to shrink much more slowly than the population. Declining communities tend to suffer from a dearth of employment opportunities, which in turn lead to social problems, such as crime, that can be exacerbated by the presence of vacant housing units. Immigration into declining areas can have minimal impacts on housing prices, as there are surplus housing units to begin with, and yield quality-of-life improvements to the extent that their presence reduces vacancy and deters crime.

While these extensions of a traditional fixed-capital, manufacturing-based model seem sensible, there remain empirical questions regarding the magnitudes of these effects. Are outsourcing decisions significantly sensitive to expansion of the domestic labor force? Is the expansion of opportunities in construction and the service sector, coupled with effects in traditional manufacturing industries, sufficient to match the increase in the number of workers?

Data

To answer these questions, Census Bureau data on almost every county in the United States were collected for the decennial enumerations in 1970, 1980, 1990, and 2000, as was the American Community Survey five-year sample of 2006–2010. These data provide five snapshots of conditions in over 3,000 areas nationwide, including information on the native- and foreign-born population, median owner-reported housing values, and housing unit characteristics including the type of structure (single-family detached house, attached row house, apartment building, etc.), the number of units in multi-unit structures, and the year of construction. For purposes of analysis, housing prices were converted to 2010 dollars using the Consumer Price Index.

As noted in the introduction, counties comprise a sensible unit of geographical analysis, as their borders rarely change and they are defined for nearly the entire population and land area of the United States. Counties that changed boundaries between 1970 and 2000—including rare cases of counties splitting in two or being merged into one or counties in Virginia absorbing or ceding territory to independent cities—were excluded from the analysis. The analysis also excludes data for Alaska, which does not have reliably defined counties, as well as Hawaii, which suffers from other data reporting issues. Finally, some sparsely populated counties were excluded from the analysis because the Census Bureau did not disclose key variables for those counties in one or more years. The ultimate sample for analysis consists of 3,091 counties—or county equivalents, including parishes in Louisiana and independent cities in several states—observed five times between 1970 and 2010.

The analysis of manufacturing trends couples the census-based data with information from the County Business Patterns (CBP) data set. The CBP records are derived from business filings with the Social Security Administration, identifying the business's industry and employment level. The CPB split the manufacturing industry into approximately 20 different sectors, such as primary metals or rubber and plastics. The CBP data are often redacted to protect the identity of individual employers. In a small county with a single steel mill, for example, the CBP might provide only a range for the actual number of employees. In some counties there is only one manufacturer over-all, in which case the CBP redacts total employment figures; in other counties there is no manufacturing whatsoever. The analysis excludes counties for which the total manufacturing employment value was redacted in either 1970 or 2010, the years used for purposes of analysis. The resulting data set includes 2,156 counties.

Methods

As noted in the introduction, the simple strategy of comparing immigration to a county with trends in housing prices, native population, or manufacturing employment will tend to yield misleading answers, since immigrants can be expected to gravitate toward host communities with better opportunities. A correlation between immigration and community vitality, in other words, might reflect causality in either direction.

In scenarios such as this, with the potential for reverse causality (vitality leading to immigration rather than vice versa), IV analysis can provide a strategy to isolate causality running in one direction rather than the other. The key is to identify an instrument, in this case a variable that predicts whether immigrants locate in a given county but bears no other relationship with measures of community vitality.

Several prior studies of immigration have used measures of the historical size of the immigrant population in a local area as an instrument for future immigration flows to that area, based on the tendency for immigrants to gravitate toward areas where individuals of their own nationality already reside.[2] The strategy, known as a "shift-share" methodology, can be credited to Joseph Altonji and David Card, who first used it to study the impact of immigration on the labor market.[3] Two prior studies have used this strategy when examining effects in large cities and American states.[4]

To implement this strategy, data are first used to forecast the number of immigrants in a county as of a particular census year after 1970. This prediction is based on the number of immigrants of each nationality observed in 1970 and the nationwide trend in population for immigrants of that nationality in subsequent decades. Counties that had a large population of Scandinavian immigrants in 1970, for example, would be forecast to witness less growth in the foreign-born population than counties with an equivalent number of Latin American or Asian immigrants.

Rather than estimate a single regression model where the outcome of interest—housing prices or the native population—is modeled as a function of the foreign-born population and controls, the IV procedure involves the estimation of two regression models. The first regression model relates the actual number of immigrants in a county to the forecasted number. Because forecasts can be expected to become less reliable over time—based on 1970 data, for example, we would expect more accurate forecasts in 1980 than in 2000 or 2010—the relationship between the forecast and the actual number is permitted to vary over time. The second model uses predicted values from the first model in place of the actual foreign-born population. Thus, the potentially "tainted" data on the immigrant population ends up replaced by a scaled version of the constructed forecast variable.

The IV analysis permits the use of additional control variables. In this case, it is desirable to include variables that are potentially important determinants of the outcome variables. For the native population and housing price models, each regression incorporates housing market information from the previous census—that is, prices or population in one decade is estimated as a function of housing prices, housing stock size and average age, the housing vacancy rate, and the proportion of single-family detached homes in the prior decade. The analyses also control for a set of year fixed effects, which account for nationwide trends in home prices or population. Finally, each model includes a set of county fixed effects. These account for all permanent differences across counties—acknowledging, for example, that Manhattan is persistently more dense and expensive than Loving County, Texas.

The often arcane subject of functional form is consequential for this analysis. When analyzing variables that are always positive—such as housing prices or population—econometricians typically transform variables using logarithms. In this case, the analysis would estimate how the logarithm of housing prices, for example, reacts to the logarithm of the immigrant population. There are technical reasons to prefer logarithmic transformations, but a log-log specification also yields a sensible interpretation: when the coefficient on a logarithmic independent variable equals x, it implies that a 1 percent increase in that variable leads to an x percent increase in the logarithmic dependent variable.

Is it reasonable to think that a 1 percent increase in the immigrant population should have a uniform impact on housing values, as would be implied by a log-log specification here? Bear in mind that a 1 percent increase in the immigrant population means something very different in counties of different sizes. A log-log specification in this case would imply that the effect of adding 1 immigrant to a base population of 100 in a sparsely populated rural county would be exactly the same as adding 1,000 immigrants to a county that already had 100,000: both would increase housing values by a fixed percentage.

An alternative linear specification would imply that the effect of adding 1,000 immigrants is 1,000 times greater than the effect of adding one, regardless of the base population. Moreover, the effect would be measured in dollars rather than percent. While readers may have differing opinions regarding which of these interpretations seems most plausible, a common empirical method of choosing among them simply looks at which model best fits the data, as measured by the R^2 statistic. Here the answer is clear: a linear specification works best.

Table 2.1 shows the results of the first-stage model. The significant positive coefficient on the shift-share forecast demonstrates that the strategy of imputing immigrant population on the basis of preexisting populations and national immigration trends is at least somewhat accurate: on average, every 1,000-immigrant increase in the forecast foreign-born population raises the actual foreign-born population by 372. The forecast is not perfect—as would be expected, given the importance of other factors in determining immigrant location decisions—but it is statistically robust.[5] The forecast is approximately as accurate in 1990 as it is in 1980; in later years, however, the accuracy declines. By 2010, raising the forecast by 1,000 yields an actual increase of only 247. The effect continues to be statistically robust. As the table shows, the first-stage regression also controls for the variables to be included in the second-stage model. Coefficients show that the foreign-born population tends to be higher in counties with cheaper, younger, and more abundant housing in the previous census. Immigrants are also attracted to counties with a higher proportion of apartment-style housing and where vacancy rates were lower in the preceding census.

The manufacturing analysis uses slightly different methods while employing the same basic IV procedure. Because of missing CBP data issues, only two years are used: 1970 and 2010. The dependent variable is defined as the change in a county's manufacturing employment between 1970 and 2010 relative to expectations, where expectations are computed using a variant on the shift-share methodology. For each county, a predicted change in manufacturing

Table 2.1. First-stage regression.

Independent variable	Coefficient (Std Err)
Shift-share based forecast	0.372 (0.021)
SSBF × 1990	0.018 (0.007)
SSBF × 2000	−0.061 (0.013)
SSBF × 2010	−0.125 (0.014)
Lagged median housing value	−0.029 (0.005)
Lagged median age	−21.26 (21.51)
Lagged housing stock size	0.647 (0.005)
Lagged vacancy rate	−7017 (2216)
Lagged proportion single-family detached	−726 (2194)

Year and county fixed effects included; R^2=0.864; balanced panel of 3,091 counties.

employment is computed by examining the distribution of manufacturing jobs across industries in 1970, then comparing nationwide employment trends in that industry over the next forty years. Predicted county-level manufacturing job losses are particularly strong in counties dominated by the worst-performing industries, such as primary metals, in 1970. By contrast, counties concentrated in the best-performing industries, such as rubber and plastics, were forecast to exhibit slow declines or even increases in manufacturing employment. The dependent variable is then the difference between the actual and predicted job losses: positive numbers indicate that the county did better than expected.

The change in manufacturing jobs is modeled as a function of the change in foreign-born population. The actual change in foreign-born population between 1970 and 2010 is replaced with a predicted change based on

Table 2.2. First stage, manufacturing analysis.

Independent variable	Coefficient (Std. Err.)
Shift-share based forecast	0.304
	(0.007)
Manufacturing employment 1970	−0.200
	(0.046)
N=2,156; R^2=0.696.	

shift-share methods. Table 2.2 shows that the shift-share forecast is again robust: a predicted increase of 1,000 immigrants maps onto an actual increase of 304 foreign-born residents. The specification also controls for 1970 manufacturing employment levels; the first stage shows that immigrants tended to avoid counties with higher levels of manufacturing employment in 1970.

Results

Effects on Housing Prices

Table 2.3 presents results of the second-stage IV analyzing housing prices in inflation-adjusted 2010 dollars. The results indicate that the addition of one immigrant to a county's population increases housing prices by 11.6 cents. One thousand new immigrants, by extension, would raise prices by $116. The estimated effect is statistically significant with a t-statistic over 5. The second-stage regression also shows that housing prices tend to be higher in counties with a younger housing stock, more housing overall, higher vacancy rates and lower prices in the previous Census, and a higher proportion of single-family detached homes.

Certain of these results may seem counterintuitive: other things being equal, we would generally expect the more expensive locations of ten years ago to continue to be more expensive today; likewise, we would expect high vacancy ten years ago to predict lower prices today. The key to understanding these findings lies in the use of county fixed effects. These added control variables force the analysis to examine only fluctuations around long-term averages in each county. In counties that had above-average housing prices ten years ago, there must be some tendency to mean-revert (otherwise the

Table 2.3. Median home value results.

Independent variable	Coefficient (Std. Err.)
Foreign-born population (instrumented)	0.116 (0.022)
Lagged median housing value	−0.391 (0.013)
Lagged median age	−452 (60.73)
Lagged housing stock size	0.106 (0.025)
Lagged vacancy rate	12,475 (6276)
Lagged proportion single-family detached	117,015 (6185)

Year and county fixed effects included; R^2=0.483; balanced panel of 3,091 counties.

mean would have been higher to start with). Likewise, in counties that had high vacancy rates relative to the long-run average ten years ago, we must expect lower vacancy and higher prices this time around.

Effects on the Native-Born Population

Table 2.4 shows IV estimates of the impact of the foreign-born population on the native-born population. When the immigrant population increases by 1,000, the native population increases by an estimated 423. The estimated effect is statistically significant, with a t-statistic over 24.

Some portion of the estimated increase in the native-born population might reflect immigrants bearing children in the United States. To assess the likely magnitude of this effect, Integrated Public Use Microdata Series data were used to estimate the number of native-born children residing with immigrant parents. Results indicate that the ratio of native-born children of immigrants to immigrants is roughly 15 percent—for every 1,000 immigrants, then, we can expect the native population to increase by 150 due to immigrant childbearing alone. The remainder of the effect, attributable to location decisions on the part of natives themselves, amounts to 270 natives per 1,000 immigrants.

Table 2.4. Native population results.

Independent variable	Coefficient (Std. Err.)
Foreign-born population (instrumented)	0.423
	(0.017)
Lagged native population	0.875
	(0.011)
Lagged median age	−77.35
	(27.69)
Lagged housing stock size	−0.293
	(0.029)
Lagged vacancy rate	2234
	(2890)
Lagged proportion single-family detached	11251
	(2834)

Year and county fixed effects included; R^2=0.483; balanced panel of 3,091 counties.

The remainder of the coefficients shows some interesting contrasts with the first-stage results, implying that natives and immigrants are attracted to different types of counties in general. Whereas immigrants tended to avoid counties with a high proportion of single-family detached homes, natives move toward them. Natives show a stronger aversion to older housing stock and actually show a tendency toward counties where vacancy rates had been higher in the previous census.

Effects on Manufacturing Employment

Table 2.5 reports the results of the IV specification for manufacturing employment. Results indicate that the addition of 1,000 additional immigrants to a metropolitan area over the 40 years between 1970 and 2010 results in the addition or retention of 46 manufacturing jobs. The effect is statistically significant, with a t-statistic around 15. The regression also shows that the manufacturing industry tended to perform worse, relative to expectations, in counties with the highest manufacturing employment levels in 1970.

Table 2.5. Manufacturing employment results.

Independent variable	Coefficient (Std. Err.)
Change in foreign-born population (instrumented)	0.046
	(0.003)
Manufacturing employment 1970	−0.321
	(0.006)

N=2,156; R^2=0.739.

Conclusion

These results generally support the argument that immigration results in a net increase in economic opportunity for natives in the local labor market. Any negative effects caused by the foreign-born "taking" jobs is offset to some extent by a reduced tendency for employers to shift operations overseas, as seen in the manufacturing specifications, and by the creation of opportunities to provide services and durable goods to new neighbors. While the specifications here do not directly provide evidence of this latter set of opportunities, the tendency for natives to flow into rather than out of counties experiencing immigration points indirectly to their existence.

The positive estimated impact of immigration on housing prices carries mixed implications. Among those who own American housing, immigration has created wealth. The net impact on American wealth can be estimated as follows. Each immigrant raises housing prices by an average of 11.6 cents in her or his county of residence. The average immigrant resides in a county with 800,000 housing units, implying an average total windfall gain of over $90,000. Multiplying this value by the estimated 40 million immigrants currently residing in the United States reveals a net impact of $3.7 trillion. In 2008 after the bursting of the American housing bubble, total housing wealth in the United States amounted to just over $25 trillion.[6] Thus, immigration accounts for about 15 percent of all housing wealth in the United States and roughly 7 percent of total household net worth.

For those who rent rather than own housing, immigration translates into a rent increase rather than a boost to wealth. When considering total impacts on household well-being, one must consider this rent increase in tandem with the increase in local economic opportunity made apparent in other specifications.

Do immigration-induced rent increases harm the nation's most vulnerable households? Several observations suggest otherwise. The prospective impacts of immigration on housing values are greatest in the areas receiving the most immigrants. Between 2000 and 2010, the largest imputed housing price increase—brought about by the greatest increase in the foreign-born population—occurred in Harris County, Texas, the area around Houston. Houston is a relatively affordable city, with housing prices substantially below the national average. In 2010, the median home was worth just $131,700. By contrast, the most expensive counties in the United States can attribute very little of their cost to immigration since 2000. Manhattan and San Francisco, the nation's two most expensive urban cores in 2010, both witnessed a decline in the foreign-born population over the prior decade. In the greater New York area, the greatest impact of immigration on housing values occurred in the Bronx, which in general does not appear on lists of the most expensive urban regions in the United States. Similarly, in the San Francisco Bay area the strongest impacts of immigration occurred in the less expensive East Bay, not in the city of San Francisco or the exclusive enclaves of Marin County.

Additional evidence suggests that the price increases caused by immigration to areas such as the Bronx are accompanied by significant improvements in quality of life. While New York City has received much attention for the dramatic declines in crime over the past twenty years, analysis of precinct-level data reveals that the greatest drops in crime occurred in the areas experiencing the strongest inflows of immigrants.[7] In general, evidence shows that price increases in neighborhoods experiencing revitalization along these lines are modest relative to estimates of what most households would be willing to pay for them.[8]

It is important to state that the evidence presented here does not disprove the theoretical possibility that immigration might decrease native living standards. Conceivably, there may be some cases where immigration to a community does not lead employers to shift job opportunities into that community and where the impact of additional population on demand for services is slight—for example, because immigrants prefer to use their income to send remittances to their home country. What the empirical evidence shows, however, is that the predominant pattern contrasts with this bleak image. On average, immigration appears to create opportunities that attract rather than repel natives.

CHAPTER 3

Immigrants, Housing Demand, and the Economic Cycle

Gary Painter

The widespread impact of immigration on housing markets has been documented in the literature by many.[1] The primary difference between immigrants and native-born households has been related to their higher rates of mobility and their lower rates of household formation.[2] A challenge to modeling changes in immigrant housing demand is the fact that most longitudinal data do not have sufficient numbers of immigrants. In this chapter, I use changes in headship and changes in the rate of adult children living with parents to better understand how housing demand shifts for immigrants across the economic cycle. Finally, I discuss how these trends can play a role in metropolitan revitalization.[3]

Research has documented the widespread impact of immigration on housing markets.[4] However, not all analysts connect the impact that immigrants have had on metropolitan housing markets to urban revitalization. Analysts have typically focused on the potential that immigrant entrepreneurs can have on economic growth.[5] However, immigrant housing demand can have a critical impact on markets that are in decline, as implied by the work of Albert Saiz on the link between house prices and immigrants.[6] In this chapter, I focus on understanding the determinants of immigrant housing demand and how this may have changed over time.

Most of the research on immigrant housing demand has focused on the change in size of the population across the United States[7] or on the determinants of home ownership.[8] Less attention has been placed on changes on household formation or headship, which is an important determinant of housing demand because it affects the number of units occupied directly. Painter and Yu have noted that immigrant headship is lower than the headship rate of native-born adults and that this difference persists even after controlling for resources and other differences.[9]

Early papers in the housing literature on household formation noted the role of house prices and rents in their models of household formation.[10] More recently two papers revisited the issue, motivated in part by the increase in home ownership rates in the early part of the decade of the 2000s and differences in home ownership rates across immigrants.[11] They noted that the increase in home ownership rates may have been due to shrinking household formation, and the work confirms that household formation did play a role.

Recently, the recession has highlighted the fact that the rate of household formation does change due to economic shocks.[12] Lee and Painter provide evidence of how young adults adjust their rate of leaving home during a recession and times of higher unemployment.[13] Choi and Painter estimate how such shocks in unemployment impact household formation over time and the length of time it takes household formation to return to normal levels. The Choi and Painter paper suggests that this adjustment process can take over two years but that the rate of household formation will eventually return to normal even without a change in unemployment rates.[14]

Unfortunately, most of the recent work on household formation does not focus on how immigrant headship may change over the cycle (Painter and Yu estimate headship models at two points in the cycle, but the focus of the paper is not on changes in housing demand over the cycle).[15] One contribution of this chapter is to focus on how one might measure the changes in immigrant housing demand over the most recent cycle. To do so, I focus on changes in the headship rate and the rate of children living with their parents over the economic cycle. Below, I also provide context for these changes by displaying data on changes in the immigrant population and trends in home ownership and headship over the past four decades for both native-born and immigrant households.

Change in the Composition of the Immigration Population in the United States, 1980–2010

One of the impacts of the immigrant population on housing demand can be seen by viewing the scope of change in the immigrant population in the United States over the past four decades. Figures 3.1–3.4 display changes in the immigrant population in the top 150 metropolitan areas as measured by overall population. In the figures, the population is stratified by quintiles based on the size of immigrant population in 1980. The changes in shading represent higher quintiles.

Figure 3.1 displays the trends in the overall immigrant population. In 1980, the metropolitan areas in the highest quintile, with an immigrant population over 19 percent, were limited to the tip of Texas, Miami, New York, and southern California. The geographic distribution of the immigrant population was little changed by 1990. Concentrations of immigrants increased in primarily Texas, Florida, and California. Other small increases were in Chicago, near New York, and in the Northwest. However, increases in the immigrant population became a national phenomenon by 2000. These geographic shifts further accelerated through 2010. The recession may have been expected to reduce these trends because of job losses that may have shifted immigrants back to metropolitan areas with the strongest economies, but this did not occur.[16] By 2010, there were significant concentrations of

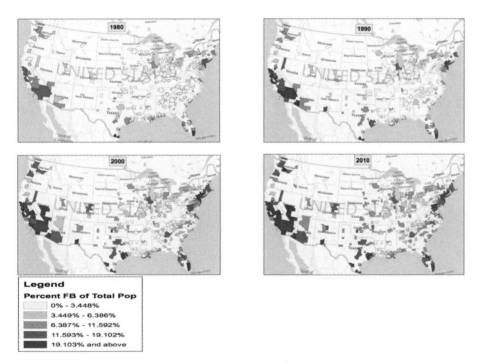

Figure 3.1. Percent foreign born of the total population.

the immigrant population across the Eastern Seaboard, a large swath of the South, and the entire Northwest and Southwest in addition to the areas that already had significant numbers of immigrants in 1990. Importantly, in 2010 there were almost no metropolitan areas from 1980 that were still in the lowest quintile.

The pattern displayed in the overall immigrant population is largely the same as in the Latino population alone (Figure 3.2). This is not surprising because the largest numbers of immigrants from 1980 to 2010 came from Latin America. In 1980, the only areas in the highest quintiles were southern California and the southern tips of Texas and of Florida. By 1990, New York City, Chicago, and the Northwest started to become Latino immigrant destinations. By 2000 and increasingly so in 2010, the Latino population had spread in large numbers throughout the United States.

The pattern for Asian immigrants is similar over time, but there are some differences in the pattern of migration over time in the metropolitan areas. There is also a difference in the size of the immigrant population from Asia.

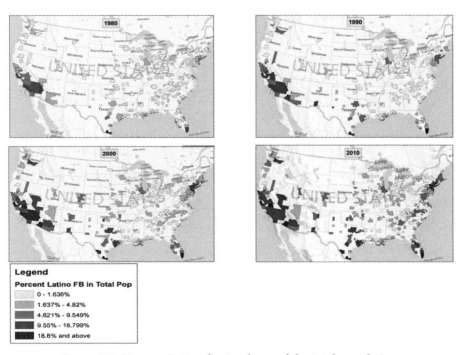

Figure 3.2. Percent Latino foreign born of the total population.

Figure 3.3.   Percent Asian foreign born of the total population.

As noted in Figure 3.3, the beginning of the highest quintile of the Asian immigrant population was only 4.4 percent of the population in a metropolitan area. In 1980, the highest quintiles were only in California. In 1990, the Asian immigrant population had increased in the Northwest, Houston, and New York City. In 2000, increases were seen across the Eastern Seaboard, Minneapolis, Atlanta, and Texas. By 2010, most metropolitan areas were in the highest quintiles as measured by the 1980 population distribution.

While Figures 3.1–3.3 are instructive concerning changing demographics, they do not say much about housing demand. If immigrants have housing demands similar to those of the native population, then changes in the demographic makeup of the population should not matter. However, research has shown that immigrants are less likely to be home owners if they have been in the country fewer than ten years.[17]

Figure 3.4 displays the percentage of the immigrant population that has been in the United States from fewer than 10 years but does not indicate the size of that population. In 1980, the geographic distribution of the newness

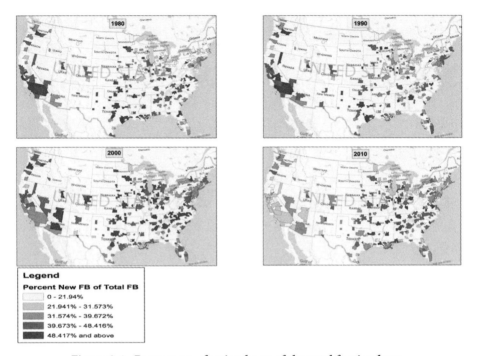

Figure 3.4. Percent new foreign born of the total foreign born.

of the immigrant population was fairly evenly distributed. The places with the fewest new immigrants were in New York and Miami. By 1990, half of the immigrant population (the highest quintile) in California was new. This pattern was also true in the Northwest. There were some small changes in the geography of the immigrant population across other metropolitan areas in 1990. The changes in where new immigrants were likely to reside began in the 1990s and accelerated in the 2000s. The location of new immigrants began to occur in higher proportions in the middle and southern parts of the country so that by 2010 less than 30 percent of the immigrant population in the California metropolitan areas had been in the country fewer than ten years. In contrast, in most metropolitan areas of the middle of the country and the South, over 40 percent of the immigrant population had likely been in country fewer than ten years, and in some places it was well over 50 percent.

The shifts in the immigrant population have important implications for those metropolitan areas in the Rust Belt that have experienced population losses. Without the influx of the immigrant population, these metropolitan areas would have been even harder hit. While some have been concerned about the negative implications of the increases in rents because of immigration, as noted in the work of Albert Saiz,[18] the influx of immigrants in declining cities has played an important role in stabilizing the housing market. This sustaining influence has also prevented local property tax revenue from falling as fast as it would have without the arrival of immigrants. However, these immigrant populations may not have as much of an immediate impact beyond the housing market due to the fact that they were much more likely to be new to the United States. Over time, though, these new populations will contribute to the revitalization of these declining cities.

Housing Demand, 1980–2010

Home Ownership

One of the most commonly used measures of housing demand has been home ownership. Implicit in a study of home ownership is that the analysis assumes that the choice to become a household is exogenous, since measures of home ownership are at the household level. However, it would be expected that households can adjust housing demand by having larger numbers of people living in larger units or by splitting up into small of numbers of people in smaller units. An alternative to measuring home ownership at the household level would be to measure it at the person level. This has the advantage of accounting for changes in headship and home ownership over time, but the disadvantage is that it is less consistent with practice.

Figure 3.5 displaces the home ownership rate for both native-born populations and immigrant populations for the population aged 18–65. I have chosen to display the data across different groupings of metropolitan areas because the research of Painter and Yu suggests important differences in the housing outcomes of immigrant groups across gateway and smaller metropolitan areas.[19] Part of these differences is due to housing cost differences, and part is due to the composition of immigrants across the metropolitan areas. The data for the entire nation is displayed in the last columns of the figures.

Figure 3.5 displays what might be a surprising trend in immigrant home ownership for some readers. Nationally, immigrant home ownership increased steadily from 1990 to 2010. This increase is partially due to the increase in immigrant home ownership before the Great Recession, but

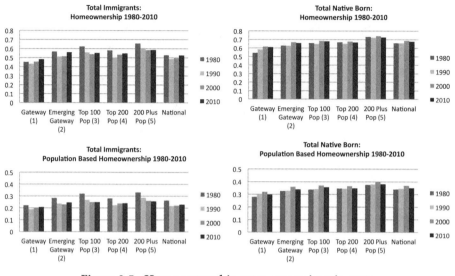

Figure 3.5. Home ownership rates among immigrants
and native born (total).

immigrant home ownership fell less after the crisis than did native-born households.[20] The rates (53 percent) are much lower than that for native-born households (67 percent), but the trend has been increasing. This trend is true in almost all regions of the United States and is also true in the places (gateways and emerging gateways) where most immigrants reside. Home ownership for native-born households went up in 2000 but fell back in 2010 after the housing crisis.

Population-based home ownership has a lower rate for both groups, because all adults are now included in the calculation instead of just household heads (25 percent nationally and 35 percent nationally in 2010 for immigrants and native-born adults, respectively). The increase in the population-based home ownership rate for immigrants is lower. This suggests that part of the gains in household-based home ownership was due to fewer independent households. This is also observed in the native-born population, as the fall in population-based home ownership rates from 2000 to 2010 was larger than the decline in the household-based measure.

Figures 3.6–3.9 display the same trends for each of the four racial/ethnic categories that are studied here. For the sake of completeness I included a

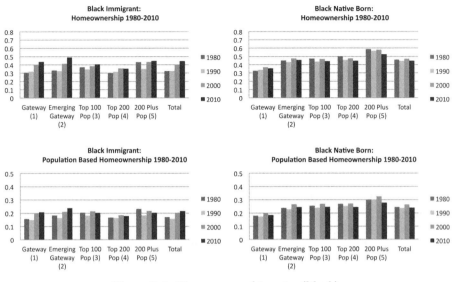

Figure 3.6. Home ownership rates (black).

sample of black and white immigrants, but their numbers are too small to be a focus of analysis here. The home ownership rates (Figure 3.6) of the black native population moved up in the large gateway metropolitan areas from 1980 to 2000 but then fell back again. The rates of home ownership are very low (35 percent) in those metropolitan areas. Nationally the pattern was a bit different, and the decline after the 2000–2010 period is more pronounced. The population-based home ownership rates are noticeably different in 1990 versus 1980 in the gateways, and the decline from 2000 to 2010 is larger than the household-based measure.

The pattern for the white population again reveals slight differences between 1980 home ownership based on household heads and the rate based on the population (Figure 3.7). White home ownership increased over the four decades when measured by the household-based rate but declined over the same period when using the population-based measure. The decline is not large, but the difference is interesting and is not well appreciated in the housing literature.

Now I turn to the immigrant population, which is the focus of this study. Figure 3.8 displays the two home ownership measures for the Latino native

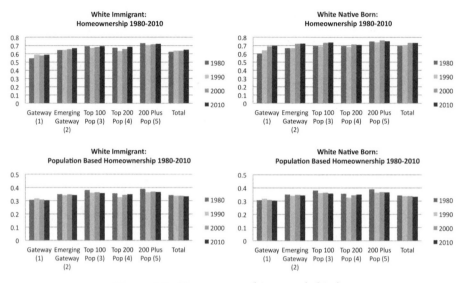

Figure 3.7. Home ownership rates (white).

and immigrant populations. While the Latino immigrant home ownership rate is lower than the rate for Latino native populations, the gap has closed over time and is quite small in some of the smaller metropolitan areas. There is a striking difference in the last decade as the home ownership rate of Latino immigrants increased, while the home ownership rate of Latino natives declined after the housing crisis. Painter and Yu have suggested that a shift of Latino immigrants into lower-cost areas and a reduction in immigration flows due to the Great Recession may have contributed to the higher immigrant home ownership rates.[21]

The differences in the patterns over time between the population-based measure and the household-based measure are quite small for Latino immigrants but are worth noting for Latino native-born adults. This suggests that headship rates are likely similar for Latino immigrants over time. However, the flat to declining population-based home ownership rate suggests that headship rates have fallen for Latino native-born adults.

Figure 3.9 presents the data for both measures of home ownership for Asian adults. Asian home ownership is higher than that of Latinos. There has also been a dramatic increase in the home ownership rates of Asian households over the past four decades. The increase from 2000 to 2010 was quite large in the face of the housing crisis. It is now the case that the home

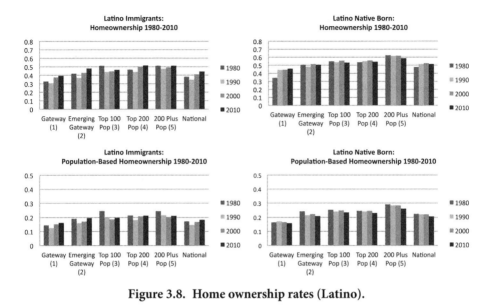

Figure 3.8. Home ownership rates (Latino).

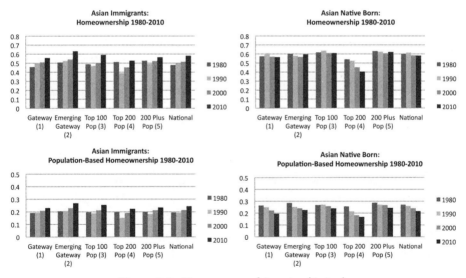

Figure 3.9. Home ownership rates (Asian).

ownership rate of Asian immigrants is higher than that of Asian native-born residents in many places in the United States. Home ownership rates for Asian native-born households have been largely flat or declining over the period. As with the Latino population, the patterns of home ownership rates over time are quite similar for Asian immigrants across the two home ownership measures. The same is true for Asian native adults. The results suggest a larger decline in home ownership when measured at the population level.

Headship

The data on home ownership suggest interesting differences between the population- and household-based measures of home ownership. In order to more directly measure changes in the number of independent adults over time, I next turn to a set of figures that display the headship rate. The headship rate is simply the number of household heads divided by the number of adults age 18–65. Figures 3.10–3.14 display changes in the headship rate from 1980 to 2010.

Headship rates among native-born populations rose across much of the nation from 1980 to 2000 but fell back to levels found in 1980 in 2010 (Figure 3.10). The only exception to this general pattern was in the largest immigrant gateway cities, but the decline from 2000 to 2010 was the same. The results nationwide suggest increasing housing demand from 1980 to 2000, as adults were more likely to occupy additional units as a percentage of the adult population. This could be due to many factors—higher divorce rates, lower marriage rates, and fewer adults living with parents or children.[22] However, the trend reversed after 2000 as the rate of headship fell dramatically from 2000 to 2010.

The changes for immigrants were different from native-born households. The 1980 headship rate of immigrants was very similar to native-born households in 1980 but were about 8 percentage points lower from 1990 to 2010. These differences between natives and immigrants have important implications for housing demand as immigrant populations have grown across the United States.[23] As Painter and Yu have noted, the headship rate for immigrants did not decline much, if at all, for immigrants from 2000 to 2010, which is partly attributed to a changing composition of that population over time.[24]

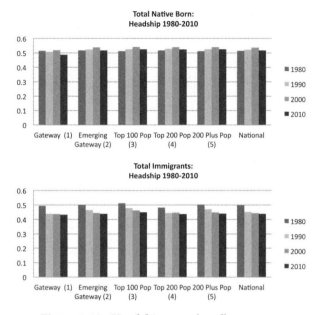

Figure 3.10. Headship rates (total).

I next decompose the native-born headship rate into the rate for the black and white population separately (Figure 3.11). It is first notable that the headship rates of the white and black populations are quite similar. The literature on household formation points to the role of resources as an explanatory variable in describing different rates of household formation.[25] Despite fewer resources, the black population has a headship rate similar to that of the white population, which may have important implications for wealth accumulation and other social predictors. Overall, the pattern of change in the headship rate of the two populations is similar at the national level. The increase in the headship rate of the black population was larger in 2000 but fell back to the level of the white population in 2010.

I next turn attention to headship among the Latino population. As is evident in Figure 3.12, Latino headship fell among both immigrants and native-born adults after 1980, which coincided with the large wave of migration in the 1980s. In the gateway metropolitan areas, the headship rate is about 40 percent among immigrants and less than 40 percent among native-born adults. The second panel reveals that this difference between immigrants and native-born adults can be a bit misleading and is partially due to

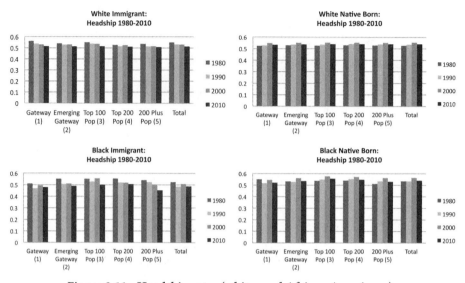

Figure 3.11. Headship rates (whites and African Americans).

how the children of immigrants that are U.S. citizens are classified. If these children are reclassified as immigrants when they live with their immigrant parents, then the headship rates of immigrants falls dramatically, and there has been relatively stable headship among native-born Latinos. This suggests that the third-generation young adults are much more likely to live independently than the second generation. Notably, the rates of headship are still lower than those of the white or African American population but are closer to 50 percent.

The headship rates of Asian immigrants (Figure 3.13) and native-born adults are low or lower than the Latino population. The headship of immigrant adults is around 40 percent over the forty-year period, with a decline in 1990 and an increase over the next two decades. The headship rates of native Asian adults fell dramatically over the period, with the biggest declines in the largest metropolitan areas. However, this phenomenon was largely due to second-generation Asian young adults living with their immigrant parents. When I reclassify this group as immigrants, the figure shows that immigrant headship has been fairly constant over the period, with a small decline from 2000 to 2010, but that native-born headship is around 50 percent in the gateways and emerging gateways. Again, this suggests a large difference in housing demand between the second and third generations.

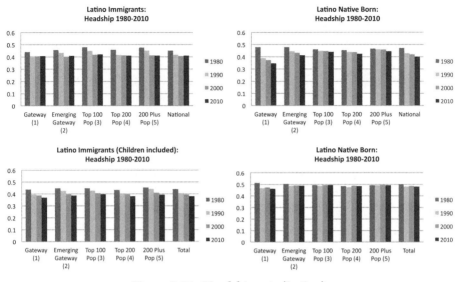

Figure 3.12. Headship rate (Latino).

It is worth noting that the headship rates of Asian and Latino adults are very similar despite different average resources. Further, there are interesting geographic differences in headship rates across groups. For both groups of Latinos (see Figure 3.12) headship is lowest in the gateway metropolitan areas, which is not surprising due to housing costs being much higher there. However, this is not the case for all Asian adults. When we restrict the attention to native Asians that are not living with immigrant parents (see Figure 3.13, panel 4), headship is higher in the gateway metropolitan areas than in many other metropolitan areas. The difference across places for Asian immigrants is also smaller than for Latinos. All the above suggest interesting dynamics for housing demand across race/ethnicity and place that needs to be accounted for in an analysis of housing demand.

Adult Children Living at Home

I next investigate how the percentage of adult children living with parents has changed over the four decades. This is only one component of how headship rates may change, but it could also be the most sensitive to changes in the

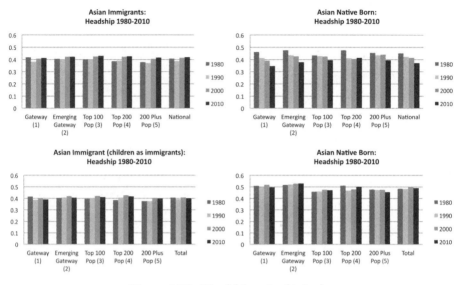

Figure 3.13. Headship rates (Asian).

economy. Figure 3.14 displays the change in rate over time for the four racial/ethnic groupings, and Figure 3.15 displays these changes by immigrant status. The rates of adult children living at home were lowest for the Latino population until 2010. For all groups, the rate of children living at home rose dramatically in 2010 versus 2000, but the jump was largest for Latino children. Overall, the rate of adult children living with parents is highest for the black population and lowest for the white population.

There are clear differences between the rate of adult immigrant children living with parents and that of native-born children (see Figure 3.15). The differences are particularly pronounced for Latino and Asian adult children. Over half of native-born Latino and Asian young adults aged 18–30 live with their parents, about 20 percent points higher than that of immigrant young adults. It is worth noting that many of these children are in the second generation and are living with their immigrant parents.

Measuring Changes in Housing Demand over the Cycle

Finally, data over the most recent cycle are presented in Figures 3.16–3.20. As is well appreciated, the traditional home ownership rate fell for all groups

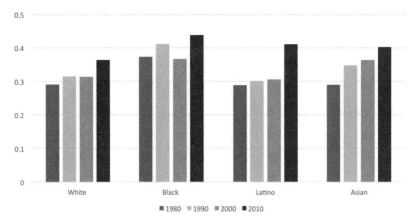

Figure 3.14. Percentage of adult children living with parents (among 18–30-year-olds).

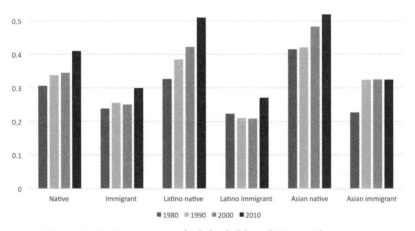

Figure 3.15. Percentage of adult children living with parents, natives vs. immigrant (among 18–30-year-olds).

during the recession (Figure 3.16). The rate declined the most for Asian native-born households (5 percentage points), but most groups experienced at least a decline of 3 percentage points. It is interesting to note that the decline in home ownership began in 2007 for the white and black populations but began in 2008 for the other groups.

Figure 3.17 demonstrates that there has also been a dip in headship across all racial and ethnic groups. Plotting data from the period 2006–2011,

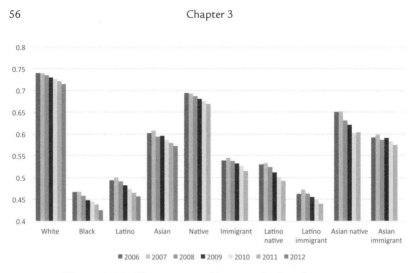

Figure 3.16. Home ownership rates during downturn.

we note that headship rates for black adults fell the most (from almost 55 percent to 53 percent), with no signs yet of recovery. Headship rates for the Latino population fell over 1 percentage point but started to tick up in 2011. The changes in immigrant headship rates are less stark and are harder to interpret. There was a dip in the headship rates of Latino immigrants in the middle of the period, but the headship rate have been stable across the period, which may be due to fewer new immigrants arriving in the United States during this period.[26] There was a slight decline in the headship rates of Asian immigrant adults, but the decline among native-born Asian adults was much larger.

As demonstrated previously, how one classifies second-generation young adults can alter the assessment of how the recession impacted Asian and Latino immigrant native-born populations. As is evident in Figure 3.18, the decline among native-born adults is not as large when one classifies second-generation young adults living with immigrant parents as immigrants instead of natives. This suggests that a sizable number of second-generation young adults were living with their immigrant parents.

Part of the decline in headship was certainly due to an increase in the rate of children living with parents (Figures 3.19 and 3.20). The rate of adult children not living independently increased the most for the Latino population, beginning at 30 percent in 2006 and increasing to 43 percent in 2011. This rate was highest for the black population in 2011 (46 percent) but had started the recession at 40 percent. The rate of change in childship over the recession

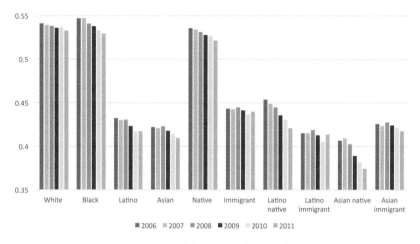

Figure 3.17. Headship rates during downturn.

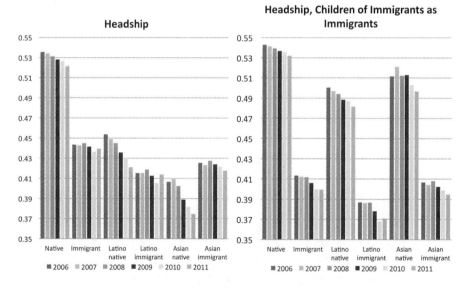

Figure 3.18. Headship differences based on classification.

was much smaller for the white and Asian populations, but there were no signs of this rate going down as of 2011.

Figure 3.20 demonstrates that while there were increases in the percentage of adult children living with parents among natives and immigrants, the rate of increase between the immigrant and native populations was quite similar. As noted in Figure 3.15, native adult children were much more likely to live with parents than were immigrant adult children. The rate of change

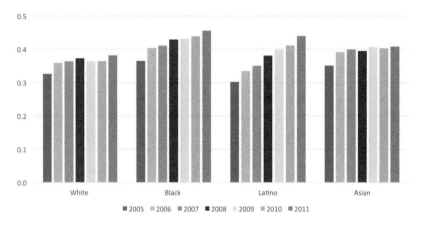

Figure 3.19. Percentage of adult children living with parents (among 18–30-year-olds).

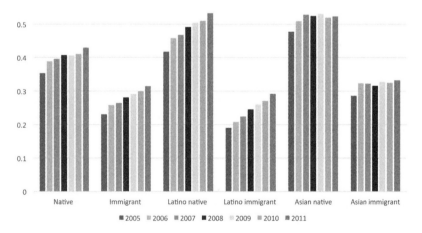

Figure 3.20. Percentage of adult children living with parents, natives vs. immigrant (among 18–30-year-olds).

for Asian adult children from 2006 to 2011 was quite small, and the rate of increase for Latino adult children was about 10 percentage points. This suggests an increasing burden on these families and a reduction in housing demand for Latino families.

Analysis of Headship

Next, I estimate simple probit models to determine the correlates of headship and the rate of adult child living at home with parents. Table 3.1 displays the estimates of headship in a sample of 80 metropolitan areas that were chosen to be comparable to recent research.[27] Column 1 displays the evidence for the entire population. Columns 2 and 3 display this information for native-born persons and immigrants, and the final column drops white and black immigrants from the sample.

After controlling for other characteristics, Asian adults have the lowest headship, and Latino and African American adults have headship rates lower than whites but similar to each other. The raw data hinted at the finding for Asians, who have relatively low headship despite higher incomes than other minority groups. As would be expected, young adults are less likely to be a household head, and this rate of headship increases over the life cycle. Also as expected, higher headship is present for divorced and widowed adults. Higher headship is also present for the most educated adults, but this is hard to interpret because higher income does not lead to higher headship. These variables are clearly correlated with each other and require further analysis. The number of children under age 18 in the household increases headship, and the number of workers in the household decreases headship; however, these should be true because of how headship is define.

The housing market affects headship in mixed ways. Lee and Painter demonstrate that higher rents reduce headship, as is found here.[28] However, in this simple model, higher house values increase headship. This later finding is likely related to the decision to own and thus is difficult to interpret. The analysis also indicates that living outside of the gateway metropolitan areas increases the likelihood that an adult is a household head. It is unclear what this finding is representing, since housing costs are already accounted for. As expected, higher unemployment rates reduce headship. Finally, all else being equal, immigrants are less likely to be independent household heads, which was not always apparent in the raw data.

Table 3.1. Probability of Living as an Independent Head of Household, 2010.

Dependent: Head of Household Sample:	(1) All	(2) Native	(3) Immigrants	(4) Immigrants (2)
Ethnic group (ref = white)				
Hispanic	−0.0836***	−0.118***	−0.0729***	
	(0.00571)	(0.00703)	(0.0105)	
African American	−0.0888***	−0.0916***	−0.0229	
	(0.00563)	(0.00614)	(0.0149)	
Asian	−0.163***	−0.167***	−0.118***	
	(0.00743)	(0.0135)	(0.0103)	
Other	−0.0415***	−0.0270*	−0.0473	
	(0.0130)	(0.0146)	(0.0290)	
Age (ref = 24–34)				
18–24	−0.815***	−0.823***	−0.704***	−0.728***
	(0.00705)	(0.00774)	(0.0165)	(0.0174)
35–44	0.161***	0.166***	0.168***	0.137***
	(0.00536)	(0.00621)	(0.0101)	(0.0107)
45–54	0.302***	0.313***	0.316***	0.251***
	(0.00535)	(0.00606)	(0.0105)	(0.0116)
55–65	0.360***	0.376***	0.332***	0.267***
	(0.00584)	(0.00656)	(0.0117)	(0.0132)
Marital status (ref = single)				
Married	−0.143***	−0.138***	−0.169***	−0.148***
	(0.00517)	(0.00588)	(0.0104)	(0.0109)
Divorced or separated	0.332***	0.327***	0.352***	0.363***
	(0.00644)	(0.00723)	(0.0136)	(0.0143)
Widowed	0.453***	0.522***	0.211***	0.274***
	(0.0162)	(0.0191)	(0.0296)	(0.0317)
Education (ref = less than high school)				
High school	0.118***	0.251***	0.0469***	−0.0176
	(0.00728)	(0.00958)	(0.0103)	(0.0115)
College+	0.506***	0.661***	0.374***	0.284***
	(0.00730)	(0.00954)	(0.0106)	(0.0120)
Number of children	0.146***	0.139***	0.173***	0.163***
	(0.00185)	(0.00217)	(0.00335)	(0.00352)
Number of workers	−0.175***	−0.180***	−0.185***	−0.177***
	(0.00216)	(0.00252)	(0.00388)	(0.00412)
Log household income	−0.230***	−0.246***	−0.152***	−0.180***
	(0.00258)	(0.00298)	(0.00488)	(0.00519)

Dependent: Head of Household	(1)	(2)	(3)	(4)
Sample:	All	Native	Immigrants	Immigrants (2)
Metropolitan area				
Emerging gateways	0.0815***	0.0776***	0.0763***	0.0698***
	(0.00552)	(0.00643)	(0.0106)	(0.0110)
Small metro	0.0424***	0.0394***	0.0402***	0.0263*
	(0.00629)	(0.00717)	(0.0132)	(0.0137)
Median rent	−0.143***	−0.126***	−0.190***	−0.200***
	(0.0165)	(0.0192)	(0.0314)	(0.0326)
25th percentile house value	0.119***	0.115***	0.122***	0.119***
	(0.00818)	(0.00963)	(0.0150)	(0.0156)
Unemployment	−0.00514***	−0.00589***	−0.00302**	−0.00332**
	(0.000752)	(0.000878)	(0.00141)	(0.00147)
Immigrant	−0.118***			
	(0.00843)			
Time in the U.S. (ref = <10)				
Came to U.S. 11–20 years ago				0.0803***
				(0.00988)
Came to U.S. 21+ years ago				0.196***
				(0.0102)
Fluent English				0.132***
				(0.0105)
Ethnic group (ref = other)				
Asian				−0.0837***
				(0.00948)
Latino				−0.0312***
				(0.00968)
Constant	1.733***	1.791***	1.239***	1.520***
	(0.0680)	(0.0765)	(0.141)	(0.147)
Pseudo R^2	0.1329	0.1405	0.1082	0.1111
Observations	848,547	664,272	198,666	184,537

Robust standard errors in parentheses.
80 MSAs, Age 18–65
*** $p<0.01$, ** $p<0.05$, * $p<0.1$

I next turn to the comparison of the estimates for immigrants and native-born households. There are larger racial and ethnic differences in headship among native-born adults than among immigrants, which might be because of the lower headship overall for immigrants. The coefficient estimates for immigrants are smaller than those for native-born adults in most cases. The one difference is a greater sensitivity to the median rent in the metropolitan area. Finally, the evidence (see Table 3.1, column 4) demonstrates that time in country and English fluency are strongly connected to headship. For both measures of immigrant integration, higher headship is predicted with more integration. As with the full population, Asian immigrants are less likely to be household heads than are Latino immigrants.

Table 3.2 displays the correlates of the likelihood that an adult child will live at home. Nonwhite adults are more likely to live at home than are white young adults. Asian young adults are the most likely to live at home. When separating out the immigrant and native populations in Table 3.2 (columns 2 and 3), it is apparent that native-born adult children are more likely to live with parents. In fact, immigrants Latino young adults are least likely to live with parents.

The other coefficients of the model are in line with expectations. The youngest adults and those who have never been married are most likely to

Table 3.2. Logit: Probability of Adult Children Living with Parents, 2010.

Dependent: Head of Household	(1)	(2)	(3)	(4)
Sample:	All	Native	Immigrants	Immigrants (2)
Ethnic group (ref = white)				
Hispanic	0.320***	0.493***	−0.284***	
	(0.0182)	(0.0174)	(0.0437)	
African American	0.477***	0.458***	0.155**	
	(0.0208)	(0.0188)	(0.0605)	
Asian	0.653***	0.605***	0.209***	
	(0.0277)	(0.0310)	(0.0446)	
Other	0.363***	0.276***	0.293***	
	(0.0384)	(0.0349)	(0.0935)	
Age	−0.234***	−0.236***	−0.238***	−0.237***
	(0.00215)	(0.00201)	(0.00471)	(0.00470)
Marital status (ref = single)				
Married	−1.377***	−1.753***	−0.854***	−0.857***
	(0.0193)	(0.0204)	(0.0361)	(0.0360)

Dependent: Head of Household	(1)	(2)	(3)	(4)
Sample:	All	Native	Immigrants	Immigrants (2)
Divorced or separated	−0.155***	−0.221***	−0.0506	−0.0538
	(0.0376)	(0.0357)	(0.0853)	(0.0854)
Widowed	−0.530**	−0.838***	−0.131	−0.139
	(0.242)	(0.253)	(0.386)	(0.386)
Education (ref = less than high school)				
High school	−0.179***	−0.324***	0.414***	0.412***
	(0.0163)	(0.0156)	(0.0388)	(0.0388)
College+	−0.685***	−0.915***	−0.0590	−0.0674*
	(0.0169)	(0.0161)	(0.0409)	(0.0408)
Number of workers	0.0880***	0.198***	0.0872***	0.0894***
	(0.00741)	(0.00691)	(0.0135)	(0.0135)
Log household income	0.865***	0.979***	0.438***	0.434***
	(0.0109)	(0.00950)	(0.0203)	(0.0202)
Metropolitan area				
Emerging gateways	−0.460***	−0.372***	−0.546***	−0.539***
	(0.0212)	(0.0206)	(0.0442)	(0.0441)
Small metro	−0.585***	−0.468***	−0.731***	−0.728***
	(0.0235)	(0.0226)	(0.0530)	(0.0530)
Median rent	−0.628***	−0.924***	−0.00646	−0.0104
	(0.0629)	(0.0602)	(0.129)	(0.129)
25th percentile house value	−0.103***	0.108***	−0.353***	−0.347***
	(0.0303)	(0.0293)	(0.0608)	(0.0608)
Unemployment	0.0493***	0.0380***	0.0548***	0.0554***
	(0.00378)	(0.00359)	(0.00792)	(0.00791)
Immigrant	−0.476***			
	(0.0197)			
Ethnic group (ref = other)				
Asian				0.129***
				(0.0395)
Latino				−0.368***
				(0.0375)
Constant	1.567***	−0.273	4.771***	4.842***
	(0.266)	(0.252)	(0.591)	(0.592)
Pseudo R^2	0.266	0.327	0.193	0.192
Observations	218,246	177,060	41,186	41,186

Robust standard errors in parentheses.
80 MSAs, Age 18–65
*** $p<0.01$, ** $p<0.05$, * $p<0.1$

live at home. Households with higher incomes provide more resources for an adult child to live at home, and children with less education are more likely to live at home. Higher housing costs, whether rentals or single-family homes, increase the likelihood that a child will live at home. Finally, unemployment rates increase the likelihood of a young adult living at home.

Conclusion

This chapter has demonstrated that understanding immigrant housing demand is more complicated than simply estimating differences in home ownership rates. There are important differences in household-based and population-based home ownership rates that suggest the need for future research in tracking changes over time. The headship rate is another related measure that has implications for housing demand, but as the regression analysis has shown, it is hard to interpret the coefficient of the model because the decision to own and live independently are interrelated. This suggests that more careful empirical studies are needed like the type in Lee and Painter,[29] but there are challenges to replicate such a study for immigrants because there are not enough immigrants in these longitudinal data sets.

One dynamic measure that is available in cross-sectional data is the rate of adult children living with parents. Arguably, this rate is less contaminated by the endogeneity bias that exists in the headship rate regression models. We find that Latino immigrant adult children are the least likely to live at home and that Asian adult children are the most likely to live at home. However, over the economic cycle, the biggest changes in this rate were among Latino young adults. Future research should explore the other contributors to headship rate changes over the cycle.

The role of immigrants in urban revitalization is well established.[30] Furthermore, the role of housing in urban revitalization is not in dispute. This chapter highlights how immigrants express housing demand and how one can use census data to determine dynamics in the housing market. The fundamental elements of population growth, headship, and time in country are strong predictors of how much housing is demanded.[31] This chapter adds an important component to the work of Saiz[32] in determining how population increases influence demand and therefore provides a foundation for urban revitalization.

PART II

Revitalizing Diverse Destinations

CHAPTER 4

Revitalizing the Suburbs: Immigrants in Greater Boston Since the 1980s

Marilynn S. Johnson

Since the 1990s, we have seen growing attention to immigrants as agents of urban revitalization. In cities from New York to Los Angeles, post-1965 immigration has coincided with the restructuring of metropolitan economies in which immigrants have contributed to both the top and bottom ends of the new service economy. Moreover, scholars have shown how immigration has often helped revitalize declining manufacturing centers by reversing long-term population losses and revitalizing declining urban housing, neighborhoods, and shopping districts.[1]

But while immigrants have contributed to urban economies in many places, the improved fortunes and success of some cities have led to new problems. Since the mid-1980s, gentrification and growing income inequality have made some cities increasingly unaffordable, forcing newcomers out to surrounding suburbs. Indeed, Asian, Latino, and Caribbean newcomers in the 1970s and 1980s were often the leading edge of urban neighborhood transition and higher housing costs that ultimately drove immigrants out and reduced their presence in up-and-coming central city neighborhoods.

Since the 1980s, then, more immigrants have been settling outside of central cities in older inner-ring suburbs and in growing edge cities. Most of the research on this so-called suburban immigrant nation has focused on the South and West—emerging gateway regions such as Atlanta, Dallas, Phoenix, and Washington, D.C. In such places, immigrant suburbanization has spread across sprawling metropolitan areas that developed mainly after World War II. In these newer and rapidly growing areas, revitalization has been a less significant topic than sheer growth and expansion across nearby deserts, farms, and orchards. Moreover, many of these metro areas had little experience with large-scale immigration in the past and thus lacked the social and political infrastructure to help accommodate newcomers. Indeed, resistance to immigrants in these areas has often been bitter, despite their importance to robust and expanding regional economies.[2]

But suburban immigration has been an equally important force in the older metropolitan centers of the Northeast and Midwest, where immigrants have long played a central role in urban life. In fact, most of these older cities were surrounded by a network of mill towns and outlying industrial communities dating back to the early nineteenth century. For a variety of reasons—some familiar and some new—these are precisely the places where newer immigrants have been settling. How have immigrants fared in such communities, and to what extent have these older suburbs been revitalized as a result?

This chapter explores these issues through an examination of immigrant suburbanization in greater Boston.[3] In an effort to document the diversity of migrant destinations, I look at several types of suburbs—older industrial centers, affluent western suburbs, and the so-called one-step-up communities—to see how and why new immigrants settled there.[4] Looking at the latter, I examine three older suburbs to see how they have changed over time and how new immigrants have successfully built their communities on the foundations of the old, diversifying and revitalizing these communities in the process.

As one of the nation's oldest cities, Boston has a distinctive metropolitan history and form—one that is not well suited to traditional notions of city and suburb. Given its early economic development and geographic constraints, the city decentralized quite early. Some of the state's oldest and largest industries, such as textiles and shoes, were located outside Boston to take advantage of rural labor and waterpower from local rivers. These ranged from more distant mill towns such as Lowell and Lawrence to those closer to Boston along the Charles, Sudbury, and Mystic Rivers. Such industrial towns soon attracted immigrant workers, and several developed distinct ethnic neighborhoods for Irish, French Canadian, Italian, and other workers. Because Boston's attempts to annex its neighboring communities ended rather early (essentially by the 1870s), the city's land base remained small. New industry and population thus began moving to these surrounding areas after 1890, filling in vacant areas within the preexisting patchwork of older towns and manufacturing centers. The Boston metro area thus has a particularly long history of suburban development, one in which immigrants have played a vital part.[5]

After World War II many of the smaller manufacturing centers experienced a precipitous decline, as did New England industry more generally. At the same time, with federal support for higher education, home loans, and highway building, burgeoning middle-class suburbs grew up along and beyond what would become the Route 128 beltway west of the city. As middle-class whites (often second-generation Irish, Jews, and Italians) moved out of Boston and Cambridge, rising vacancy rates created housing opportunities for new immigrants arriving in the 1960s and 1970s. Beginning in the 1980s, however, Boston's renaissance as a high-tech, medical, education, and financial services center attracted more affluent workers who pushed rents and property values back upward. Many new immigrants were thus compelled to look outside the city; by 1990, more of them were moving to the suburbs and nearby cities than were settling in Boston itself. In many cases, they moved in or around the old inner-ring manufacturing centers that had long been home to immigrant workers. More skilled and educated migrants, by contrast, moved to more prosperous suburbs near Boston and Cambridge or along Route 128.

By 2010, twenty-five towns and small cities in the metro Boston area had foreign-born populations that were larger than the statewide average, ten of which had higher shares than the city of Boston itself. In recent years, both academics and the press have heralded the rise of immigrant suburbanization, noting that some migrants have been moving directly to the suburbs, bypassing the traditional urban immigrant enclaves. Although this has certainly been true in the Boston area, it does not mean that immigrant suburbanization was a uniform process or one that has simply reproduced the earlier experience of upwardly mobile European immigrants (or more often their children). Exactly why this movement has occurred and what it means is a more complicated story.

First, a significant proportion of new immigrants moving outside Boston have gravitated toward the Commonwealth's older mill towns and industrial communities—places such as Chelsea and Lynn. Built around burgeoning shoe and garment factories in the nineteenth century, these cities saw their industrial production and population peak in the 1920s, followed by protracted decline. The downturn in manufacturing in the decades following World War II was particularly devastating to these communities, bringing staggering population losses between 1940 and 1980—38 percent in Chelsea, 20 percent in Lynn. Beginning in the 1980s, thousands of foreign-born new-comers took up residence in such neighborhoods as West Lynn and Chelsea's downtown district. By 2010, the foreign-born population of Chelsea reached 45 percent—the highest in the state—while Lynn's immigrant population reached 30 percent, the fourth highest (Table 4.1). These rates matched or exceeded those cities' foreign-born population rates in 1910, showing that new immigrants were settling in many of the same places as their predeces-sors a hundred years earlier.

Unlike European immigrants who flocked to the mills, however, jobs were not the decisive factor for newcomers choosing these destinations. While struggling local industries sometimes recruited Puerto Rican and Dominican workers in the 1960s and 1970s, newcomers arriving after 1980 were more likely to commute to construction or service jobs in surrounding communities. Their own cities, meanwhile, suffered from continued job loss and unemployment as well as high crime rates, failing schools, and ongo-ing fiscal crises. As such, these older mill towns were not obvious choices for settlement. Relatively lower housing costs, however, made them popular sites for refugee resettlement, including federally subsidized programs for Cubans and Southeast Asians in the 1970s and 1980s. In many cases, these resettlement programs planted the seeds of the region's growing Southeast Asian and Latino communities outside Boston. A 1990 study of Chelsea highlighted the city's appeal for Latino families, noting that 87 percent of Chelsea's Latino households had children under age 18, compared to 73 per-cent of such households in Boston. The supply of relatively affordable housing in these old manufacturing centers—including thousands of aging or vacant triple-deckers—together with some migrants' preference for living in smaller communities provided a strong draw for working-class immigrant families.[6]

These Massachusetts communities are part of a larger group of second-tier industrial cities in the Northeast that have become increasingly import-ant centers for poor and working-class immigrants. The exodus of many Latino, Cambodian, and other impoverished migrants from central cities such as Boston should therefore not be confused with classic patterns of suburban migration and upward mobility. Although some observers have claimed that new migrants are simply following in the footsteps of the old, the larger restructuring of the metropolitan economy means that the new arrivals have few job prospects near their homes and live in depressed communities where economic disinvestment has led to substandard housing, schools, and

Table 4.1. Percentage foreign born in Boston and selected suburbs.

Town/City	1910	1970	1980	1990	2000	2010	Top Groups in 2010
State	31	9	9	10	12	14	China, Dominican Republic, Brazil, Portugal, India, Haiti, Vietnam
Boston	36	13	15	20	26	27	Haiti, China, Dominican Republic, Vietnam, El Salvador
Chelsea	42*	14*	13	22*	36*	45*	Central America, Colombia
Framing-ham	(24)	(7)	(8)	12	21	26*	Brazil, India, China
Lynn	31	10	9	14	23	30*	Dominican Republic, Cambodia, Guatemala, Russia
Malden	(30)	10	9	14	26	41*	China, Vietnam, Brazil, Haiti,
Quincy	33	9	(8)	11	20	28*	China, Vietnam, Ireland

( ) Lower % foreign born than statewide average.
* Higher % foreign born than the city of Boston.

Source: U.S. Census of Population, 1910, 1970, 1980, 1990, 2000; 2010 data based on American FactFinder, Five-Year Sample Census, 2008–2012.

services. The situation for Latinos has been particularly dire. Since the 1980s, Chelsea and other heavily Latino mill towns and suburbs have had some of the lowest median incomes and highest poverty rates in the Commonwealth. They have become what one scholar calls "the tenements of the state"—reservoirs of lower-cost housing where migrants have struggled to build communities amid restructured economies that offer little likelihood of upward mobility or social integration in the future.[7]

In stark contrast to these poorer newcomers, educated and highly skilled migrants found homes in some of the region's most affluent suburbs. Attracted by Boston's burgeoning universities, medical centers, and high-tech industries, foreign-born professionals and technical workers began settling in Cambridge and Brookline during the Cold War era when the United States was actively recruiting foreign scientists, engineers, and researchers. Served by public transportation, both communities offered easy access to Harvard, MIT, and Boston University, and since the 1960s, they have hosted a higher proportion of foreign-born residents than the city of Boston itself. While these highly skilled migrants initially settled near centrally located universities and research facilities, some—mainly Taiwanese and Indian immigrants—began moving to affluent western suburbs as early as the 1960s and 1970s. Propelling this centrifugal movement was the growth of the high-tech sector around Route 128, where more than 1,200 corporations had located by 1973.[8] Soon, suburbs such as Waltham, Lexington, Newton, and Burlington became home to a growing cadre of high-tech workers from China, India, the Soviet Union, and Western Europe. Asian immigrants were especially visible in this movement, relocating to affluent suburbs where nearby employment and good public schools were the principal draw. Their high levels of education, English proficiency, and professional ties through local employers facilitated relatively rapid integration into these suburban communities.[9]

For highly skilled migrants, then, employment and education played an important role in where they settled, but that was not typically the case for less prosperous immigrants. Although the tech sector created both high- and low-skill jobs, very few unskilled immigrants were able to settle in the western suburbs. Fearing overdevelopment and changes in the social fabric of their communities, many of the towns along Route 128 had enacted large lot or "snob" zoning restrictions that precluded the building of affordable smaller homes or multifamily dwellings. Nor did they build much subsidized housing, except for projects designed for the elderly. As a result, very few unskilled immigrants, other than those employed as live-in domestics, settled in these areas. Restrictive housing policies, combined with discriminatory real estate and lending practices, meant that these suburbs would remain heavily white and (to a lesser degree) Asian American. The concentration of the area's foreign born in Cambridge, Brookline, and the western suburbs on the one hand and old industrial centers such as Lynn and Chelsea on the other hand reflected the class and racial divide of the dual knowledge/services economy that has developed in greater Boston since the 1950s.[10]

Although new immigrants have been concentrated at these two ends of the metropolitan economic spectrum, a growing number have also been moving into the region's more typical working-class or lower-middle-class suburbs. One scholar has characterized these communities as "one-step up suburbs," signifying their importance as centers of upward mobility for immigrants, just as many post-World War II suburbs were for earlier European groups.[11] The most popular destinations have been older inner-ring suburbs just north and south of the city, but a few of the more heterogeneous western suburbs also fit this description. These suburban communities had a long history of industrial development that attracted earlier waves of immigrants who built thriving ethnic communities. Since the 1980s these aging suburbs have been claimed by newer immigrants, who by 2010 made up as much as 40 percent of the population. Immigrant newcomers have helped revitalize and transform these communities and reinvent their economies.

To better understand this process, I'll briefly discuss three Boston area suburbs: Quincy, Framingham, and Malden. I have chosen these communities because of their varied geographic locations—south, west, and north of the city, respectively—and because they represent some of the fastest-growing immigrant suburbs between 1980 and 2010 (see Table 4.1). Moreover, the three communities felt the initial impact of the new immigration at different times: Quincy in the 1980s, Framingham in the 1990s, and Malden most notably after 2000. In all three, the new immigrants took up residence in older neighborhoods as white ethnics departed. But while the newcomers shared their predecessors' aspirations for middle-class suburban lifestyles, their movement into these communities has been shaped by different forces and has led to a rather different configuration of work and community life.

Like many inner-ring suburbs where new immigrants have settled, these three communities were older industrial centers that were home to large ethnic working-class populations prior to World War II. Capitalizing on its large granite deposits and coastal location just south of Boston, Quincy developed booming granite and shipbuilding industries beginning in the nineteenth century. Likewise, the town of Framingham—located twelve miles west of Boston along the region's main east-west railroad corridor—developed a host of manufacturing industries including carpet and woolen mills in the nineteenth century and paper manufacturing and auto assembly plants in the twentieth century. Five miles north of Boston, Malden became home to the Converse shoe factory as well as numerous manufacturers of knitted goods, chemicals, candy, and other products. Over the years, such industries attracted a diverse array of older immigrant groups, including Irish, French Canadians, Italians, Jews, Syrians, and Portuguese. These migrants built Catholic parishes, synagogues, and other religious and ethnic organizations that would help welcome new immigrants in the decades after World War II.

Like other local industrial communities, Quincy, Framingham, and Malden faced wrenching changes in the postwar period as the region's manufacturing economy shrunk, plants closed, and large numbers of older ethnic residents moved away. Unlike their industrial neighbors, however, these three communities moved aggressively—and with some success—to overhaul their decaying infrastructures and reinvent themselves within the emerging postindustrial economy. In Framingham, which suffered a string of plant closings in the 1970s and 1980s, the construction of Route 128 and the Massachusetts Turnpike (I-90) laid the groundwork for the town's emergence as a new edge city service and retail center. As retailers and malls proliferated, the town soon became home to the Golden Triangle—New England's largest suburban shopping district—as well as numerous corporate headquarters for retail and high-tech companies. During these same years, inner-ring suburbs such as Malden and Quincy also struggled with plant closings, outmigration, and eroding tax bases. But these two cities were fortunate in that both were selected as termini for expanded subway lines constructed by the Metropolitan Boston Transit Authority in the 1970s. Both cities, which had built substantial numbers of public housing units in the postwar period, now began issuing building permits for hundreds of multifamily homes and apartment buildings concentrated around the transit lines. Framingham too had dramatically expanded its housing options for working-class families in the 1960s and 1970s, rejecting restrictive zoning and building dozens of apartment complexes and a string of residential high-rises along the Route 9 commercial strip. With these new developments in place, new immigrant populations would arrive and thrive.

Quincy was one of the communities that began to grow again as Asian immigrants discovered the city, dramatically expanding its small Chinese American community. During the 1970s and 1980s the pressures of urban redevelopment in Chinatown had become critical, and many of the neighborhood's foreign-born residents began to move out. Quincy's abundant stock of rental properties attracted a small stream of these migrants in the late 1970s, many of whom later purchased homes in North Quincy and Wollaston. They did so by pooling assets and sharing homes with extended family members, typically with multiple wage earners per household. Many were restaurant or garment workers who were buying homes for the first time. According to a survey conducted in 1989, 76 percent of Asians in Quincy traveled to Boston's Chinatown at least once a week, while 40 percent commuted daily or multiple times per week; 80 percent cited the presence of the new Red Line train as a key factor in choosing Quincy.[12]

Quincy also attracted a growing number of Vietnamese families, many of whom were sponsored or assisted by the Wollaston Lutheran Church, which began outreach to the local Asian community in the mid-1980s. The church hired a Chinese- and Vietnamese-speaking pastor in 1988 and provided ESL classes, job placement, and other services for refugees and immigrants. Soon, such families were sponsoring relatives who came directly from China and Southeast Asia. Quincy's newcomers thus included a range of poorer refugees, working-class families, and middle-class business owners and white-collar workers.[13]

Affordable housing, accessible transportation, and basic immigrant services helped push Quincy's Asian American population from 330 in 1980 to 22,098 in 2010 (or 24 percent of the city's population). Along with other newcomers, they pushed the city's aggregate population upward once again. New Irish immigrants flocked there in the 1980s, Indians arrived in the 1990s, and a small but growing Arab and Muslim community coalesced around the Islamic Center in Quincy Point, a mosque founded by an earlier generation of Lebanese and Syrian immigrants who had settled near the shipyards. But the dominance of Chinese, Vietnamese, and other Asian immigrants—who comprised more than 65 percent of the foreign-born population in 2010—gave the city a distinctive Asian identity.[14]

This burgeoning community supported a growing number of Asian-owned restaurants, stores, and services that sprang up along Hancock Street in North Quincy and Wollaston. Asian cultural and social service programs were also established, some of them satellite offices of Chinatown organizations. In 2003 the city's first Asian American shopping center opened in Quincy Point, anchored by a large Chinese-owned supermarket. The opening of the mall sparked considerable attention and speculation that Quincy was becoming "Chinatown South" or "the new Flushing"—a reference to the Queens, New York, neighborhood where upwardly mobile Asian immigrants had settled a few years earlier. By 2000, in fact, Quincy's Asian American population was more than three times larger than the Asian American population of Boston's Chinatown.[15]

Like Quincy, Framingham also provided new opportunities for immigrants who arrived on the heels of the town's postwar deindustrialization and decline. As the older white working-class population abandoned downtown and the adjoining south side, migrant newcomers moved in. Puerto Ricans, who were hired at nearby farms and garden centers, first settled downtown in the late 1950s and the 1960s. Over the next two decades, they were joined by a growing number of newcomers from the Caribbean and Central and South America. Framingham's Latino population grew by 142 percent in the 1980s, making it one of the largest in the metro area. During these same years local synagogues helped resettle dozens of Soviet Jewish refugees, while high-tech firms along Route 128 began recruiting Chinese, Indian, and other highly skilled immigrant workers. Framingham's foreign-born share of the population thus expanded from less than 7 percent in 1970 to more than 26 percent in 2010.[16]

Among this new wave of immigrants, Brazilians made up the largest group. Beginning in the late 1980s, a steady stream of Brazilian migrants moved to the downtown area, where they found affordable apartments and a Portuguese-speaking community around St. Tarcisius, a Catholic parish that had served Italian and later Portuguese immigrants. Framingham was also one of the few Boston suburbs that offered bilingual education in Portuguese, an attractive option for newly arrived Brazilian families. Compared with Boston and Somerville, the other top destinations for Brazilians, Framingham attracted many more migrant families with children—14 percent of the town's Brazilian population in 1999–2001 compared to less than 9 percent of those in Boston and Somerville.[17] Moreover, rising rents in Allston (the center of Boston's Brazilian community) likely encouraged families to seek housing elsewhere. In Framingham, the typical suburban attractions of safety, amenities, and services—financed by a healthy tax base of retail business and commercial services—were enhanced by a linguistically friendly community and relatively affordable multifamily housing.

The town's Brazilian population thus grew exponentially in the 1990s, accounting for roughly 7 percent of the population by 2000 (the actual numbers were no doubt much higher, as many new Brazilian arrivals were undocumented). Researchers found that by 2003, Framingham had the highest percentage of Brazilian-born residents in the state and likely the country as well.[18] The newcomers were credited with revitalizing the old downtown area, founding more than forty new businesses by 1999, many of them occupying once vacant storefronts. Many also bought homes in the area, renovating deteriorating properties. Like Asians in Quincy, Brazilians created a thriving ethnoburb in Framingham on the remains of an older ethnic working-class community.[19]

Similar forces were at work in Malden, an inner-ring industrial city a few miles north of Boston. As in Quincy, the availability of affordable housing, accessible mass transit, and interfaith service programs for refugees began attracting Chinese and Vietnamese immigrants to Malden in the 1980s. The newcomers settled in the redeveloped areas west of downtown around the Orange Line. Many of them purchased homes, taking advantage of Malden's affordability. Its median home prices were significantly lower than those in Boston. Like Quincy's newcomers, Asian immigrants in Malden had higher incomes and educational levels than those in Chinatown but lower than Asians statewide. The Asian American population of Malden mushroomed from less than 1 percent in 1980 to 14 percent by 2000.[20]

Although Malden's Asian community grew rapidly in the 1990s, it was not as dominant as in Quincy. After 2000 Malden's foreign-born population became more diverse, attracting growing numbers of Haitians, Brazilians, North Africans, and others. In fact, the percentage of immigrants from Asia dropped from 46 percent of the total foreign born in 2000 to 40 percent in 2010, while those from Africa, Latin America, and the Caribbean increased their share from 35 to 47 percent. Such trends suggest that Malden is evolving into a polyethnic, multiracial suburb, much like its neighbors, Somerville, Everett, and Revere. Malden's more affordable housing stock and its well-regarded schools helped give it the second-highest percentage of immigrants in the metro area in 2010—second only to Chelsea.[21]

So, what do these one-step-up suburbs of Malden, Framingham, and Quincy have in common? As older industrial cities, they all had aging infrastructures and a native-born working-class population that was leaving as jobs moved to outer-ring suburbs, the Sunbelt, or abroad. Facing such decline, all three cities moved aggressively to reinvent themselves, either as edge cities or commuter suburbs with ample multifamily rental housing. Immigrants proved to be vital to this process as the native-born continued to abandon these cities in the 1960s and 1970s. Ironically, it was this depopulation and deindustrialization that made the immigrant influx possible as housing stock and commercial properties became more available and affordable. Mass transit as well as better-quality and linguistically friendly schools and churches also played a role. Ultimately, such suburbs have constituted the *new* immigrant zone of emergence where the desires of striving newcomers meshed well with the revitalization needs of local communities.

The story of these Boston suburbs, however, should make us skeptical of popular assumptions that newcomers have simply followed in the footsteps of earlier immigrants and that they will enjoy similar paths of upward mobility. That view does not take into account the reconfiguration of metropolitan economies and communities of the last fifty years. Indeed, immigrants arriving since the 1960s have encountered an opportunity structure dramatically different from earlier times. The new global economy has allowed some highly skilled immigrants to move directly to affluent suburbs, a feat rarely achieved by earlier Irish, Italian, or Jewish immigrants. Other newcomers, pushed out of the central city by redevelopment, gentrification, and soaring housing costs, settled in older working-class suburbs undergoing economic transformation; the ethnoburbs and polyethnic communities that they created played a role in metropolitan revitalization while offering the possibility of greater economic opportunity and social incorporation. These successes have tended to obscure the plight of those who have ended up in some of the region's most impoverished industrial towns and cities and who remain economically distressed and socially isolated from the mainstream. The diffusion of immigrants across the metropolitan landscape, then, has produced a diverse array of globalized communities that reflect the new polarities of the postindustrial service economy.

The suburban diffusion of immigrants seen in greater Boston has been occurring in metro areas across the country in recent decades. But the potential for suburban revitalization has been most evident in continuous and reemerging immigrant gateways, especially the older industrial centers of the Northeast and Midwest. Such metro areas have seen similar patterns of bimodal immigrant suburbanization, with high-skilled migrants settling in more affluent suburbs and working-class immigrants reclaiming housing and neighborhoods in the inner-ring industrial suburbs and older industrial sections of the outlying communities. In the Philadelphia area, immigration has figured prominently in the revitalization of older satellite industrial centers such as Norristown, whose residents find jobs in the nearby King of Prussia retail center, as well as inner-ring suburbs such as Upper Darby, once a thriving textile town that became the terminus of an east-west subway line connecting it to downtown Philadelphia.[22] Similarly, once-declining industrial cities such as Passaic and Paterson, New Jersey, and Bridgeport, Connecticut, in the New York metro area and older industrial suburbs north and west of Chicago—such places as Cicero and Skokie—have seen a major influx of immigrants in the last few decades.[23] In all of these suburban towns and cities, newcomers have boosted declining or stagnating populations and labor forces, revitalized older housing areas, and rejuvenated commercial districts by opening small shops and businesses. Indeed, without the immigrants arriving in the last forty years, the populations and workforces of most northeastern and midwestern metro areas would be shrinking.

But whether such areas become one-step-up suburbs, where immigrants can share in the metro region's wider prosperity and have access to decent schools and other services to advance the next generation, remains the key issue. This study of immigrant suburbs in Boston suggests that an ample supply of affordable housing is an important precondition but is not sufficient in itself. Access to jobs via convenient mass transit and/or the development of an economic infrastructure that can support local employment and services is critical if such communities are to become something more than just reservoirs of low-cost housing. Planning efforts must therefore be done with immigrant integration in mind rather than vilifying immigrants or falling back on familiar schemes to attract middle-class professional residents. Ultimately, though, impoverished older suburbs and mill towns cannot effect these changes alone; they will need the support of regional and statewide planning efforts to incorporate new immigrant communities into broader metropolitan economies while reducing the growing social inequalities that plague them.

CHAPTER 5

Immigrant Cities as Reservations
for Low-Wage Labor

Michael B. Katz and Kenneth Ginsburg

On weekday mornings, white jitney vans scurry along the streets of Paterson, New Jersey, stopping to pick up passengers. Their destination reads "New York City." They are owned by a Peruvian immigrant who transposed a transportation practice common in Lima. They are one of the modalities for moving Paterson's increasingly immigrant working-age population to jobs outside the city, where the large majority of them are employed.

In three immigrant cities that are the focus of our research—Paterson and Passaic, New Jersey, and Bridgeport, Connecticut—between 75 and 87 percent of the employed population work outside their city of residence. These small and medium-size cities have become the source of low-wage labor for the municipalities that surround them. Their historic function has changed: formerly exporters of manufactured goods, now they are exporters of human capital.

At the same time, these cities are also experiencing immigrant-led urban revitalization. The term "revitalization" is bandied about in urban studies literature but is rarely defined. To us, urban revitalization consists of increases in population, commerce, occupancy, leisure/entertainment venues, services, and safety. Although these features of the revitalization process form a package, population increase comes first. The process is facilitated by a distinctive type (or types) of private agency and by sets of public/private relationships, embodied often in special services districts and community development corporations (in Paterson, for example, the New Jersey Community Development Corporation and the Hamilton Partnership).

This revitalization follows on roughly a half century of *devitalization*. Devitalization refers to a decrease in each of the factors listed above. Depopulation, dying downtowns, vacant stores, disappearing movie theaters and restaurants, bank closings, and rising crime rates: together these squeezed the life and vitality out of older American cities. They are what revitalization—often led by immigrants—has begun to turn around.

Immigrant-led revitalization in small and medium-size cities does not depend on reindustrialization or even on the widespread prior availability of semi- and low-skilled work. Nor is it accompanied at first by a decline in official poverty or a rise in real estate values. Rather, at its core it is residential, driven by newcomers who increase population, form new communities, and establish small businesses and services but for the most part work outside the city.

Most of the abundant new literature on recent immigration concentrates on the traditional immigrant ports of entry and on new and emerging immigrant gateways.[1] As in urban studies literature more generally, small and medium-size cities remain relatively neglected. However, these cities house a significant fraction of the population and are home to huge numbers of immigrants. Indeed, in 2010, 61 percent of the U.S. foreign-born population lived in municipalities that numbered fewer than 200,000, with 12 percent in cities between 100,000 and 199,000, 33 percent in cities and towns of 20,000–99,000, and 16 percent in smaller places. Immigration, in fact, is transforming the demographics, economies, and spatial organization of these small and medium-size cities.

With case studies of three cities—Paterson and Passaic, New Jersey, and Bridgeport, Connecticut—we are studying the impact of immigration on urban revitalization. All three of these cities once hummed with manufacturing that kept them vibrant and prosperous. As manufacturing industries folded or decamped, the native white population also left in large numbers, leaving behind the hulks of factories along with empty stores, dying downtowns, decimated tax revenues, and high rates of crime and poverty. Immigrants have begun to turn these faltering cities around. As is well known, the repeal of the notorious nationality-based immigration quotas in 1965 and subsequent federal legislation opened the door to immigrants whose numbers matched those arriving during the late nineteenth and early twentieth centuries, only now primarily from Central and Latin America, the Caribbean, and Asia instead of Europe. Drawn by the availability of low-cost housing as well as by the presence of relatives and communities of conationals, they have moved in large numbers into small and medium-size cities, where their impact is palpable on the streets, in the schools, in the real estate market, in small businesses and urban amenities, in the labor market, and—slower to emerge—in city government. One of the questions we have asked is what role this immigration plays in redefining the function of these cities.

We hypothesized that immigration has transformed them partly into reservations for low-wage labor. To test this hypothesis, we turned to data sets that (1) show whether individuals are employed in the cities in which they live and (2) enable us to compare the occupational structure and incomes of residents who work outside the cities with those of nonresident employees in them. The data provide striking confirmation of our hypothesis. In the rest of this chapter, we present the data and discuss its significance.

The data used to test this hypothesis comes primarily from three sources: the U.S. Census Bureau, the Environmental Systems Research Institute, and the Federal Bureau of Investigation. These sources enabled us to gather and analyze demographic, economic, and crime data and permitted us to examine patterns beginning in the middle of the twentieth century through the first decade of the twenty-first century.

The basic facts about these cities are told easily and repeat a familiar story. Despite some variation in the total population from the early twentieth century through 2010, there is a similar tale of growth, decline/stasis, and growth resumed—with the turnaround in population beginning in the last decades of the twentieth century (Figure 5.1).

With an official 2010 census population of slightly more than 145,000 residents, Paterson, New Jersey, embodies a long history of immigration. Paterson was founded in 1792 by Alexander Hamilton, who envisioned the city developing a strong manufacturing sector to lead America in industrialization.[2] Its location in northern New Jersey on the Passaic River along the Great Falls of Paterson provided a source of power for manufacturing, especially before the rise of coal-powered electricity.[3] Throughout the nineteenth century, Paterson was known for manufacturing silk in addition to having a large Eastern and Southern European immigrant population and for its radical politics.[4] Its silk industry remained strong through World War II and declined afterward.[5] Much like the silk industry, other important industries, notably firearm, aircraft, and locomotive manufacturing, declined along with population and the general quality of life in the city.

Bridgeport, Connecticut, a city of just under 110,000 residents in 2010 located along the Pequonnock River in Fairfield County, also boasts a substantial immigration history. It was settled by Englishmen in 1639 who

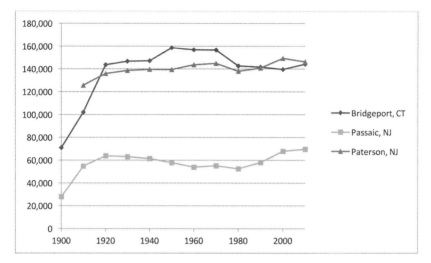

Figure 5.1. Total population.

Source: U.S. Census Bureau.

bought the land from the Paugussett tribe and was incorporated in 1821.[6] Before the industrial revolution, the city's economic strengths included whaling and shipbuilding.[7] By the mid-1800s the city developed into a manufacturing center that attracted a large immigrant population. The city became a center for producing a number of items, including sewing machines, saddles, milling machines, corsets, carriages, and ammunition.[8] The city's economic reputation built on its ammunition industry, which thrived during World War I and World War II. In the late 1800s and early 1900s, this booming industry attracted a large number of immigrants at the peak of immigration during this period.[9] Many of these immigrants were East Europeans and Italians, resulting in a large Catholic population within Bridgeport in the first half of the twentieth century.[10] Following the conclusion of World War II, Bridgeport experienced significant population decline and deindustrialization.

Passaic, a city with a population of approximately 63,000 residents in 2010, has a long history of immigration that has continued to the present day. The city was founded by Dutch settlers in 1679 on the Passaic River in present-day northeastern New Jersey and initially was named Acquackanonk after the Native American tribe who originally inhabited the area. Starting in the nineteenth century, Passaic developed into a metalworking and textile center throughout the industrial revolution. With its growing economic prominence and increase in population, Passaic received a city charter in 1873. It continued to grow economically and demographically, thriving on the influx of immigrants in the late nineteenth and early twentieth centuries, and attracted a large Orthodox Jewish population.[11] However, by the post-World War II era, it became apparent that Passaic's manufacturing was in decline along with other aspects of the city.

Population growth coincided with the in-migration of foreign-born residents into each of these cities. Early in the twentieth century, each housed a substantial number of immigrants—in 1910, the foreign-born populations were between 36 percent and 53 percent of their populations. Adding in the second generation—the children of immigrants—boosts the foreign-stock population to between 73 and 82 percent. Truly, these were immigrant cities. With the nationality-based quotas of the 1920s, the Great Depression, and World War II, immigration largely dried up. In each city, the proportion of foreign-born residents reached its nadir in 1970, about the same time as the lowest point in its population history. The growth of immigrant populations in each city rebounded with the national upsurge in immigration in the decades after the 1965 repeal of the quota legislation (Figure 5.2). Today, these are once again immigrant cities. Foreign-born residents—between 26 and 46 percent of their official 2010 populations including undocumented immigrants—would raise the percentage a substantial but indeterminate amount. Adding in the children of immigrants age eighteen and under shows the foreign-born stock at between 35 and 62 percent. Unfortunately, a limitation of the American Community Survey is that it fails to include adults whose parents are foreign born, which undoubtedly deflates the percentages provided above.

In the early twentieth century, the immigrant populations of these cities originated primarily in Europe. Today they come from Central and Latin America, the Caribbean, and Asia. Bundled together, the largest group is Hispanic—about half the population—although this label masks the diversity in the population's origins, lumping together quite demographically and socially diverse groups—in Paterson, for example, Dominicans, Peruvians, and Puerto Ricans.

It was manufacturing jobs that attracted immigrants in the early twentieth century. With no public transportation in the age before the automobile, immigrants needed to walk to where they worked. This meant that these cities, of necessity, were places of both work and residence for their new arrivals. The availability of work attracted and held them. In 1910, 48 percent of

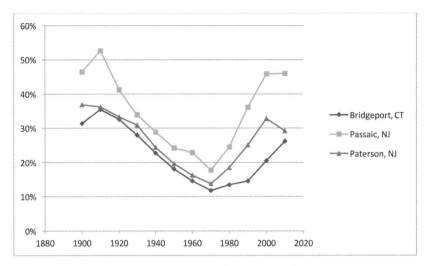

Figure 5.2. Foreign-born population.

Source: U.S. Census Bureau.

Bridgeport residents, 50 percent of Paterson residents, and 63 percent of Passaic residents worked in manufacturing.[12]

In the late twentieth and early twentieth centuries, this relation between work and residence changed. The availability of manufacturing work no longer served as the principal source of attraction. In fact, the proportion of the population employed in manufacturing continued to decline, dropping to around 6 percent in 2010. Instead, immigrants worked most often in service-sector jobs, transportation, and construction. The widespread availability of buses and private automobiles enabled them to find work outside the cities in which they lived. And this is what they did (Figure 5.3). The proportion of employed residents working elsewhere in 2010 ranged between 75 percent and 87 percent. In Paterson in 2010, 40,314 of the 50,330 employed residents worked outside the city.

Why did the foreign born decide to settle in these cities as opposed to living closer to work? Undoubtedly, various factors were at play. Low rent certainly was one attraction. In all, rents were about 16 percent lower in these cities than in surrounding municipalities (Figure 5.4). Low rents resulted from the exit of middle-class whites and some blacks, along with deindustrialization and the consequent population decline. Early immigrant arrivals established nascent communities attractive to new immigrants and their

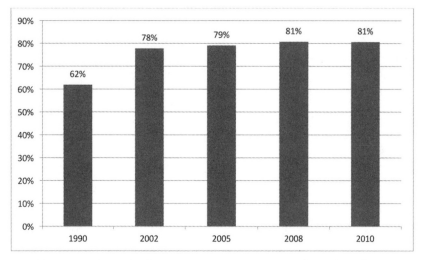

Figure 5.3. Percent of residents working outside place of residence, average of the three cities.

Source: U.S. Census Bureau.

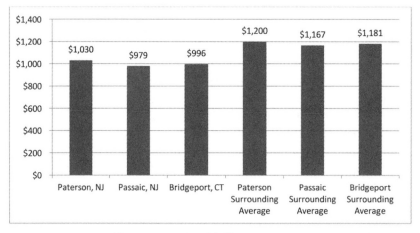

Figure 5.4. 2010 Median gross rent.

Source: U.S. Census Bureau.

families who received preferences under U.S. immigration law. A large but indeterminate number of undocumented immigrants found support in local ethnic communities. At the same time, an extensive public transportation network enabled workers to find and reach employment outside the cities.

A substantial number of immigrants did open small businesses—restaurants and enterprises providing local services to meet the needs of the new ethnic communities. It is not clear how many of these ethnic businesses are owned by city residents and how many by ethnic entrepreneurs who live elsewhere. They do, however, provide a modest amount of low-skilled employment for local residents. As part of our larger project, we are analyzing the size and geography of businesses in these cities. At this point, we can say that most of the businesses in these cities are truly small. Taking the three cities together, in 2010, 50 percent of businesses employed at most one person; 29 percent employed two to five, and only 11 percent employed more than fifteen (Figure 5.5). From their names, it is clear that many served the immigrant community: El Tempano Restaurant, the Gonzalez Travel Agency, the Turkish Grill and Café, the De Leon Money Transfer, Arab Voice, and Oficina Del Voto Dominicano.

Drive into Paterson from the west, and the main street is lined with small businesses serving the local population. The lack of vacant storefronts is remarkable. Similarly, the automobile traffic downtown is heavy; most,

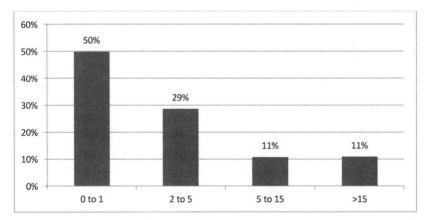

**Figure 5.5. Number of paid employees for all businesses,
average of three cities.**

Source: Environmental Systems Research Institute.

although not all, storefronts are occupied with low-end retail and services
that are surviving despite a new downtown mall. Continuing through the
immigrant neighborhoods, the observer is struck by tidy small homes and
neighborhood bodegas with a vibrant Arab quarter centered around the
southern section of Main Street. The new residents sustain these small businesses, bring life to the streets, and inject cash into the economy. But for the
most part they leave the city to work. We cannot identify the ethnic origins
and birthplaces of the workers who leave these cities for employment. However, there is no doubt that a high fraction of the workers exported by these
cities are foreign born. Indeed, during the period of immigration growth the
average percentage working outside their city of residence increased from 62
percent in 1990 to 81 percent in 2008.

The labor force exported by these cities works primarily at low-wage jobs
in retail, health care, and human services as well as in construction and transportation. In Paterson, 16 percent of residents who work outside the city are
employed in goods-Producing industries, which include construction work
and small-scale goods production as well as more conventional manufacturing; 27 percent work in trade, transportation, and utilities, which encom-
passes retail; and 58 percent work in all other services, which is where health
care and human services workers are found (Figure 5.6).

The working population can be divided into three groups: residents who
work outside the city, nonresidents who work in the city, and residents who
work in the city. In economic terms, the nonresidents do best; the residents

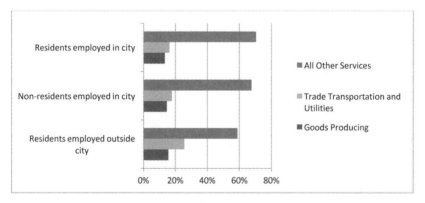

**Figure 5.6. Industry by relation of work and residence: three cities, 2010
(average of percentages).**

Source: U.S. Census Bureau.

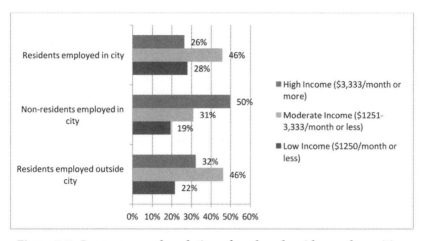

Figure 5.7. Income group by relation of work and residence: three cities, 2010 (average of percentages).

Source: U.S. Census Bureau.

who remain in the city do the worst. The data allow us only to divide the workforce into three groups by income: $1,250 per month or less, $1,250–3,332 per month, and $3,333 per month or more (Figure 5.7). For purposes of discussion, we will call these low, medium, and high—although the latter is high only in this context. A quarter of the residents who work outside the city earn low incomes, and 24 percent earn high incomes. By contrast, 46 percent of nonresidents working in the cities earned high incomes, while only 21 percent of residents working in the city are in the top income category, and 31 percent find themselves in the lowest income category.

The immigrant residents who leave the city for work each day by and large lack the education needed for the city's better jobs, and they may be hindered by a lack of language skills as well. But they are welcome—indeed, needed—by the restaurants, nursing homes, supermarkets, construction, and unskilled or semiskilled manufacturing in the towns and cities within commuting distance. Despite their recent arrival, marginal English-language ability, and limited schooling, the labor force participation rates of foreign-born men are higher than those of either native-born whites or African Americans. In a sample drawn from northern New Jersey cities for 2011, among eighteen- to sixty-four-year old men, labor force participation was 88 percent for the foreign born compared to 84 percent for native whites and 67 percent for African Americans. These participation rates reflect national trends;

immigrants show consistently higher rates than do other population groups.[13] At the same time, bundling incomes within households partially offsets the low wages paid to immigrants. Indeed, taking the median for these three cities, foreign-born household heads earn about 55 percent of total household income compared to 69 percent for the native born.

These cities always have produced and exported products. In the late nineteenth and early twentieth centuries, manufactured goods were their primary export. Today it is people—human capital, largely for low-skilled and semiskilled jobs. Most accounts of the history of urban economies trace a trajectory from manufacturing to service. While this is valid, for these small cities another coexistent trajectory also captures their history: the transition from an economy based on the export of goods to one based on the export of human labor.

The exchange of workers between municipalities shows that it is not only a deficit in jobs that motivated residents of our study cities to look elsewhere for work. In Paterson in 2010, 28,011 members of the workforce lived outside the city. These cities contain, in fact, many solid middle-class jobs, such as teachers, police, firefighters, municipal officials, and health care technicians, to name some of the most obvious. Anecdotal evidence—which is the best we have right now—supported by the income and occupational data shows that the better jobs by and large go to workers who enter these cities from other municipalities. In Paterson, we were told, most of the teachers, police, and firefighters lived outside the city. So did the attorneys who flocked to the city because it is a county seat. The young staff of a community development corporation we interviewed either lived outside the city or hoped to depart soon. In Paterson, anecdotal evidence is clear and consistent: departure for residence, if not always work, in the suburbs usually accompanies economic mobility. (One exception is city politicians. One of the upwardly mobile young city politicians with whom we talked lives in one of the old factory buildings converted into lofts.)

Industrious, family-centered, often entrepreneurial immigrants did more than provide these formerly manufacturing cities with a new export— human labor. They also reduced crime. Indeed, immigration has exerted an astounding impact on crime rates within these cities. Figure 5.8 traces the correspondence between the growth of an immigrant population in the 1990s and the decrease in crime. Taking the average of the three cities, crime rates per 100,000 population plummeted from just over 8,000 in 1990 to 4,000 in 2010. Other scholars, notably Robert Sampson and John MacDonald, have

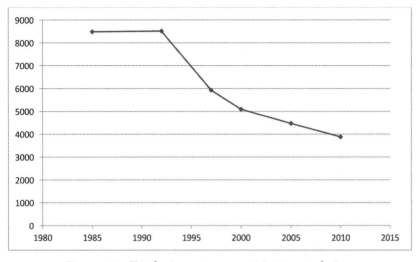

**Figure 5.8. Total crimes, rate per 100,000 population,
average of three cities.**

Source: Federal Bureau of Investigation.

discovered similar reductions in crime associated with the growth of immigrant populations—reductions larger than in cities lacking large numbers of immigrants.[14] The reasons why crime has declined await more analysis. Clearly, though, they must include fear of deportation, high labor force participation, immigrant culture, higher marriage rates, and improved policing.

What is the significance of these trends? Why does it matter that extraordinary proportions of residents work outside the cities in which they live? First, the pattern we have excavated points to a historically unprecedented shift in the relation between place of work and residence among working-class immigrants in small and medium-size cities that, in an ironic twist, have taken on some of the historic functions of suburbs. In post-World War II America, middle-class and affluent suburbs became classic bedroom communities. Now this function has been assumed by these new immigrant municipalities, although it is more appropriate to think of them as reservations for low-wage labor than as bedroom communities.[15] (We use "reservation" in the dictionary sense of an area of land set aside for occupation.) The price of housing in neighboring municipalities acts as an informal market-led agency of exclusion—preventing the entrance of an immigrant working class through the high cost of housing. Working-class immigrants are not forced into the small and medium-size cities that have become their homes—as Native Americans were forced onto reservations—and are not excluded from more affluent municipalities by explicitly segregationist mechanisms. The barriers, instead, are "neutral" market mechanisms. But they have the same effect of concentrating them in space and leaving them few residential alternatives.

Second, the proximity of a nonresident low-wage labor force serves nearby municipalities well. They do not have to educate the children of immigrants, pay for affordable or subsidized housing, pick up the local costs associated with poverty, or manage ethnic diversity. Instead, they can draw as they need on a ready flexible pool of reliable workers to care for their elderly, work the cash registers in supermarkets, wash dishes in their restaurants, clean the rooms of their hotels, and tend their lawns—all with minimum responsibility for their well-being.

Looked at another way, however, the picture does not appear either as bleak or as exploitative. From the viewpoint of the struggling cities in which they live, these immigrant workers—regardless of where they are employed—bring population growth, increased tax revenues, commercial revival, and cultural vitality, and they lower crime rates as well. Immigrants compose the key engines driving these cities on the road to revitalization.

Revitalization means more than population and economic growth. It also embraces civil society and civic life. Take, for example, Union City, a small northern New Jersey city, long ago a center of the lace-making industry and now primarily Hispanic and poor—a city much like nearby Paterson and Passaic. In his gripping account of the stunning about-face of the city's deteriorating public schools, *Improbable Scholars*, David L. Kirp points out that despite its grim statistical portrait, "Union City remains vibrant." Within the city "civil life" thrives nourished by immigrant enclaves, each with its own associations and institutions. "Despite the grim figures, Union City would surely rank high in a survey of personal happiness."[16]

From the point of view of immigrants, these cities offer inexpensive housing, the security and comfort of living among coethnics, proximity to jobs, and an opportunity to bundle the incomes of household members. They also hold out the promise of social mobility for the second generation. These small and medium-size cities may be reservations for low-wage labor, but they also provide the first tentative steps toward the realization of the American Dream.

PART III

The Politics of Immigration
and Revitalization

CHAPTER 6

Old Maps and New Neighbors:
The Spatial Politics of Immigrant Settlement

Jamie Winders

In a study of the role that images play in urban transformation, Sharon Zukin and her coauthors ask, "Can the meanings of place have as 'real' an impact on growth and decline as material factors?"[1] This chapter raises a related question. Can contests over the social or cultural meanings of place revitalize neighborhoods undergoing demographic changes? Here, I mean "revitalize" in a very basic sense—to give new life or vigor. The contemporary *and historic* meanings of place can be driving forces in efforts to revitalize neighborhoods, particularly when those historic meanings are understood to be in danger of disappearing. In situations where the neighborhood's contemporary reality contrasts sharply with dominant versions of its past, that past can be revitalized, in the sense of resurrected, and former understandings of neighborhoods can become ways to intervene in an unfamiliar present. This chapter examines that process of revitalizing old neighborhoods in the context of immigrant settlement in Nashville, Tennessee.

Throughout the twentieth century and into the twenty-first century, immigrant settlement has been a key way that urban neighborhoods change and that the links between place and identity, present and past, fuse and fray. Since most immigrants in the United States live in metropolitan or suburban areas, the city, especially the neighborhood,[2] has been the primary lens through which immigration has been understood.[3] Although other sites of daily life, such as workplaces and public spaces, also shape immigrant experiences,[4] the neighborhood is where the rubber meets the road, so to speak, in the politics of immigrant integration. Immigrant settlement can revitalize declining neighborhoods by creating new businesses, housing demands, and enrollments for public schools.[5] It can change a neighborhood's physical environment in ways that are sometimes framed as revitalization and sometimes as a loss of identity or heritage.[6] In still other cases, one immigrant group can replace or join another in models of ethnic succession that both echo those from Chicago and challenge us to think anew about the spatial politics of immigration.[7] In all these ways, the picture of immigration and urban change in America, as seen from the perspective of the neighborhood, is complex.

This chapter explores a portion of that complicated picture of immigration and urban dynamics in a part of the United States that has been marginal in discussions of both topics. Southern U.S. cities have been largely ignored in research on American cities in part because they have not always played key roles in the South's development and in part because many classic urban processes, such as industrialization, were minor players in the South's economy through the late twentieth century.[8] Similarly, the South has been almost entirely absent from discussions of immigration until very recently. Throughout the twentieth century, people, especially African Americans, mainly *left* the South, making it a region of out-migration more than in-migration. Only in the last two decades have immigrants come in large numbers to the South.[9]

This chapter thus adds to understandings of the relationship between immigration and U.S. cities by considering it from a different place. In 2000, Mike Davis examined "the consequences of putting Latinos where they clearly belong: in the center of debate about the future of the American city."[10] Nearly two decades later, thinking about where Latino/as belong in debates about American cities involves a much greater range of places, especially in the South and Midwest. Through a case study of the spatial politics of neighborhood change and immigrant incorporation in Nashville, Tennessee, in the late 2000s, this chapter shows how struggles over the social and cultural meaning of neighborhoods experiencing immigrant settlement can be understood as struggles over competing versions of urban revitalization, of how to bring a neighborhood (back) to life.

In the late 1990s and early 2000s Nashville, like many southern and midwestern cities, saw the arrival and settlement of Latino immigrants, both directly from Latin America and through secondary migration from such places as Chicago and Houston.[11] A majority of Latin Americans in Nashville came from Mexico, but many also came from various parts of Central and South America, making its Latino population diverse in terms of nationality, class, and other factors. Because Nashville had been a prominent refugee relocation site since the 1960s, its international community also included smaller groups of refugees from global hot spots around the world.[12] By the late 2000s Nashville's population was between 10 and 12 percent foreign born, and the Music City was marching to the beat of an increasingly diverse band.

The research presented here draws on eighteen months of qualitative fieldwork (2006–2008) in southeast Nashville, the quadrant of the city where most foreign-born residents settled in the 2000s. Historically, southeast Nashville was white and working class, with small pockets of black settlement. Its northernmost neighborhood, Woodbine, developed in the 1920s and boomed in the 1950s and 1960s as the prime postwar suburb in a growing city. The southernmost part of southeast Nashville, Antioch, experienced explosive residential and commercial growth a decade later in the 1970s, when Nashville, like many southern cities, began to sprawl outward. By the 2000s Antioch was one of the few remaining spaces for development in Nashville, and seemingly everyone in search of (reasonably) affordable housing was moving there. By the time of this study, Woodbine was increasingly known as Nashville's "Little Mexico" and Antioch was known as "Hispanioch," making both areas synonymous with the city's growing foreign-born, especially Latino, population, even as both areas also remained home to long-term white (and, to a lesser extent, black) residents.

This chapter focuses on interviews and ethnographic fieldwork with long-term white and black residents and new Latino immigrants in Woodbine and Antioch. Through a discussion of this material, it highlights how long-term residents in particular mobilized collective memories of their neighborhoods to make sense of local changes, including but not limited to immigrant settlement. In its main, the chapter points to an unexpected way that immigrants can revitalize cities—in this case, by becoming a motivation to reanimate, or bring back to life, *old* maps of neighborhoods as a response to a new social reality shaped by immigrant settlement and other urban transformations. In Nashville, neighborhood responses to immigration were bound up with not just the ways that immigrants occupied and reconfigured the city's *present* landscape, as many studies have shown.[13] Such responses were also bound up with the ways that an immigrant presence articulated with collective memories of a local *past*. As a number of scholars have suggested, immigrant belonging in host communities is "geographically mediated" through the social spaces within which immigrants and long-term residents encounter one another.[14] This chapter adds to these arguments by showing that the spatial mediation of immigrant belonging also takes place through symbolic contests over *historical* sites and collective memories that new immigrants inadvertently redefine. When new immigrants and old neighborhoods collide, elements of local histories can become a means to revitalize those old neighborhoods and to transform their public images in ways that shape immigrant incorporation and exclusions.

Recalling Neighborhood

In assessing neighborhood revitalization, the first question to ask is, *the neighborhood according to whom?*[15] Whose version or understanding of neighborhood is being brought to life or revitalized? In Nashville, long-term black and white residents and Latino immigrants saw and understood neighborhood in different ways, even when they lived side by side. As a result, the question of neighborhood change was particularly hard to answer. Many long-term residents had lived in southeast Nashville for decades or had a regular presence in it since childhood. When they described their *present* neighborhood, they often called on place-names and neighborhood boundaries from as early as the 1930s. A mental map of the neighborhood "as it was" remained central to their own present sense of place, even as material evidence of that past was fading from the built environment.

Burton, for example, a white man born in 1926, moved with his family to the southeast Nashville neighborhood of Radnor in 1929. He lived in Radnor until 1956, when he moved his own young family farther south in the county, in a pattern replicated for many white residents of his generation. Despite moving away from Radnor, Burton maintained a daily presence in southeast Nashville through his business there until retirement in 1993. Like many long-term residents, he described Radnor as a tight-knit community. "We were so close up on the street there [in] Radnor," Burton explained. "I could name every kid going up one street and another." Although he moved away in 1956, Burton's sense of Radnor as a distinct neighborhood continued to shape his understanding of self and community, and he continued to see himself as from and intimately tied to Radnor as a neighborhood.

Many Latino immigrants living in the same part of Nashville, by contrast, knew very little about the boundaries, identities, or histories of where they lived. A passage from an interview with a young man from Mexico demonstrates this trend:

Sandra: I have another question ... What is the name of your neighborhood?

Arturo: The—?

Sandra: The name of your neighborhood?

Arturo: Oh, the one I live in now? Well, it is a nice neighborhood more ...

Sandra: No, what do you call it?

Arturo: It is a more peaceful place, that's the only thing I can tell you because ...

Sandra: What name does that place have? What is the name you know it by?

Arturo: Well, it is a ... They are apartments. I don't really know what they are called. ... No, I can't remember, but it is a nice place compared to the other one.

At the time of this 2007 interview, Arturo had lived in Nashville for a year. He was not unusual in struggling to answer a question about neighborhood. Arturo knew that his current apartment complex was a "nice place" in comparison to where he had lived before, but he did not see it as a bounded neighborhood with a definitive meaning, as did the long-term white residents living around him. Although Arturo lived in a neighborhood in one sense, in another he did not simply because he did not see his current place of residence as a neighborhood proper.

Sometimes, questions about neighborhood became questions about immigrant networks more generally. Carlos, for example, an older Mexican man who had lived in Nashville since 2002, could only explain that his neighborhood "belongs to Davidson [County] ... near I[nterstate]-24." When asked about his neighborhood's boundaries, he stretched them to include his wider daily path and social connections throughout Nashville and beyond: construction and cleaning work sites across Middle Tennessee, his friends' homes "even outside of Nashville," and Indianapolis, Indiana, where he had friends as well. In this way, "neighborhood" for Carlos was not the geographic area where he lived but the spatially dispersed social network he maintained—a community without propinquity.[16] Thus, for Latino immigrants living in southeast Nashville, the very features that defined neighborhood for many long-term white residents—neighborhood names, boundaries, landmarks, or local histories—were invisible. Residents living side by side in this changing part of the city both did and did not live in the same neighborhood, which they defined and understood in different ways.

Narrating Neighborhood Transitions

> Goodness, I don't know what to tell you. I guess—I don't
> know. Maybe in the 1970s? I don't know. I really can't—
> it's hard to tell.
>   —Burton, long-term white resident, in response
>   to a question about when Radnor peaked

A surprising finding in interviews with long-term black and white residents in southeast Nashville was the difficulties many of them faced when asked to narrate neighborhood change, as this quote from Burton shows. Although long-term residents could recall much about their neighborhood's history, many were unsure about how to describe neighborhood change and, in particular, how immigrant settlement in the late 1990s and early 2000s related to wider transformations in their neighborhoods. Most long-term residents were certain that their neighborhoods had changed over time. They were less clear, though, about when those changes began, what precipitated them, and how, if at all, neighborhood decline was related to immigrant settlement. As public discourse around immigration and its threat to local communities grew shrill in the late 2000s, from the perspective of the neighborhood, immigration's effects were hard to tease out amid wider urban transitions in Nashville. Even in a study of the effects of immigrant settlement on neighborhoods, it was difficult to overlook the fact that the people most directly impacted by this phenomenon were unsure what it meant for their neighborhood.

A handful of historical sites and events, however, helped bring clarity to many long-term residents' narrations of neighborhood change and immigrant settlement, providing anchor points in the interpretive scaffolding used to frame and make sense of demographic and neighborhood change. Although many studies point to the "appropriation of social space" as "a critical means of empowerment for Latino immigrants,"[17] this appropriation becomes particularly salient when it takes place within sites that are historically meaningful to host communities. When immigration's *spatial* manifestations take place on the grounds of key *historical* memories for receiving communities, the politics of immigrant reception get caught up in the politics of nostalgia. In a new destination such as Nashville, the spaces in which immigrants interacted with local memories became central to the process of immigrant incorporation.

This interaction between immigrant presence and local past can be seen in debates over an informal day-labor site along a major thoroughfare in southeast Nashville, Murfreesboro Road. The site where Latino day laborers gathered near a gas station on Murfreesboro Road anchored many narrations of neighborhood change for long-term white and black residents. Across interviews, its transformation into a "little Mexican town" was, in the words of an African American teacher from the area, a flashpoint in Nashville's immigration politics. As early as 2001, for example, it was described as "ground zero"[18] for change in the area. In 2004, representatives for local neighborhood and business groups raised concerns over day labor's impact on business growth, and in 2005 local ordinances to stop street-side solicitation of work were suggested.[19] In 2006 metro police in Nashville identified the area as the city's heaviest concentration of Latino residents, and by 2007 it was the subject of much concern for police and local residents.[20]

For many long-term residents, the gas station on Murfreesboro Road stood out not only because of the visibility of Latino day laborers gathering there but also because of what the site had previously been. Through the early 1970s,[21] the space where the gas station now stood had been home to the Crescent Drive-In Theatre, a popular gathering place for area teenagers and the heart of the local community. A *current* point of gathering and departure for Latino men seeking work, it was a *former* point of gathering and departure for local teenagers seeking diversion. According to interviews with long-term residents, the bus stop at this intersection was often the starting point for narrations of what the neighborhood had been, as residents described mile-long transects from the bus stop into surrounding neighborhoods along which they could identify every house and family. Now these same paths charted dramatic change, as they saw houses with families they no longer knew *at the same time* that they saw Latino men gathering around the gas station. By the 2000s, most long-term residents had abandoned businesses around the gas station on Murfreesboro Road and avoided contact with Latino day laborers. Nonetheless, the site remained deeply meaningful, linked as it was to their recollections of and claims to the neighborhood they remembered. In this way, the day-labor site became the place associated with the greatest and most contested change in southeast Nashville not only through the arrival of Latino day laborers but also through the perceived loss of a neighborhood landmark that itself was gone long before Latino immigrants arrived. The Latino men gathering at the gas station were unaware of what that space meant to long-term residents, as they were of how their presence articulated with a local past now experienced as a loss for some.

Perhaps the strongest *event* through which long-term residents narrated neighborhood change associated with immigrant settlement was the advent of busing schoolchildren across Nashville from the 1970s to the late 1990s to create racial balance in public schools. As was the case in many U.S. cities,[22] in Nashville a complicated pairing of public schools bused children between white inner suburbs and the city's black center in an effort to undo ingrained patterns of racial segregation across neighborhoods. Over time, federally mandated busing in Nashville led to white flight from the county itself, the closing of some public schools, and fierce debate over how to intervene in urban geographies of inequality.

In the eyes of many long-term white residents, busing brought substantial change to southeast Nashville. It fatally "fragmented" neighborhoods, as one long-term resident described the "trauma" of a 1971 school closing associated with busing.[23] Another long-term white resident, Arnold, pointed to the busing of white children out of the neighborhood as beginning "the change" in Glencliff and the dispersal of his friends to Davidson County's rural fringes. Busing, though, did more than explain the roots of neighborhood change in southeast Nashville. Several long-term residents also used their experiences with busing in the 1970s to frame their responses to Latino immigrants in the 2000s. Carl, for example, a white resident who had lived in southeast Nashville for decades, explained that to understand how immigrant settlement had changed his neighborhood's residential dynamics, "you've got to go back before that. In our city, it goes back to school busing. Whether you're for it or against it . . . , one of the most detrimental effects of that was that it destroyed our neighborhood's relationship with our children." For Carl and other white residents, understanding immigration's impacts on neighborhoods in the 2000s meant understanding busing's effects on the neighborhood in the 1970s. Immigrant settlement, from this perspective, was part of a longer history of neighborhood change that began, in the eyes of some residents, with busing.

Part of busing's role in narrating immigrant settlement, of course, is bound up with its class and racial politics. Court-ordered desegregation of

public institutions such as schools was designed to address racial inequalities between blacks and whites. In the process, however, it sometimes aggra-
vated class divisions among whites.[24] When busing began in Nashville in
1971, for instance, some white families left southeast Nashville or the county
altogether. White working-class residents of southeast Nashville, however,
often lacked the socioeconomic mobility to move elsewhere and possessed
a strong cultural connection to where they lived. This pairing of limited economic mobility and strong cultural ties to place left them with the sense that
they had little say in their neighborhood's fate and that they simply had to
accept changes to it. As Carl explained at a neighborhood meeting where the
topic of immigrant residents came up, in the 1960s and 1970s when school
integration in Nashville began, he had to learn to accept life with black residents—"and that was fine." Now, in the 2000s, he was learning again, this time
to accept immigrants in his neighborhood. In this way, the historical memory
of busing offered a frame of reference for making sense of southeast Nashville's current condition—a template for understanding contemporary ethnic diversification brought about by immigrant settlement as another change
over which long-term white residents felt they had no control. Busing, in
the eyes of some long-term residents, began the death of the neighborhood.
Immigrant settlement made what was left of its social fabric unfamiliar. As a
result, some long-term residents sought ways to bring back the old neighborhood by resurrecting old maps of it.

Bringing Back the Neighborhood

Wendy Cheng argues that branding campaigns can have material effects
across cities and that in publicly marking and marketing urban spaces, they
can privilege certain economic and social classes over others.[25] In the 2000s,
the changes that southeast Nashville experienced—immigrant settlement,
residential turnover, suburban development, new ethnic businesses, and so
on—led two neighborhoods to develop a *re*branding campaign that was,
more accurately, a revitalization of old neighborhood names and territories.
In the process they, like the communities Cheng studied, privileged particular versions of the past to make sense of and intervene in the present.

Although the northern part of southeast Nashville was home to multiple
small neighborhood associations representing areas such as Woodbine, in
2000 a new organization emerged—the Flatrock Heritage Foundation (FHF).

This new organization was different from existing groups in important ways. First, it called on a different, and older, neighborhood name. Through the late 1930s, this part of southeast Nashville was called Flatrock. In 1939, however, local residents voted to change the name of their neighborhood to Woodbine, which became the more common name for this northernmost part of southeast Nashville on city maps and for local businesses. Flatrock remained a colloquial term that circulated locally among older residents, but it did not often appear publicly or officially. Thus, in calling itself the Flatrock Heritage Foundation, this group resurrected a name that had been out of print for 60 years. By putting the word "Heritage" in its name, it explicitly referenced this early twentieth-century history of the area.

Second, the FHF drew on a larger swath of southeast Nashville than did most neighborhood associations. Although Flatrock's borders were hotly contested by local residents, there was general agreement that they engulfed Woodbine as well as other small neighborhoods such as Glencliff and Radnor. Thus, when the FHF was founded in 2000, it rescaled this part of Nashville to a larger designation. According to its creators, the FHF was an effort to create a wider, more unified image for southeast Nashville, a way to be visible in a city full of active neighborhood associations. It also, however, intervened in the increasing conflation of Woodbine and "Little Mexico" in public discourse by revitalizing a name that predated an immigrant arrival by decades. As Spanish-language signage, Mexican restaurants, and other indications of an immigrant presence became increasingly prominent "spatial icons" in Woodbine,[26] some long-term residents worked to reanimate specific elements of the local past under the new/old bigger name of Flatrock.

In some ways officially revitalizing Flatrock was not necessary, since memories of it remained central to many long-term residents' understandings of place. As early as the 1980s Flatrock festivals or reunions were held in the area, and older long-term white residents continued to describe their neighborhoods as Flatrock, despite the 1939 name change.[27] Nonetheless, Flatrock as a formal territory remained off institutional maps of Nashville and out of view for the broader city until the FHF began activities such as Nights Out Against Crime and neighborhood cleanups in the name of Flatrock. In 2007, Flatrock became even more visible when the FHF unveiled a large mural proclaiming the southern entrance to the "Flatrock Community" painted onto old railroad trestles running through the area. With this formal marking, Flatrock returned to contemporary maps and public awareness with an official "gateway to our community" visible to anyone driving in or out of this part of the city. Although long-term residents debated the gateway's location outside Flatrock's traditional boundaries, its dedication ceremony stressed that the FHF was working "to change the face" of the area. Speeches at the dedication referenced the mural's power to contribute to "the community" of Flatrock, whose *contemporary* presence and border were now marked for all to see. In Flatrock, as in many urban communities across the United States, organizers recognized "the social power exercised by cultural symbols on material forces"[28] and took steps to put a new/old cultural symbol back in circulation.

As the gateway to Flatrock opened in 2007, another resurrection of an old community was taking place farther south in Antioch. In the midst of Antioch's spectacular growth and demographic transformation into what some called "Hispanioch," an old community was being reborn. Like Flatrock, this revitalized community was returned to contemporary maps of Nashville to address changes that had made the local past invisible to long-term residents and the local present increasingly unfamiliar. The reanimated neighborhood in Antioch was Cane Ridge.[29] A rural community in the midst of greater Antioch, Cane Ridge had roots in the early nineteenth century, when it began as a small tight-knit settlement.[30] Over time Cane Ridge was engulfed by Antioch but was not forgotten by older residents, many of whom continued to describe where they lived as Cane Ridge. In 2007, Cane Ridge's existence as a formal place separate from Antioch was reestablished. Mail could now be sent to Cane Ridge, and properties within its boundaries were listed as Cane Ridge, not Antioch.[31] Although the small road signs that marked Cane Ridge's formal borders as a community or neighborhood paled in comparison to the colorful mural that welcomed drivers to Flatrock, for its (re)creators Cane Ridge was a means, and a space, through which to intervene in Antioch's bad public image. Cane Ridge was (re)designed to "run out the riffraff," in the words of an African American resident familiar with the campaign, by running Cane Ridge's borders around them.

It is important to stress that Cane Ridge, like Flatrock, was not solely, or even mainly, a response to immigrant settlement.[32] An important community symbol for older residents, Cane Ridge meant something to those who lived and grew up in it, and this meaning did not necessarily link to an immigrant presence. Instead, the collective meaning of Cane Ridge was grounded in a shared history of schools, churches, and other community institutions and was reproduced through a strong local identity for residents. Cane Ridge's community club participated in events at the state fair and other agricultural venues, and people still gathered monthly at the old Cane Ridge School to meet and eat. Because Antioch received a bum rap across Nashville, however, Cane Ridge was formally resurrected and remapped, its creators explained, to trace the line between home owners and "everything else." Concerned that they were "painted with a broad brush" that mixed renters and home owners, community members and "riffraff," Cane Ridge's designers created new boundaries for the old community to distinguish it from Antioch. Those borders "came to us gradually," according to one organizer. What emerged in that gradual process was a neighborhood map designed to include those residents for whom Cane Ridge was meaningful and to exclude those for whom it was presumed not to be. Those areas left out included strip development and nearby apartment complexes, where "Cane Ridge doesn't mean anything" to residents, in the words of one Cane Ridge resident.

This exclusionary definition is clearest in notes from an interview with two older white women who had lived all their lives in Cane Ridge.

Both women first noticed Latino/as in the Antioch area around 2000, when they started seeing them at work—mowing lawns, working in construction, doing general labor. They think most Latino/as live on Nolensville Road but are also interspersed in Antioch. They're starting to see Latino/as in the subdivisions but not much. Hispanics don't have much money to live here, they explained, until their families from Mexico come. There are no Latino/as in Cane Ridge. There are more, though, in Antioch—"*all over.*"

I asked what neighborhoods Latino/as lived in, or what was the name of the area where Latino/as lived. Latino/as live in the apartments up and down Bell Road, they said. "*What's its name?*" I asked again. One woman finally explained, "*That area doesn't have a name. It's where the Mexicans live.* They live by Home Depot. If you leave early in the morning, you can see the kids catching the bus for school."

In this passage, the contemporary presence that some Cane Ridge residents were concerned would "swallow" their neighborhood becomes clear. With Cane Ridge as an official place, "we won't disappear" amid the urban development and change that threatened to engulf Cane Ridge and its (semirural) way of life, an organizer stressed. When I asked where Hispanics lived, he, like many others, named spaces beyond Cane Ridge—main corridors in Antioch, apartments by a local mall, and a major thoroughfare in Woodbine. When I asked what those areas were called, he replied "just Antioch."

Cane Ridge thus became a spatial strategy, in the words of an organizer, "to preserve our identity" against an unnamed but obvious presence "all over" Antioch. In Antioch, the areas of high density where many Latino immigrants settled were a spatial other to Cane Ridge's small farms and subdivisions, the residential structures that allowed Cane Ridge's creators to find the line between Cane Ridge and "just Antioch." Equally important, these areas beyond Cane Ridge's territory were the unfamiliar presence that revitalizing this old community was meant to overwrite. By settling near Cane Ridge and challenging its historic identity as rural and largely white, Latino immigrants problematized what being from this area meant for long-term residents, leading to the return of an old map to redefine an increasingly unfamiliar new reality.

Latino residents living close by knew little of Cane Ridge or their exclusion from its territory. Débora and Jaime, for example, moved to Nashville from El Salvador in 2003 and 2004, respectively. After living separately in various parts of southeast Nashville, they married and moved into an apartment complex along Bell Road, just beyond the sign marking Cane Ridge's borders. When asked what their neighborhood was named, Débora replied, "I just know it is Bell Road," making no mention of Cane Ridge, which was literally across the road from their apartment. Elena and Flor, roommates in the same complex, were equally unfamiliar with Cane Ridge. Elena came to Nashville in 2005 from El Salvador, and Flor came from Mexico with her brother in 2004. Like Débora and Jaime, they lived across anchor points in Nashville's immigrant neighborhoods before coming to "La Bell Road." For Flor, as for designers of Cane Ridge, her neighborhood, just outside Cane Ridge, was simply "Antioch."

Conclusion

Cheng, along with other scholars, has examined "how struggles over race, geography, and history are intertwined in the contemporary identities of places and integral to the shaping of civic landscapes."[33] This chapter adds to these arguments by showing how efforts to revitalize old neighborhoods, in the sense of bringing them back into existence, can be responses to neighborhood revitalizations associated with immigrant settlement—a younger immigrant population, more children in local schools, new businesses catering to immigrants, and so forth. In southeast Nashville, both new Latino immigrants and long-term residents were revitalizing and reanimating neighborhoods. They did so, however, through understandings of neighborhood that mapped different boundaries and drew on different moments in history. They were, in essence, revitalizing two different understandings of neighborhood in the same place.

To see these dual revitalizations, this collision between old maps and new neighbors, this study had to frame immigrant settlement within a longer historical trajectory and a wider set of neighborhood transitions than is often seen in migration studies. In doing so, it revealed the ways that the cultural politics of immigrant settlement in Nashville were simultaneously the cultural politics of memory and the past. The spatial overlap in Nashville neighborhoods between Latino immigrants and long-term residents—a sense of shared social spaces apparent to both groups—was also a *temporal* overlap between an immigrant present and a remembered past for long-term residents. This temporal overlap, however, was not apparent to Latino immigrants, who often unknowingly transformed key sites of shared memories for long-term residents. As long-term residents responded to these transformations by revitalizing old maps of neighborhood, Latino immigrants were excluded, sometimes literally, from these new/old maps of neighborhood. Flatrock and Cane Ridge—as places distinct from Woodbine and Antioch, respectively—were invisible to Latino immigrants who, as recent arrivals in Nashville, were unfamiliar with the city's history. As a result, revitalizing neighborhoods by returning to old maps produced an immigrant exclusion that was inadvertent but potent.

At the same time, Latino immigrants themselves charted new maps of community that were hard for long-term residents to see. When asked about neighborhood relations in southeast Nashville, for example, an area pastor for a Latino congregation explained that "the Hispanic community . . . would have community amongst their own family and their friends more than in neighborhood." In this way, Latino residents made friends at work, saw neighborhood as including friends in other cities, and connected Nashville to Latin America through remittances, videos, and phone calls. These (trans) local projects created new maps of community that stretched far beyond the confines of neighborhood but remained unseen by long-term residents. In this way, *both* Latino immigrants *and* long-term residents understood and enacted neighborhood in ways that the other group could not see. Both revitalized neighborhood in different ways.

Nonetheless, these two groups increasingly lived side by side. Within shared social spaces and amid competing maps of neighborhood, some new and old residents unknowingly mirrored each other in their feelings about life in Nashville. Field notes from interviews with a Honduran man and with a white elderly resident illustrate this overlap:

> Bernardo doesn't know much about his . . . neighborhood. He describes it as quiet place to raise a family. He said there is no communication among neighbors aside from "hi," and he doesn't know their names.
>
> Since he has moved to Nashville, however, his life has changed because he has something of his own, a house with a backyard. . . . Although he dreams of returning to Honduras, he now considers Nashville a home.
>
> Arrived in Nashville in 2006

> Don doesn't spend much time outside in his neighborhood anymore. There are only a few people he still knows in the neighborhood, and he mainly speaks to them when an ambulance shows up. "I really don't know" when all this changed. They [immigrants] "just keep to themselves," and so does he. . . . "At first we accepted them. Then, they came in droves." Given all these feelings, I asked why he stayed. "I don't know. This place is home to me. This place was willed to me. Here seems like forever."
>
> Born in Nashville in 1929

Immigrants who could not see the past that was the bedrock of long-term residents' understanding of place and long-term residents who could not understand a present defined by Latino claims to place met in the intimate spaces of neighborhood. Here, both groups claimed home, *and* both groups felt out of place. Our understanding of these sites, and the politics they produce, must account for these competing, yet overlapping, maps and meanings of neighborhood and their articulations with the past.

By definition, new immigrant destinations such as Nashville have little or no experience with foreign-born populations and lack recallable histories of immigrant settlement. Thus, in most new destinations, long-term residents struggle to narrate immigration's impacts. The kinds of interpretive frameworks seen in places with long histories of immigration such as New York and Los Angeles are not available in such cities as Nashville. With little sense of how their city or neighborhood became attractive to immigrants and with no obvious way to place immigrant settlement in local histories, long-term residents in new destinations make sense of immigrant settlement through a local lens that draws on specific events and sites in their neighborhoods' histories. In doing so, the narratives and maps they create can inadvertently become mechanisms of exclusion, reinforcing immigrants' location as outsiders and inhibiting immigrant abilities to claim place.

What role did anti-immigrant sentiment play in these efforts to revitalize and resurrect old neighborhoods in southeast Nashville? Certainly, in the mid to late 2000s anti-immigrant rhetoric was on the airwaves, in the newspapers, and in local public discourse in Nashville, as in many other American cities. Chalking these remappings of neighborhood up to anti-immigrant attitudes or xenophobia alone, however, is too simplistic. To be sure, anti-immigrant sentiment could be found in these neighborhoods. At the same time, though, immigration was rarely, if ever, the sole explanation offered by long-term residents for how and why their neighborhoods had changed or declined. Especially in Cane Ridge, commercial development and the construction of apartment complexes were often greater issues than immigrant settlement in the minds of many long-term residents, even as both trends were strongly associated with an immigrant presence. No one could deny that Latino immigrants *had changed* neighborhoods in southeast Nashville or that long-term residents were often at a loss as to how to make sense of these transformations. Both Latino immigrants and long-term black and white residents were invested in making a place in Nashville and its neighborhoods. They did so, however, by understanding the neighborhood, its boundaries, and its history in different ways. In the process, immigrant incorporation into the neighborhood—understood in these competing ways—was inhibited because the two groups involved worked with and through different maps.

CHAPTER 7

Transforming Transit-Oriented Development Projects via Immigrant-Led Revitalization: The MacArthur Park Case

Gerardo Francisco Sandoval

Urban revitalization efforts in the United States have historically led to either forceful removal or displacement of low-income communities and communities of color.[1] Many communities of color view large-scale revitalization efforts as simply catalysts for neighborhood transition and gentrification. In MacArthur Park near downtown Los Angeles, by contrast, the working-class Latino immigrant community was able to transform a large-scale, initially top-down infrastructure project into a more community-led project consistent with existing regeneration efforts and benefiting existing residents.

The MacArthur Park case demonstrates that immigrant low-income neighborhoods can withstand the pressures of large-scale redevelopment and actually benefit from top-down transit-oriented development (TOD) and other infrastructure projects. It shows how endogenous forms of capital that exist within low-income immigrant Latino communities serve as assets that immigrant communities rely on to place political pressure on local politicians and reshape planning projects that threaten their communities. In some cases, as in MacArthur Park, these forms of political, financial, and cultural capital provide opportunities for revitalization without substantial gentrification as these communities stand up to big state-led projects.

MacArthur Park's low-income Central American and Mexican immigrant community was able to transform the large-scale transportation infrastructural project into an immigrant-led revitalization effort that improved the community for a number of key reasons. First, progressive community-based organizations (CBOs) in the area were well organized. They had a strong history of neighborhood activism from two decades of struggle to maintain the neighborhood's identity in the face of pressures from large-scale urban redevelopment and also advocated for community benefits. These organizations partake in labor organizing, teach English as a second language, and engage in refugee human rights organizing (since the horrific Central American civil wars of the 1980s); they organize for immigrant rights advocacy, tenant rights, and housing issues, among other organizing work that positioned them to mobilize the community.

Second, the local city council office controlled by progressive Latinos was proactive in pressuring developers and other planning institutions to increase affordable housing projects in the area. Los Angeles City Council members have land-use jurisdiction in their districts. Hence, developers had to negotiate with the councilman's office for any projects that would change the zoning requirements in the area. The progressive councilman used that as leverage to encourage mixed-income and affordable housing projects.

Finally, the immigrant cultural capital that existed in the neighborhood served as an anchor for Latino place making and neighborhood resistance. Immigrant place making in the neighborhood is evident via Latino-serving local businesses that contribute to urban vibrancy and in active public spaces where cultural celebrations take place within the park. The park itself was transformed from a passive recreational space (which historic preservationists have fought to maintain) to an active public space filled with street vendors, informal soccer fields, Central American cultural celebrations, and immigrant rights protests. MacArthur Park demonstrates that some immigrant neighborhoods possess vibrant forms of capital that help them resist and transform large-scale state-led projects to more community-oriented revitalization efforts that benefit the existing community and do not lead to gentrification.

Large-Scale Transportation Infrastructure Projects in Low-Income Communities of Color

Beginning in the 1950s and 1960s, it was common practice in the United States to build major highways through low-income communities and communities of color.[2] Federal transportation policy mostly consisted of allocating large amounts of money to build interstate highways. These types of transportation policies and practices, which were also linked to racialized urban renewal policies targeting low-income communities of color, led to the destruction of thriving neighborhoods and large-scale displacement.[3] These racist urban policies targeted Latino barrios (neighborhoods) just as they destroyed African American and old immigrant neighborhoods in U.S. cities. As David Diaz and Rodolfo Torres have argued, "From the beginning of eminent domain in the post-World War II era of redevelopment and transportation route designations, the state has viewed barrio space as vulnerable and expendable." Razing Latino barrios meant "the demolition of massive amounts of affordable housing, the dismantling of zones of minority property ownership, and radical reconfigurations of space, . . . carried out with a dismissal of minority concerns that express a racist contempt for marginalized communities."[4] Chavez Ravine in Los Angeles serves as a key example of a vibrant historical Mexican American community that fell victim to the bulldozers to make room for the construction of Dodger Stadium.[5]

Contemporary East Los Angeles is the product of freeway after freeway extensions that divided the community and led to forceful displacement of Latinos.[6] In 1961, Los Angeles Assembly member Edward F. Elliot recognized the economic and physical impacts that freeways were having on the eastern side of Los Angeles and decried the way in which the downtown area "had become encircled, cut up, and glutted by freeways."[7] In the Boyle Heights area, freeways displaced one-tenth of the local population. The freeways that dissect the area in many ways continue to reproduce the spatial segregation that created the East Los Angeles neighborhoods.

Urban historians and legal scholars have shown how freeway locations in U.S. cities are rooted in the politics of urban renewal era "Negro removal," often designed to reinforce racial segregation.[8] The identification of blight had racial undertones whereby findings of blight were associated with a certain percentage of nonwhite population.[9] These racist policies led to the destruction of many vibrant low-income communities of color especially in the 1950s and 1960s. Institutional racism and low levels of political power historically prevented many of these communities from opposing government plans for the destruction of these neighborhoods.

But communities of color have also fought back to protect their neighborhoods from these racist urban policies. The highway revolts of the 1960s and early 1970s were a turning point in urban transportation policy, as many neighborhoods throughout the country, with the help of high-level transportation planning, opposed new highway constructions.[10] Community opposition has prevented large-scale displacement and other inequitable effects. For example, in 1972 individuals and organizations concerned about households that would be displaced by the proposed I-105 freeway in Los Angeles filed a lawsuit against state and federal government officials. In 1982, the Ninth Circuit Court of Appeals required that the state and federal defendants provide freeway displacees with 3,700 units of decent, safe, and sanitary replenishment housing by either rehabilitating existing structures or constructing new ones.[11]

Chicano Park in San Diego's Barrio Logan is a key example of community opposition in low-income Latino communities leading to the creation of a public space in protest of freeways that sliced up the historical Mexican American neighborhood.[12] The neighborhood was initially cut in half by the construction of Interstate 5 and then again cut in fourths by the construction of the Coronado Freeway Bridge. The final straw was a proposed California Highway Patrol staging area that was to again separate the neighborhood under the freeway by creating more barriers. Activists in the neighborhood protested and fought off this plan and created a public space underneath the freeway. Chicano Park is now considered the umbilical cord of Aztland (the mythical Chicano homeland of the Southwest). Chicano murals painted on the freeway pillars depict the Chicano movement and highlight the neighborhood's struggles for self-autonomy against racist state interventions.[13]

Today, forceful displacement of communities of color via eminent domain has given way to more market-driven displacement, often primed and supported by public infrastructure investments. Large-scale transportation and urban redevelopment projects are carried out as catalyst projects that change land-use patterns, encourage more private developer investments in low-income neighborhoods, and have the danger of leading to gentrification.[14] Gentrification is generally characterized as "the process by which higher income households displace lower income residents of a neighborhood, changing the essential character and flavor of that neighborhood."[15] From the perspective of incumbent communities, gentrification manifests as displacement of housing and retail businesses due to increased rents.

Gentrification in U.S. cities is closely related to residential relocation, including immigration but especially the "back to the city" flow patterns of suburban middle-income residents relocating within metropolitan areas for environmental and lifestyle urban preferences, which in turn is linked to expanding transit options for higher-income residents.[16] Due to the

perception that increased property values and improved neighborhood amenities—including transit infrastructure—signals community revitalization,
middle-income residents generally upgrade their housing conditions for personal consumption.[17] The gentrification process is commonly associated with
physical property improvements, property value increases, a demographic
shift from low- to higher-income levels, and more young and professional
households. There is also a racial aspect to gentrification, so demographic
changes in a community are also important to consider when identifying
areas of potential gentrification. While some gentrifying neighborhoods
absorb vacant properties, others displace households that are no longer able
to afford increased housing costs.[18]

Transportation infrastructure investments aimed at spurring revitalization continue to play an important part in gentrifying and displacing low-
income immigrant and migrant communities of color. Some of the most
common reasons for transportation-related gentrification are (1) an increased
desirability of an area because of transportation investments such as extensions of commuter rail lines, (2) a new or improved train service or station, or
(3) the addition of a highway ramp or exit. Gentrification associated with new
investments and new housing and commercial services and increased access
to regional transit for higher-income populations is often most targeted and
dramatic in TOD projects that explicitly seek to reshape land use, ownership,
and development around transportation hubs, especially rail, light rail, and
subway stops, as in the case of MacArthur Park.

A TOD Project in an Immigrant Gateway Neighborhood

MacArthur Park became a Central American immigrant community between
the mid-1980s and the mid-1990s, a time when most Angelenos associated
the area with crime, drugs, and lawlessness. It was known as one of the most
dangerous areas of Los Angeles, serving as the hub of the city's drug traf-
ficking market and having the largest concentration of illegal drug activities.
MacArthur Park saw the emergence of violent street gangs (for example,
MS-13) and had the most corrupt police station in Los Angeles (the Rampart
Division). The neighborhood had a reputation as a place with no regulations
and with lawlessness unprecedented in any other part of the city. Much of this
criminal activity was carried out by people who did not reside in the neighborhood but used the lawlessness in the area to their criminal advantage.

When newly appointed Los Angeles Police Department chief William Bratton, former head of the New York and Boston police departments, took a tour of the park in October 2002, he contended that "This is the toughest police environment I have ever faced."[19]

Yet, Central American and Mexican immigrants kept coming because the area served their housing and labor needs and represented one of the largest immigrant gateway communities in Los Angeles. Another reason immigrants decided to locate in MacArthur Park was because they were not asked for documentation such as Social Security cards or formal ID cards when looking for housing. Most important, however, it emerged as a gateway immigrant community because people felt at home there. Most residents were not faced with a language barrier, for instance. By the late 1980s, the area had become a neighborhood mainly consisting of Mexicans and Central Americans (Figures 7.1 and 7.2). This occurred simultaneously with the long, dreadful, and violent civil wars that plagued both Guatemala and El Salvador,

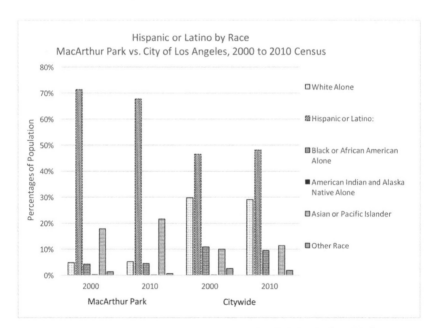

Figure 7.1.   Percentage of Latinos living in MacArthur Park compared to the city of Los Angeles.

Source: U.S. Census Bureau, "Social Explorer Fact Sheet—Table SE: T15," 2000; U.S. Census Bureau, "Social Explorer Fact Sheet—Table SE: T55," 2010.

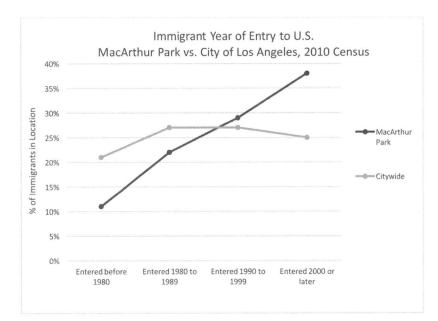

Figure 7.2. Years of arrival in the United States of immigrants in MacArthur Park and the city of Los Angeles.

Source: U.S. Census Bureau, "Table B05005," 2009.

as more Central Americans migrated to the United States to escape the wars. In fact, most of the Central American CBOs that emerged in MacArthur Park focused their work around issues related to amnesty, political asylum, and human rights. CBOs such as El Rescate, the Central American Resource Center (CARECEN), the Salvadoran American Legal and Education Fund (SALEF), Clinica Romero, and others emerged in MacArthur Park during that turbulent and violent time in Central America to work with refugees and immigrants.

MacArthur Park in the mid-1990s reached a climactic point as its increasing density packed 35,000 people into a few blocks. Homicide rates peaked at 150 per year near the park. The Rampart police corruption scandal reached the front pages of *Time* Magazine.[20] The city councilor representing the area was arrested for buying cocaine in the park. A terrible fire exposed the housing code violations of absentee landlords. Rioting spread throughout the neighborhood following the Rodney King verdict. MacArthur Park in the early to mid-1990s resembled Lawrence Veiller's descriptions of New York's immigrant slums at the turn of the ninwteenth century. Hector Tobar's award-winning novel *The Tattooed Soldier* (1998) takes place in MacArthur Park and demonstrates the chaotic environment that existed there throughout the 1990s and into the mid-2000s.[21] Tobar's fictional story is a tale of revenge as a Guatemalan immigrant meets (in MacArthur Park) the man who killed his family during the civil war. In the climactic final scene, the protagonist is running near MacArthur Park as rioting is taking place, and he seeks the opportune moment to carry out his revenge on the Tattooed Soldier.

In this context of a gateway immigrant neighborhood that was growing but had big, dramatic problems, the Los Angeles County Metropolitan Transportation Authority (MTA) first proposed, in the early 1980s, the MacArthur Park metro as a mixed-use, transit-orientated development (TOD) project consisting of new high-density housing and retail uses. Initially, the top-down redevelopment project did not take the local community into consideration and actually aimed to change the demographics in the neighborhood by bringing in luxury condos and higher-end retail.[22] The plan called for a large commercial development around the planned subway station and had no provision for affordable housing. Initially the TOD called for taking four blocks in the neighborhood and building the new development next to the subway station. Like most subway expansions, the project took many years during which it underwent dramatic changes. Community members opposed the initial TOD plan, and with the help of local Latino politicians they were able to change the project into a Latino immigrant-led revitalization effort.

Located above the MTA Redline Subway Station in Westlake/MacArthur Park, the TOD project is adjacent to one of the most significant public parks in Los Angeles. The ultimate developer of the MacArthur Park TOD was McCormack Baron Salazar, a firm that specializes in building affordable housing and mixed-use development around transit stops. The project's goal became to build multifamily affordable housing above MTA's MacArthur Park station to help address the need of the community for safe, decent housing. The project's final plan consisted of two phases: 90 affordable apartments catering to large families, 15,000 square feet of commercial retail space, and 249 parking spaces, including 100 for commuters, completed in June 2012, and another 82 affordable rental units, 17,000 square feet of retail space, and 83 residential parking spaces by early 2015 (Figures 7.3 and 7.4).

The MacArthur Park TOD is now seen as a model for building similar development to benefit low-income communities, even as it also supported a subsequent market-rate development boom, including the revival of old

Figure 7.3. The TOD is located across the street from MacArthur Park, a regional public space in Los Angeles.

Credit: Photo by Gerardo Sandoval.

Figure 7.4. MacArthur Park TOD. The affordable housing units are directly across the street from the MacArthur Park subway station.

Credit: Photo by Gerardo Sandoval.

theaters and hotels. The Community Redevelopment Agency of the City of Los Angeles saw the community benefits of this project as building affordable housing units, encouraging TOD, creating jobs through local hiring practices, and increasing retail services in the neighborhood. Former Housing and Urban Development secretary Shaun Donovan toured the site and claimed that "this [is a] model that the rest of the country should be looking to. Putting housing close to transit is part of President Barack Obama's Climate Action Plan."[23]

Political Capital: CBOs and Local Latino Politicians' Advocacy for Community Benefits and Affordable Housing

The process through which the MacArthur Park TOD became a community-led project to benefit the working-class immigrant community illuminates the key role that immigrant civil society and political leadership often play in community revitalization and preservation. CBOs and local Latino politicians' advocacy in the neighborhoods served as important forms of endogenous political capital that ensured that the initially top-down TOD project took the community's well-being into consideration. The relationships between the CBOs and between the CBOs and politicians and their respective capacities and ties to the community and to public institutions helped them succeed in engineering this transformation.

MacArthur Park has a long history of community activism and a strong involvement of neighborhood leaders in community improvement efforts. The CBOs in MacArthur Park initially started their activism work covering human rights abuses and advocating for refugee status during the civil wars in Central America in the early 1980s to mid-1990s. After the civil wars in Central America ended, the CBOs in MacArthur Park started to turn their attention toward immigrant rights and local neighborhood issues. This positioned local civil society to effectively oppose, transform, and advance its own TOD plan.

Roughly fifteen to twenty diverse CBOs advocate for immigrant rights and community development in the neighborhood. These organizations range from the CARECEN, founded in 1983 and focused on immigration, refugee, and educational advocacy, to Mama's Hot Tamales, a more recent organization that worked to help formalize the street vendors in and around the park. An example of CARECEN's community development work is its day-labor center, located two blocks from the TOD site, that helps educate day laborers on workers' rights and serves as an intermediary between day laborers and contractors. Another key CBO in the neighborhood is the SALEF, which provides educational scholarships to students in the community. SALEF has also contributed to the Latino place-making efforts in the neighborhood by spearheading the petition for construction of a new Monsignor Oscar Romero plaza across the street from the TOD site. In this eight-year effort, SALEF led a collaborative network of CBOs in the neighborhood to pressure local officials for a space significant to the Latino community.

The interactions between the local city councilman's office and these networked CBOs were extremely important in making sure the TOD and the revitalization of the neighborhood included specific community benefits. The progressive Latino council member made it a point to gain buy-in and even fund community projects via these networked CBOs. Staff members from the councilman's office said that the role that community organizations and activists played in the negotiations over the TOD were critical. The councilman's office purposely reached out to these CBOs because the organizations could put political pressure on other city entities that were not doing enough to improve the neighborhood. A former councilman for the district stated that "We started bringing community organizations into the city bureaucracy, they were great advocates, and we started forcing other city government services to listen to them. We started working with building and safety and police, and recreation and parks."[24] A different, and also former, city councilor of the area recalled how the councilman's office collaborated with these CBOs:

We were trying to empower the community. We had what we called More Advocates for Safe Homes, MASH units. They were small neighborhood groups that were basically fighting for their communities. And we worked with them to bring attention to issues in the community. There were immigrant organizations like Churlock, CARECEN, One-Stop Immigration and we worked through them. I had a policy where I would not call a press conference, but I went to their press conferences and I supported them so that people would know who they were.[25]

The collaborative relationships between CBOs in MacArthur Park and the local councilman's office notwithstanding, some CBOs kept up pressure on the office to make sure affordable housing was being implemented both in the TOD site and in other revitalization efforts in the community. One such group, Collective Action, used grassroots activist techniques to maintain accountability from local officials. The group's staff was very aware of displacement pressures that might occur because of the new investments in the community, and they wanted to maintain close ties to the city's planning and transportation agencies. One of Collective Action's leaders explained their rationale for placing pressure on city officials and staff, as urban development was fundamentally a political process, and thus political engagement was necessary throughout the entire process:

> We want to create a plan that we can take to the Fair Housing members, or the zoning administrator and say, this is what we want. And also for developers, as more developers start coming in. Say, "that's nice, your condo development looks great, but this is what we want." For us it's a process because we are process . . . . We influence developers and elected officials; we bring people to the table who know what they are talking about, who understand policy, because you know, *it's not rocket science; it's just political.*[26]

Local Latino politicians also played key roles in developing political capital for Latino neighborhood interests. The role that these politicians played in the TOD project's transformation and ultimate development cannot be understated. They were the link between the community organizations, residents, merchants, and the city's organizations involved in the process. They used their political capital to advocate for community benefits linked to the TOD. This ensured that the process moved forward, that key funding was available, and that the community's needs were addressed.

MacArthur Park belongs to the first district of Los Angeles, a district developed in the early 1980s from community activists' efforts and lawsuits that advocated for more Latino political representation in the city. The Voting Rights Act served as the legal platform to create the first district, an area with a high concentration of Latino immigrants and others living in poverty. A city official with a long career in City Hall described the history of the first district's creation:

> The voting rights act gave us a platform by which to advocate for a new district of leftover neighborhoods. The city council essentially

threw away a bunch of neighborhoods and said, here, we don't want these, this is where the crime is, this is where the poor people live, this is where the infrastructure is broken, and this is where no one wants to invest. That is the history of the first district.[27]

Elected out of the first district was longtime Los Angeles supervisor Gloria Molina (1991–2014), a community activist who came out of the Chicano movement. Her leadership was key to the opposition and transformation of the initial top-down TOD project in the neighborhood.[28] This initial TOD plan called for large-scale transformation of the neighborhood. The plan had no affordable housing allocation, called for high-end retail and condominium units, and lacked connections to the community. Molina described her initial impression of the large-scale TOD project:

The project that they initially wanted was too dense for the area. When they first presented it to the community, it wasn't built for the community, it was built for the people that were going to go through there; the park and ride and creating the parking. If you are going to have commercial development you have to think, what is the benefit for the community? If they want a market and you are saying, no it doesn't fit, then you are not meeting their need. The entire project was built for the commuter, the person that would go through the system; create a little coffee shop for them, it was really bizarre. I thought they were very arrogant; they didn't have a good understanding of the community. They weren't opening up the process.[29]

Molina was worried about the potential issues of displacement and the lack of community input into the initial TOD project in the area. But it was not until she became county supervisor and formally sat on the committee that controlled the MTA's budget that she was able to stop the project, forcing the transportation planners to go back to the drawing board and also providing more community input into the TOD's development plans.[30]

The leadership of council member Ed Reyes (2001–2013) was likewise crucial to the form that the TOD ultimately took. Reyes was an urban planner with a master's degree from UCLA who championed affordable housing linked to new developments in the neighborhood. According to a former staff member, Reyes focused on building community capacity and local leadership in his district:

We hire people because they came from the neighborhood. We want to see the improvements. Gloria [Molina] hired people from the neighborhood, Mike [Hernandez, another former council member] hired people from the neighborhood, and Ed [Reyes] hires people from the neighborhood. And we are educated Latinos, we understand right from wrong. We understand the injustices, but we also understand how to make it right. Now with Antonio [Villaraigosa] as mayor, [we had] another tremendous opportunity [at the time].[31]

With his planning background and focus on neighborhood development, Reyes successfully pushed for many affordable housing projects in the neighborhood. His staff remembered that every project requesting a zoning change had to go through review by the council office, and Reyes would invariably use this opportunity to advocate for affordable housing.

Local Latino politicians also played an important role in helping the informal businesses in the neighborhood earn some legitimacy, a significant step in the preservation of the immigrant community's economic vitality. A plethora of formal Latino-owned small businesses surround the park, providing goods and services ranging from groceries to money transfer for remittances to neighborhood residents' families and communities in Mexico and Guatemala, and businesses support the local business improvement district that cleans sidewalks and graffiti and offers educational programming for entrepreneurs. Yet the neighborhood's informal economic system is equally vital, including hundreds of street vendors who have sold their goods illegally in and around the park and especially next to the subway station. The street vendors sell food that caters to the Mexican and Central American community such as tamales, corn, etc. They also sell medicines from Mexico that were familiar to residents, electronic products, clothing, movies, and other products catering to the low-income Latino community. The usual response to street vending by the city has been to try to end those activities by either ticketing or arresting individuals, which has usually ended up displacing vendors. In MacArthur Park local officials' response has been different, even though public health department crackdowns on some vendors in the neighborhood have continued.

The local councilman at the start of the TOD project, Mike Hernandez (1991–2001), decided to establish the first legitimate street vending district in the city of Los Angeles. His staff viewed street vendors from an assets perspective instead of as criminals. The street vendors program started by

Councilman Hernandez and continued by Councilman Reyes relied on a CBO, Mama's Hot Tamales, to be the mediator between the city and the street vendors.[32] Mama's Hot Tamales served as a kitchen incubator where the vendors would cook their food, and this facility could be regulated by the city.

The councilman's office gave these informal activities a chance to thrive because it understood the important functions of informal financial capital in the neighborhood. A representative of the councilman's office explained why these informal financial activities were critical to the community's growth, stating that his "approach was not based on large real estate, it was based on the flow of capital as defined by small wallets. That's the MacArthur Park way. That's every city in the third world. I've been to El Salvador and all these cities that have all these intense informal activities."[33] He recognized that street vendors, day laborers, informal medical clinics, miqueros (who sell false identification papers), and some swap meet activities are all part of the economic engine driving these types of neighborhoods. He also understood that when the government tries to discourage those economic activities, it contributes to the displacement of the Latino low-income immigrant community in general because vendors, service providers, workers, and consumers are interlinked and dependent upon each other. Another council staff person stated, "the informal economy is the formal economy for this community."[34]

In 2014, the council district collaborated with three community organizations to develop a *mercado*, a type of community market where street vendors could sell their goods and not be worried about harassment from police officers or the city. In fact, the market was located in front of the police station in the neighborhood. The city encouraged street vendors to move from neighborhood alleys to this *mercado*, where they could be better regulated. Subsequently, the Los Angeles City Council once again took up the question of legalizing street vending. Hence, both the councilman's office and key community organizations in MacArthur Park have demonstrated how important forms of financial capital, even though they might be informal, can still be supported and encouraged to maintain some form of affirmative regulation.

Immigrant Cultural Capital: An Anchor
for Neighborhood Resistance

The large-scale TOD project did not lead to the wholesale gentrification of MacArthur Park in large part due to the cultural capital[35] space being transformed to an active one, the informal economic activities around the TOD, and the cultural events and celebrations occurring in the neighborhood.

One key example of how cultural capital has contributed to the revitalization of the neighborhood is the park itself, which has been transformed from an aesthetic passive park to an active space filled with Latino kids playing in new playgrounds and informal soccer leagues that host tournaments attended by hundreds of spectators (Figure 7.5). Establishing the soccer field was not an easy task, as the council district had to formally designate the field as a meadow to appease historic preservation activists, who sought to keep the park a passive space. Thus, both the soccer fields and goal posts are not permanent, and the soccer fields transform back to meadows on a daily basis. A community leader explained this process:

> Daniel is the leader of the informal soccer leagues. I met him in the late 1990s and I would tell him to hang in there because we are going to change this [situation]. But the historic preservationists did not want to change the use of the park. They wanted to keep the historic image of the 1950s and they moved to make the park a historic monument. It was their way of keeping the immigrant kids out of the park. We said we would make it into a meadow. We would make it an artificial turf because we did not stripe in the soccer fields or establish the goals. With Daniel's help, as well as working with all the families, we raised the money through Prop K and the community redevelopment agency. We designed it with the immigrant kids in mind. So the band shell, the meadow (the soccer field), and all the functional areas you see today, we brought them in so that we would keep the historic character of the park. We never used the word "soccer field." We knew that the natural forces of the community were going to take it over anyways and we weren't going to police that takeover. We weren't going to arrest the kids.[36]

Other important expressions of cultural capital in the neighborhood include festivals and celebrations that take place in the park. Both Feria Agostina (an annual Salvadoran celebration in early August) and a Central American Independence Day celebration and parade (September 15) are important cultural celebrations that draw people from throughout the Los Angeles region. As Kelly Main, who has studied the park extensively as a public space, describes:

Figure 7.5. MacArthur Park after the revitalization investments.

Credit: Photo by Gerardo Sandoval.

The events provide an opportunity for park-goers to experience both traditional and hybrid culture. Feria Agostina takes place around the time of Las Fiestas Agostinas and la bajada, when thousands of Salvadorans gather in the streets of San Salvador to celebrate the transfiguration of the Divine Savior of the World, El Salvador's patron. On Central American Independence Day, Costa Ricans, Salvadorans, Guatemalans, Hondurans, and Nicaraguans celebrate their independence in MacArthur Park. Together, these events are attended by thousands, as food and information booths, bandstands for music, carnival rides, and speeches fill the segment of Wilshire Boulevard that cuts through MacArthur Park.[37]

These types of cultural celebrations help to anchor an ethnic group to a community via their cultural capital.

Another example of how cultural capital is used as an anchor and a form of resistance can be seen in the establishment of Monsignor Oscar Romero Plaza, across the street from the TOD. Romero was a Catholic archbishop who was assassinated in El Salvador during its civil war because he spoke

Figure 7.6. Statue of Monsignor Oscar Romero in MacArthur Park.

Credit: Photo by Gerardo Sandoval.

out against human rights violations, and he subsequently became an international symbol of resistance to the atrocities committed by Central America's
repressive regimes. The Salvadorian community wanted to celebrate his legacy by dedicating a statue in his honor. The Central American Roundtable, a
coalition of neighborhood CBOs, led the eight-year effort. In November 2013
the Salvadoran community celebrated the construction of the plaza, whose
statue of Monsignor Romero is the first thing people see directly across the
street as they exit the MacArthur Park MTA subway platform (Figure 7.6).
This was a form of Latino place making and another example of how cultural
capital manifests and serves as an anchor for immigrant-led revitalization.

Transforming Low-Income Latino Immigrant Communities by Building on Their Assets and Forms of Capital

The MacArthur Park case demonstrates that immigrant low-income neighborhoods can withstand the pressures of large-scale redevelopment and actually benefit from top-down transportation infrastructure projects such as

TODs. The endogenous forms of political, financial, and cultural capital that exist within low-income immigrant Latino communities serve as assets that contribute to immigrant-led revitalization efforts.

Local Latino politicians sustained the political capital in the neighborhood, seeing it as being in their best interest to make sure the TOD projects would not displace the existing Latino low-income population. Politicians such as Gloria Molina, Mike Hernandez, and Ed Reyes and his chief of staff Jose Gardea, who also represented District 1 in Los Angeles, advocated for community-oriented design measures at critical points in the project's decision-making process. Because of this, the project was better incorporated into the existing community, limiting its potential to displace residents. The politicians maintained important ties to the local CBOs and also involved them in the TOD planning process, especially in advocating for affordable housing. Reyes's staff clearly understood the vital role that the informal economy played in the neighborhood and took steps to protect and support it.

The CBOs' long history of community activism and capacity to organize the community also served as a form of political capital that influenced the project. The CBOs were already networked and united around local and transnational immigrant rights issues. Given the strength of their ties with the community and with one another, the local council office understood that it was important to collaborate with them on issues such as affordable housing, community policing, and physical improvements to the park. MacArthur Park's CBOs demonstrate that the political capital of civil society can play critical roles in opposing, supporting, and shaping large-scale revitalization plans and projects.

Financial capital was evident in both formal and informal ways throughout the park. Local politicians and CBOs took steps to support and affirmatively regulate financial capital, as opposed to upgrading and displacing it. Preserving the economic vitality and cultural dynamism fostered by small formal businesses and by street vending was crucial to perpetuating the endogenous revitalization occurring within the working-class immigrant community.

Cultural capital also played a key role in the community's resistance and adaptation of the TOD plan for neighborhood revitalization. The infrastructure investment's design interventions benefited from a Latino cultural framing as they incorporated Latino place-making features when the TOD transitioned from a top-down to an immigrant-led project. MacArthur Park's Oscar Romero Plaza, for example, represents an important place-making cultural icon in the Los Angeles Salvadorian community. The preservation of immigrant community-serving retail and uses of public space likewise helped sustain community ownership and identity. The availability of culturally specific food in the neighborhood, the cultural celebrations and parades, and the physical reminders of Mexico and Central America that immigrants feel when they are walking through the neighborhood[38] are all cultural expressions of capital within the neighborhood. The ability to transform the TOD project in a large way can be partly attributed to the savvy way stakeholders were able to communicate the positive expressions of the cultural capital within the community.

The MacArthur Park case is an example of Latino immigrant-led revitalization. The case helps to reframe how low-income Latino immigrant communities are perceived, from being viewed as blighted neighborhoods to being understood as dynamic communities. Working-class immigrant communities encompass various forms of endogenous political, financial, and cultural capital that can help them resist and transform large-scale infrastructure development projects to benefit their community. The dreadful history of racist redevelopment interventions in communities of color does not need to be painfully repeated and perpetuated. The MacArthur Park case demonstrates how a more equitable and community-oriented approach can improve a neighborhood and provide an alternative to the historical transportation and revitalization policies that destroy and displace communities.

PART IV

Urban Revitalization
in Transnational Context

CHAPTER 8

Migrantes, Barrios, and *Infraestructura*: Transnational Processes of Urban Revitalization in Chicago

A. K. Sandoval-Strausz

For those who lived in big cities during the depths of the urban crisis, the signs of distress were all around. Elevated subway and commuter trains confronted riders with panoramic views of semiabandoned neighborhoods, television news broadcasts brought nightly accounts of rising crime, and municipal leaders struggled to explain the severity of fiscal calamity. Indeed, the sense of doom became so pervasive that even the mass-market movies of the era were predicated on conditions of urban violence and decay, as exemplified by *The Warriors* (1979, based on a 1965 novel), *Fort Apache, The Bronx* (1981, allegedly drawn from a 1976 book), and, most creatively, *Escape from New York* (1981, from a 1976 screenplay), in which a future Manhattan has been emptied of its civilian population and converted into a vast maximum-security prison. The subsequent recovery in many (though by no means all) parts of urban America means that today's city dwellers are confronted with something much like the opposite problems—excessive competition for urban space that has led to housing shortages, gentrification that is making some working-class neighborhoods unaffordable for longtime residents, and the rapidly escalating prices of many urban goods, services, and amenities—while they also face the persistence of older problems such as deindustrialization, public disinvestment, and stagnant or falling real wages.[1]

This turnabout in the fortunes of urban America coincided with a period of rapidly increasing arrivals from other countries, leading people to inquire into the connection between immigration and metropolitan revitalization. The scholars who contributed chapters to this volume have offered a broad range of empirical findings, social scientific analyses, and historical perspectives on the intertwined fates of newcomers to the United States and the nation's cities, suburbs, and towns. I hope to add two things to the discussion. The first of these is an emphasis on the transnational factors that have motivated, conditioned, and sometimes limited the actions of the immigrants and migrants who have so powerfully shaped metropolitan areas; the second is the proposition that this transnational perspective should change the way we think about urban transformations and the policies required to manage and perhaps leverage them.

In this chapter, I approach the question of immigration and metropolitan revitalization through a historical analysis of the Little Village neighborhood in Chicago. The Windy City offers a very useful site of inquiry, since it has long been the nation's preeminent laboratory for urban studies. Little Village is almost precisely coterminous with the South Lawndale community area that University of Chicago researchers delineated in the 1920s and still serves as a unit of analysis in the city. I will contextualize Little Village at three geographical scales—locally, hemispherically, and ultimately globally—in an effort to suggest how the neighborhood and its city operate within transnational systems. My hope is that these findings may also have some broader applicability, since many other places in the United States and abroad are being transformed by the same kinds of processes described herein.[2]

I will make the case that the revitalization of Little Village was made possible because its new residents incorporated it into an emergent transnational urban system. This urban system was not simply a response to the needs of capital, however—it was built from below by migrants and immigrants who were able to shape at least some of the conditions of their everyday existence. We therefore need to rethink the analytical frameworks that are often used to explain how and why things work in U.S. cities; this includes decentering the United States and seeing revitalization in a hemispheric context in which migrants' motivations, efforts, and actions have been determined on an ongoing basis by conditions in their home countries. It also means recognizing the ways that urban revitalization has both depended upon and shaped urban areas far from the cities of the United States—and seeing that it was strongly influenced by government policy making, a considerable amount of it by foreign officials. In sum, metropolitan migrants and immigrants have been the most important contributors to a process of revitalization that was fundamentally transnational.

To propose that an urban process is transnational is only the first part of a larger question, however; the subsequent inquiry must ask *what kind* of transnationalism it represents. The first generation of scholars who attempted to explain urban development in transnational terms did so under rubrics such as "globalization" and "world cities." They tended to focus on high-level private actors in capital markets, corporate boardrooms, and international financial institutions, assigning preeminent influence to the work of elite executives and suggesting that the associated developments "on the ground" followed in the causal train of these top-echelon decision makers.[3] About a decade later, a different group of scholars criticized their predecessors for what they said were oversimplified, elitist, and deterministic depictions of urban change. Instead, they emphasized contingency, historical specificity, and complex causation as key elements of transnational processes, and, crucially, they proposed that there was more agency at work in the choices of everyday people than could be captured by approaches so focused on the rarefied environs of big capitalists.[4] As we shall see, a specifically historical approach is essential to evaluating competing explanations for how cities work, because each type of transnational analysis is based on particular renderings of chronology and causation.

Metropolitan Revitalization in the United States

Chicago's Little Village neighborhood may be the nation's most thoroughly researched and remarked-upon example of the connection between immigration and metropolitan revitalization. A variety of people, from local residents to nationally prominent scholars to the city's top elected official, have observed, and sometimes outright celebrated, the trajectory of the neighborhood and in the process have clearly emphasized the role of Latinos, predominantly Mexicans, in improving conditions there. While the area still faces ongoing difficulties, including crowded and substandard housing, limited incomes, overcrowded schools, and ongoing gang activity, it has garnered a justifiable narrative of immigrant-led urban revival.

From early on, South Lawndale was a point of entry for immigrants. The area was settled in the late nineteenth century by people from Central and Western Europe and by the early twentieth century was known as a strongly Czech and Polish neighborhood. The area's dependence on these immigrants is suggested by both the preponderance of the foreign born and its unusually early population peak. In 1930, the census recorded that the area was so dominated by European immigrants that more than five of six residents were either foreign born (31.5 percent) or native born of foreign-born parentage (52.1 percent) and that 99 percent identified as white. South Lawndale had gained population along with the rest of Chicago through about 1920, but while the city as a whole grew to midcentury, the neighborhood began to contract after the end of the major influx of Europeans that lasted from 1880 to 1920. South Lawndale entered a decades-long period of decline during which the population fell by nearly a third, from a 1920 high of over 84,000 to a 1960 low of slightly under 59,000. Related challenges included limited investment in housing stock after the 1910s and, in the 1960s, the departure of a number of large manufacturers in the area, which deprived the neighborhood of many well-paid employment opportunities. Looking back on the 1960s from 1991, longtime resident and real estate broker Richard Dolejs recalled that "all the European people were moving out," so much so that "single-family homes were selling for $12,000 and half-blocks were selling for $50,000." There were more than a hundred vacancies along the main shopping street, and the local chamber of commerce reportedly offered to pay to wash the windows of vacant stores. "It looked so ugly," remembered Dolejs, "everyone was moving out."[5]

The recovery from this slump was driven first and foremost by immigrants from Mexico who would lift the neighborhood's population to levels not seen in many decades. The Windy City had been home to large enclaves of ethnic Mexicans since early in the twentieth century, but the Great Depression and the forcible repatriation of many immigrant Mexicans and U.S. citizens of Mexican ancestry had severely attenuated the size and cohesion of the communities.[6] A certain number of Mexicans came to the area in the 1950s, but it was the agricultural crisis that began in the 1960s that most dramatically increased the scale of migration from Mexico. In South Lawndale, non-Hispanic whites continued to move out but were succeeded by the newcomers. The area's population grew very slightly, from 58,643 in 1960 to 59,478 in 1970, but this apparently small increase understates the importance of the new immigrants: in the latter year the neighborhood was already more than one-third Hispanic, so without Latino migrants, South Lawndale would have shrunken in the 1960s even faster than Detroit in its worst-ever decade of depopulation. (On a related note, in 1962 the neighborhood's "old immigrant" residents led the way in unofficially renaming the area Little Village in an effort to distinguish it from North Lawndale, which had become a predominantly African American neighborhood.) The Latino-led repopulation of the area continued apace thereafter: it grew to over 70,000 inhabitants by 1980, over 75,000 by 1990, and over 80,000 by millennium's end—a dynamic that was also reflected across the Chicago metropolitan area and in countless cities and towns across the United States.[7]

Quite apart from the basic question of population loss or gain, clear signs of improvement in South Lawndale gradually emerged in the form of statistical data on key indices of neighborhood well-being. The aspect of the urban crisis that created the most public alarm was the soaring rate of violent crime. In Chicago, the murder rate—the statistic least subject to disparities in reporting—rose throughout the 1960s and stayed high throughout the 1970s and 1980s before reaching an all-time peak in 1992, when there were 934 murders in the city. But thereafter homicides fell almost continuously for more than two decades, and by 2013 the number of murders, 415, was at its lowest point since 1965, nearly half a century earlier.[8] In Little Village, a systematic survey of crime in 1999–2001 revealed that despite being a low-income neighborhood with a young population, the homicide rate was no higher than for the city as a whole, and according to the *Chicago Tribune* tally of crime in the city, as of mid-2014 South Lawndale ranked thirty-seventh of seventy-seven community areas with regard to violent crime (on a scale in which the first-place neighborhood was the most dangerous), forty-first in quality-of-life crime, and fifty-fourth in property crime.[9]

Economic conditions in Little Village also made noticeable improvements beginning in the 1970s. As the commercial strip along 26th Street became populated with a growing number of Latino-serving stores, Little Village became a prominent shopping destination for Mexicans throughout the upper Midwest. Storefront vacancy rates dropped, business boomed, and by the turn of the millennium business journalists began reporting a statistic produced by the city's tax authority that has since become by far the most quoted number about Little Village: its shopping district was generating $900 million in sales annually, making it the most active commercial corridor in Chicago other than the Magnificent Mile along Michigan Avenue. Accompanying these changes was a consistent rise in local property values. The median value of a home in the South Lawndale community area more than doubled between 1990 and 2000, and median rents increased by 50 percent or more over the same period. With the economic crisis that began in 2007 and became known as the Great Recession, local real estate values crashed, but as Chicago historian Bradford Hunt has pointed out, even then "Little Village had far fewer boarded-up buildings or vacant lots than other low-income communities."[10]

Sociologists increasingly pointed out the remarkable change of fortune in Little Village in their research on Chicago. In 2002, Eric Klinenberg's *Heat Wave* featured the neighborhood's strong social networks, active commercial landscape, and vibrant street life as part of his explanation of why remarkably few Hispanics died of heatstroke while so many black people and whites—almost thirty times as many in absolute terms and eleven times more as a proportion of the city's population—lost their lives during the devastating heat wave of 1995. Four years later in *There Goes the Neighborhood*, William Julius Wilson and Richard P. Taub incorrectly described Little Village as a place with little social capital but nonetheless suggested that the area's preponderance of Latinos created a zone of relatively low intergroup conflict that could shelter young Hispanics and others from the stress of racial conflict that was felt in many other parts of the city. And in *Great American City* (2012), Robert J. Sampson, on the basis of painstaking analyses of huge data sets analyzed in conjunction with Geographic Information Systems mapping, repeatedly cited Little Village as a place where the influx of immigrant Mexicans led to local economic growth, abundant collective civic events, and falling crime rates (the latter of which is the subject of a large scholarly literature on the inverse relationship between immigration and crime).[11]

The idea that Little Village had made a significant comeback was by no means limited to scholars; a variety of community members, commentators, business groups, and public officials have for years held the neighborhood up as a metonym for a new and improved Chicago, often by quoting the 26th Street-Magnificent Mile statistic in reports and pamphlets and on websites. In 2010 *Images of America*, a series of illustrated neighborhood histories written by local people, published its volume on Little Village. The book's final chapter, titled "Bienvenidos a Little Village," celebrates the influx of Mexicans into the neighborhood over the past four decades, emphasizing the newcomers' "reputation of being hard workers," "entrepreneurial spirit," "traditional values," and "American patriotism" and explaining that "Mexicans have come to Little Village to achieve the American dream and have been successful in doing so." The Little Village Chamber of Commerce subsequently initiated a publicity campaign featuring a new slogan, "Tu México, Tu Chicago," that it featured in pamphlet literature, on its website, and, most visibly, in a series of banners installed on light posts along the 26th Street shopping corridor (Figure 8.1). And in 2012, the city's mayor visited

Figure 8.1. The slogan "Tu México, Tu Chicago," which exemplifies
the transnational character of the Little Village neighborhood,
was emblazoned on banners all along 26th Street as part of the local
chamber of commerce's effort to promote area businesses.

local leaders in the neighborhood, where he "suggested changing the name
of 26th Street . . . to Second Magnificent Mile" and proposed a campaign "to
market it that way."[12]

Broadly speaking, then, Little Village seems to correspond to the findings
of the other authors in this book regarding the connection between immigration and metropolitan revitalization. We get a sense of how people coming to
the United States from abroad have repopulated and revivified a long-declining
urban neighborhood. Why, then, do we even need an approach that empha-
sizes factors such as binational and bilocal activities, dual identities, sustained
interaction between places, and mutual constitutiveness? In the next section, I
attempt to explain how key questions of urbanistic and historical causality and
agency are better revealed by a careful analysis of the specifically *transnational*
context of Little Village. I argue that as long as our interpretations follow a
framework of immigration centered on the United States, our understanding will be incomplete. In order to see the big picture we need to zoom out,
surveying a broader geography in order to be cognizant of the networks of

mobility, culture, and exchange that have been created first and foremost by the denizens of Little Village and other neighborhoods like it.

Transnational Metropolitan Revitalization

A close look at the precise chronology and activities undertaken in Little Village by Mexican migrants, immigrants, and Mexican Americans is essential to evaluating the transnational aspects of the neighborhood's development. Each theory of urban change under globalization is predicated on an explicit or implicit chronology, one that is in turn linked to particular interpretive choices and renderings of causality. Earlier versions of transnational urban theory tend to place substantial emphasis on the relatively recent past. In the most influential of these the pivotal era is the 1980s, with their market-friendly deregulation and financialization of the world economy; in other cases, the key milepost is the oil shocks and economic restructuring that began a decade earlier. Generally speaking, they portray capital as the active agent, with migrants following. Saskia Sassen, for example, portrays working-class migrants as servicing the needs of the professionals whom she suggests were drawn into the centers of global cities. In this sense, their urbanization is ancillary to the new role of cities in the global economy, which she consistently portrays as driven by new capital formations. As she puts it in the introduction to *Cities in a World Economy*, we find in world cities "not only the world of top-level transnational managers and professionals but also that of their secretaries and that of the janitors cleaning the buildings where the new professional class works. Further, it is also the world of a whole new workforce increasingly made up of immigrant and minoritized citizens, who take on the functions once performed by the mother/wife in the older middle classes: the nannies, domestic cleaners, and dog walkers who service the households of the new professional class."[13] By contrast, adherents of "transnationalism from below" are less committed to a grand chronology. They hope to find answers by aggregating place-specific studies of transnational urbanism and understanding the need to historicize each one. Transnational chronologies are often driven by model building, theory, narrativization, and other intellectual imperatives rather than being the result of historical inquiry.[14] The historian's role in debates about transnationalism, then, often involves using archival research to evaluate these chronologies empirically. (It should also be noted that historical research is needed to make clear what distinguishes transnational analyses from previous scholarly approaches, some of which make a strong claim to have been studying transnationalism avant la lettre for many years.)[15]

Our analysis might begin with demographic chronology. In Little Village, the period of greatest Latino population growth—as measured in both absolute numbers and percentage terms—preceded the era of financial globalization. The neighborhood's Latino population leaped from under 2 percent in 1960 to over 33 percent in 1970 and more than 78 percent by 1980; in absolute terms, the Latino population soared from 1,082 in 1960 to 19,967 in 1970 and to 55,151 in 1980. No decade thereafter came close to this magnitude of change: during the 1980s, the Little Village Latino population grew to 90 percent (68,002) and then in the 1990s to nearly 92 percent (74,163)—a substantial rise but a slower rate than in the 1970s. (Notably, the neighborhood's growth in the 1980s is often overestimated when it includes the rapid rise in the number of inmates at the Cook County Jail, one of the nation's largest single-site correctional facilities; calculated without the prison-dominated census tract, the pattern of growth looks rather different.)[16] This chronology is not limited to Little Village; it is essentially the same in the city's second most important and slightly older ethnic Mexican enclave, the adjacent barrio of Pilsen (less commonly known by its neighborhood area designation, the Lower West Side). Pilsen's Spanish-speaking or Spanish-origin population was 14 percent (6,914) in 1960, which climbed rapidly to nearly 55 percent (18,334) in 1970 and over 77 percent (33,735) by 1980. The Latino proportion of the population continued to grow in the 1980s to just over 88 percent and in the 1990s to slightly under 89 percent, but the latter figure actually indicated a fall in real terms, from 40,227 to 39,144, as the overall neighborhood shrank slightly. In both barrios, then, the heyday of human mobility came well before that of globalized capital mobility.[17]

The economic landscape of Little Village also defies the chronology of much global urban theory not only by showing substantial Latinization by the end of the 1970s but also by demonstrating low levels of service-sector employment even into the 1990s. According to the 1980 city directory, the neighborhood's stretch of 26th Street, which extended for twenty-one blocks, was home to at least eighty-four Hispanic businesses. Mirroring the kinds of small locally owned and locally serving establishments that had long been the backbone of shopping districts across Anglo America, Little Village's Spanish-designated businesses included restaurants, groceries, clothiers, bakeries, jewelers, shoe stores, photo studios, bridal boutiques, nightclubs, hairstylists, doctors, attorneys, real estate agents, auto parts stores, a butcher, a florist, a pet shop, a record store, an insurance agency, an upholsterer, a liquor store, and the inevitable funeral home. In a textbook example of institutional completeness, Little Village residents could obtain virtually any goods or services they needed in their own neighborhood and in Spanish.[18] The importance of local commerce and nearby industry in the neighborhood's economy persisted for more than a quarter century. In 1994, the sociologists Marta Tienda and Rebecca Raijman organized a bilingual household survey of Little Village residents. Their respondents reported that more than half of both men and women worked in the manufacturing sector; those in the service sector were far fewer (about 13 percent of men and 15 percent of women), and workers in "personal services" were fewer still (under 4 and 8 percent, respectively). In the most important immigrant neighborhood in a global city and between one and two decades after economic restructuring began, actual employment did not correspond to theoretical expectations.[19]

The patterns of development in Little Village and the importance of Mexican newcomers to the area were also recorded in official municipal reports and local newspaper coverage. Beginning in 1973, the City of Chicago commissioned a series of reports on the Hispanic population and Hispanic businesses and housing. The 1973 report noted that the labor force participation of Spanish-speaking Chicagoans was higher than non-Spanish-speaking city residents and in particular that Hispanic male labor force participation "was considerably higher than that for non-Spanish-speaking males." A 1982 report indicated a doubling of property values between 1975 and 1979, attributing it to the "deep-seated commitment of the community to upgrade South Lawndale," both in the form of mortgage lending and owner-initiated improvements; the report also specified that "South Lawndale now has the highest rate of home-ownership among Hispanics in the nation." With regard to commercial activity, the 1982 report also noted that "Many of the businesses in South Lawndale specialize in Hispanic goods and services. . . . Business in the area is reportedly very good, and merchants have been working together to improve the area and develop its distinctive Hispanic character." This, the report added, made the area "unusual in that its retail sales volume is increasing."[20] Statistics and narratives such as these soon found their way into newspaper reportage. A 1977 article in the *Chicago Tribune* titled "An Oasis of Harmony in the Inner City" explained that Little Village was "a bright spot of ethnic color in an otherwise gray area." It provided vignettes of Mexican American businesspeople such as bridal shop owner Patricia Villareal, who explained of her coethnics that

"These people want to help themselves and each other. They want to buy their own homes and fix them up." Ten years later, the same sorts of images were deployed in articles with such titles as "Enterprising Immigrants Converge on Little Village" and "Old Mexico Is a Hit in Old Chicago," the latter of which quoted a local real estate agent who recalled that "There were a lot of vacant stores in the late '60s when the Spanish began moving in. Now the commercial areas are 85 or 90 percent Mexican."[21]

Statistics and reports such as these document the precise chronology of Latinization in Little Village and other Chicago barrios, but the clearest evidence of grassroots transnationalism—with its cross-border, binational sensibilities and activities in clear evidence among Latinos who arrived a generation before full-fledged globalized capital—can be found in the words of the city's *migrantes* and *inmigrantes* themselves. In 1995, Louise Año Nuevo Kerr of the University of Illinois at Chicago assigned the undergraduates in her class on Chicano history to record oral histories with Mexican American elders who had come to the city over the previous decades. Her students often interviewed parents, grandparents, and various respected figures from their communities. These oral histories captured the stories of Mexicans who had come to Chicago in the postwar era but before the 1980s; since the source of the oral histories involved Mexican American college students, their interviewees did not include those who had come to Chicago in the most recent wave of migration.[22]

The Mexicans who moved to places such as Little Village and Pilsen displayed a variety of transnational attitudes and activities and between the 1950s and the 1970s had already begun to establish durable connections between their new neighborhoods and their places of origin. Their paths to Chicago and the plans they made demonstrate extensive experience with migration, regular border crossings, and a sense of contingency about whether to return to Mexico. Many of these immigrants had long family and community histories of circular and chain migration. Some, such as Jesús Serrato and Rosalio Torres, had been braceros themselves and were thus accustomed to traveling back and forth across the U.S.-Mexican border. Other *chicagoenses* traced their family histories in the United States back to fathers or grandfathers who had participated in the bracero program or had otherwise worked in the United States decades earlier. Agustín Delgado followed his uncle to Chicago; then, he explained, "I brought my brother. Then after my brother, I brought my wife, my sisters and my wife brought her sisters and her mother." Little Village resident Bertha Martínez followed her aunt to Texas and then to

Chicago; on the way, she recalled "various times of coming; going back and forth from Mexico to Texas."[23]

Another frequent characteristic of the interviewees was that they had worked in a number of places on both sides of the border before settling in Chicago. Miguel Ramírez moved from a small rural town to Guadalajara and then to Mexico City before arriving in Little Village in 1977. Eustolia Martínez was born in Texas to Mexican parents. As a young woman she met a bracero and moved to Mexico to marry him; they had two children born in Mexico and two born in Texas before he moved to Chicago and she joined him two years later. José Pérez left the Mexican border town of Piedras Negras, following "one of my wife's sisters" to go work in Fort Worth, Texas. He then became an asparagus and pea picker in Walla Walla, Washington, before returning to Piedras Negras. Pérez then met a group of Mexicans in Eagle Pass, Texas, and decided to go with them to work in a Chicago cannery, arriving in the city in 1956. Many of these Chicago Mexicans had come to the United States and returned to Mexico to dwell for years at a time, to say nothing of the many who had on multiple occasions been deported and returned. Throughout these peregrinations, many had intended to stay in the United States for only a year or two before returning to Mexico; their sense of place involved locations on both sides of the border. Serrato waited for a year and a half before deciding to move his family to Chicago rather than returning to Mexico. Margarita Arredondo arrived in Little Village on a bus in 1974; when her daughter interviewed her, she explained that after giving birth to another daughter in Chicago, she "had calculated that upon two years after your sister was born, I would go back to Mexico."[24]

Even after having lived in Chicago for many years, many interviewees still maintained ongoing contact with Mexico—in some cases as regular visitors to the homeland, in other cases because they still used their home communities as social, cultural, or economic resources. At the time of their interviews in 1995, Torres, the bracero who first came to Chicago in the mid-1950s, said that he returned to Mexico twice annually; Serrato, the other bracero, reported returning to his hometown in Guanajuato every year or two. And Gustavo Mellado, who came to Chicago in 1962, remarked that he had returned to Mexico every year for thirty-two years, sometimes for just two weeks and at other times, when he had been able to save up his vacations, for as many as eleven weeks at a stretch. Notably, the desire to preserve these transnational ties often led Mexicans in the United States to regularize their status precisely because it would allow them to move easily back and forth across the border.

When asked whether she had "any trouble going back to Mexico," Rosina Magaña, a *michoacana* living in Little Village, explained that she could do so easily, having become a legal resident under the provisions of the Immigration Reform and Control Act of 1986: "we fixed our papers and then from there we could just go back and forth." Margarita Arredondo said that she had decided to "legalize myself" during "Reagan's administration," explaining that "I wanted to legalize my residency because I wanted to go back and see your grandmother [the interviewee's mother] who was still alive."[25]

Some Mexican migrants found ways to take advantage of various resources in Mexico even as they continued to live most of their lives in the United States. Chicago dentist Rosa María Silva received her dental training in Mexico, flew her mother from there to the United States on occasion to help with child care, and sent her children to spend the summer in Mexico every year. Humberto Perales, a former Texas Eagle Scout and the editor of a Spanish-language newspaper, rescued his son Juan from a beating on the streets of Little Village in 1984. Upon learning that the boy had joined a gang as a means of self-protection, Perales arranged to have the fourteen-year-old sent to live with relatives in Mexico. Notably, precisely this use of Mexico as a zone of safety for wayward youths was featured by Robert Courtney Smith in *Mexican New York* (2005) as an example of Mexicans' transnational lives.[26]

As they grew older, Mexican immigrants' engagement with their homeland became even more prominent as they planned for the future. They frequently found themselves in an intermediate position between the United States and Mexico because they thought about returning south for their retirement but hesitated to do so because their children were so clearly rooted north of the border. Virtually all of the interviewees had become members of transnational families: some had married U.S. citizens, others were citizens who had married Mexican nationals, and almost all had children who had been born in the United States. When asked about her plans for the future, Margarita Arredondo, who had come to Chicago from Guanajuato more than two decades earlier, responded that "I think that with God's permission, I do plan to go back to Mexico. Maybe when your dad retires who knows what we plan to do . . . if we stay here or if he plans to buy a house over there." When pressed by her daughter Veronica, the only one of her five children not born in Chicago, whether she "fear[ed] that saying '*un día*' could lead to not leaving this country," she elaborated: "The reason that I'm here is because of my children who were born here." Similarly, Gustavo Gómez, who was born in Guadalajara but by the time of his interview had been living in the United

States for nearly forty years and had two American-born children, noted that he and his wife had "considered the idea of going back to Mexico" but concluded that "I think it is almost not possible because our children are here." Rosa Nungaray, a twenty-year resident of Chicago who had four brothers still living in her Mexican hometown of Torreón and four children living in the United States, specified that she was "planning to go back to Mexico" but that when she spoke about it with her children, "They say, sorry Mom, I'm not going to Mexico." Nungaray concluded that "if I'm going to Mexico I know that I'm going to leave half of my family here. So it's sad."[27]

The connections between Chicago and parts of Mexico already established by the 1960s and 1970s were not limited to individual examples; the city's *mexicanos* also inaugurated durable associations that demonstrated collective engagement with their places of origin. The metropolitan area's first hometown associations emerged in these years. Migrants from Michoacán formed the Club Deportivo Taxiomara in 1968–1969; the organization began as a sports club but soon took on significant social and cultural responsibilities. By contrast, the Club San Luis Potosí, formed in 1971, originated with the desire to maintain a regional identity among *potosinos* in Chicago and also to provide assistance to their communities back home. And the Club San Miguel Epejan, also founded in 1971, was initially a devotional group dedicated to the veneration of the Virgin of Guadalupe before taking on a broader range of community concerns. The sociological and anthropological literature on the multifarious activities of hometown associations represents a major focus of research on the activities of *migrantes*, especially in the 1990s and 2000s; the fact that such organizations first emerged two decades before adds further evidence to the significance of longer-established Mexican communities in the deeper history of Pan-American transnationalism. In addition, existing ethnic Mexican organizations moved to coordinate their efforts by forming the Federation of Mexican Organizations, the main goal of which was to help *migrantes* in Chicago find the kinds of services they needed to get by in the host society.[28]

This is not to say that nothing changed after the 1970s; the connections between Little Village and Mexico unmistakably became broader and more numerous and intense beginning in the early 1980s.[29] At the same time, it is essential to recognize that the newer arrivals to Little Village and adjacent barrios were drawn to an area that had already been substantially transformed in ways that made it particularly receptive to them. For example, as Xóchitl Bada has recently emphasized, when Chicago's Mexican migrants substantially stepped up the pace in creating hometown associations, they often did so with the support of local institutions led by longtime Mexican and Mexican American residents; these included community organizations and church-based groups. Many early hometown association leaders were people who had been active in community affairs locally. And as a result of the 1986 immigration act, more than 100,000 Mexican nationals resident in Chicago were able to regularize their status and thereby gain a level of security and cross-border mobility that allowed many of them to become the leaders of the next generation of hometown associations in the 1990s and 2000s.[30] Thus, while the rising mobility of capital certainly did influence a new era of migration, we should not view the newer transnationalism as driven from the commanding heights of the globalizing economy; in point of fact, at multiple points it was built upon foundations laid by immigrants and migrants themselves.

The intensifying transnational connections of the 1980s were soon evident on the streets of Little Village, and subsequently they shaped the landscapes of Mexican migrants' home communities. On 26th Street, Latino businesses went from being a strong contingent in a linguistically mixed neighborhood to easily the dominant presence in the commercial corridor. Perhaps more significant, the street's locally serving shops were increasingly joined by a new category of businesses: those that facilitated continuous connections to other countries. Travel agencies and money transfer outlets, while present previously, multiplied as more *migrantes* moved around and put through an ever-growing volume of financial transactions. The importance of this transnational orientation was concretized on the streetscape in 1987, when the United Latin American Businessmen, the Little Village Chamber of Commerce, the City of Chicago, and other backers cofunded the construction of a Spanish Colonial-style arch across 26th Street. The structure (Figure 8.2)—which one project director called "an ethnic symbol of our community" and which bore the words "Bienvenidos a Little Village"—quickly became the neighborhood's leading architectural feature. Four years later, Little Village's connection with Mexico in particular was recognized at the highest levels when Carlos Salinas de Gortari visited the neighborhood as part of his trip to Chicago, the first in more than ten years for a Mexican head of state. Salinas presented Little Village leaders with a clock that would be installed in the 26th Street arch, intended as a gift on behalf of the governors of six Mexican states.[31]

The increasing interest of Mexican officials in making connections with their citizens living in the United States was one of the hallmarks of

Figure 8.2. The Little Village arch was erected by local Latino
businessmen to emphasize the area's Hispanic character,
a gesture seconded by the president of Mexico when he formally
presented the mounted clock as a gift to the neighborhood.

a period of rising transnationalism, but it is essential to recognize that this
was in many respects an elite response to initiatives that originated from
the bottom up. Many Chicago-area hometown associations had already
begun to use collective remittances to improve infrastructure and facilities
in Mexican pueblos well before state and federal officials became involved.
As Xóchitl Bada has aptly phrased it, "when the Mexican government established an outreach program to organize the migrant communities in Chicago and other places in the United States, government officials realized
that . . . many migrant groups were already organized."[32] The establishment
of the National Solidarity Program by President Salinas in 1988, for example, was intended to harness the energies (and the earnings) of U.S.-based
migrant groups who had already been financing development projects, and
government coordination and assistance did increase the level of participation of *migrantes* in such activities. The decision of the Mexican government in 1998 to facilitate dual Mexican-U.S. citizenship was likewise
designed to use official channels to advance transnational activities that
migrantes had long pursued on their own. And most significant, the subsequent Tres por Uno program offered triple matching grants from county

and state governments and the federal government in support of by then well-established hometown association initiatives for financing a wide array of improvements in Mexican municipalities. This government involvement was undertaken in an administration friendly to neoliberalism, but as Natasha Iskander has shown more generally, these kinds of policies were not a predetermined plot or a simple bow to the "needs" of capital—they resulted from a process of political contestation and improvisation between Mexican migrants and their government.[33]

By the early 2000s, Chicago's *mexicanos* had established a multitude of connections with their places of origin, extending the revitalization effect that they had created in Little Village and other neighborhoods such that it included their hometowns in a transnational system of urban revitalization. For example, in 2004 alone, Chicago hometown associations were involved in a huge number of building projects that improved and in many cases established for the first time basic elements of local infrastructure, important public spaces, and community institutions. These included paving roads in the Mexican state of Hidalgo, building community centers in Guanajuato and Oaxaca, constructing potable water plants and a bullring in Guerrero state, improving an electrical grid and building a child welfare office in San Luis Potosí, and in the state of Michoacán alone building or improving roads, children's parks, agricultural facilities, egg incubators, playing fields and their associated observation stands and bathrooms, and a public library.[34]

The increasing integration of Little Village into a cross-border urban system appears to have followed a gradual and contingent chronology in which key points of articulation more clearly follow the patterns associated with transnationalism from below than they do with more top-down, capital-centered renderings of urban change. The neighborhood was in some sense transnational no later than the 1960s, and by the late 1970s many of its residents were regularly engaged with their places of origin in Mexico. It is certainly the case that the intensity of transnational exchange increased beginning in the 1980s, but even then the "global cities" narrative of big transnational capital provides only a generalized background for the transformations at hand, and its ideas about causality remain schematic rather than documented. By contrast, we can see clear points of articulation that depended on the activities of an earlier generation of immigrants, the organizational energy of more recent immigrants, and the decision making of Mexican and U.S. administrations and legislatures. The course of transnationalism in Little Village, in other words, has not been a grand narrative of capital but instead has been a history with a distinctive geographic and temporal context and a substantial measure of agency, contingency, and government participation.

Global Metropolitan Revitalization?

My research to date in this chapter and in an earlier article on Dallas has been based on the idea of an urban system extending across the Americas, and the insights that I think we can gain from a transnational approach to metropolitan revitalization are derived from this hemispheric perspective. But looking forward, I think that further decentering the subject matter could tell us even more about how metropolitan areas have become linked together by the movement of money, information, and especially people. After all, migrants increasingly operate within a global urban system, and a growing number of scholars have begun to use a diasporic framework for their inquiries in much the same way Donna Gabaccia began to study Italians from the standpoint of their leaving Italy for a variety of destinations rather than as arrivals in the United States.[35]

If we take this approach to Mexico—one of the world's largest exporters of people—we recognize that its *migrantes* have been predominantly located in the United States but that its reach is becoming more geographically diverse. Looking at the Mexican government's 2012 list of emigrant associations gives us a sense of the nation's emergent diaspora. There are more than 2,400 organizations listed in the spreadsheet. More than 2,200 of them are registered in the United States, but there are also nearly 200 groups in other countries throughout the world, including Argentina, Australia, Belgium, Bolivia, Canada, Chile, China, France, Germany, Guatemala, Honduras, Italy, Japan, Norway, the Netherlands, New Zealand, South Korea, Spain, Sweden, Switzerland, and the United Kingdom.

It is not yet clear to what extent Mexicans have been influencing urban areas in countries besides the United States, but given their presence as workers in so many nations, it will be fascinating to determine what effect their presence is having in a variety of different landscapes. At the very least, it is worth noting that the connections that bind Mexico to places beyond its borders are now denominated not just in dollars but also in euros, pounds, kronor, and other currencies.[36] It is quite beyond the scope of this chapter to propose that we should look at all the possible overlapping networks of people around the globe. Trying to analyze scores of overlapping transnational social fields would be a dizzyingly complex undertaking, but it would certainly give us a truer picture of the transnational component of the ongoing urbanization of the world.

Conclusion

In assessing the implications of this inquiry into the transformation of Little Village, we might begin with the basic empirical findings. There can be little doubt that the Mexican arrivals in the area were essential to the demographic and economic revitalization of the neighborhood and eventually of much of Chicago, where the population is fast approaching one-third Latino. This process was not limited to unidirectional immigration, however—it depended on ongoing transnational connections back and forth between Chicago and numerous communities in Mexico. The revivification of Little Village gradually extended beyond the barrio and its city and nation and came to include the built environments of distant pueblos as well. The advent of migrant-driven revitalization began no later than the 1960s and 1970s and in some respects was conditioned upon transnational connections that were established even earlier. The transformation of the neighborhood did accelerate in the early 1980s, but this was shaped more by *migrantes* themselves than by the transnationally operating capitalists who are more often cited as the prime movers of urban change. In sum, Little Village and adjacent barrios were transformed for reasons, and on a timeline, that more clearly reflected their agency and previous patterns of migration than they did the more recent restructuring of the global economy.

These findings furthermore suggest, at least preliminarily, a broader intervention into ongoing debates on the role of cities in globalization. The role of migrants should not be reduced to a narrative in which working people simply respond to the dictates of international capital; as Michael Peter Smith and Luis Eduardo Guarnizo have put it, "It is time to move beyond these theoretical discourses in which migrants seem to be perceived as will-less actors reacting to forces beyond their control."[37] Chicago's ethnic Mexican communities consciously and deliberately acted to maneuver before and during the most recent changes in the global economy; their actions were individual and collective and eventually elicited responses from multiple levels of governance, from municipal to state to federal. This rich history must not be shoehorned into schematic narratives in which complex human activities are subsumed within a story that in effect casts millions of *migrantes* and their political representatives as little more than helpmeets of global capitalism. We should heed the warning that Dipesh Chakrabarty issued relatively early in the development of transnational studies. He recalled the long and troubled history of thinkers in the imperial core emplotting the lives of people in the periphery into grand narratives that assigned little or no importance to their own ideas and agency.[38] If we are to avoid perpetuating some of the same kinds of ethnocentric and deterministic ways of thinking that underlay earlier versions of modernization theory, we need to be sure that our understanding of urban transnationalism takes into account the broadest possible range of evidence, experience, and perspective. For as much as globalization reflects the undeniable power and prerogative of the commanding heights, it does not determine all the possibilities for maneuver available to people on the move in different sites and on different scales and within a process whose development is not complete and cannot be confidently known.

In terms of policy, my research suggests two main directions of action. The first of these, which echoes the entreaties of the many hundreds of thousands of people who marched in Chicago and dozens of other U.S. cities in 2006, is to find ways for state and especially federal officials to assist migrants in continuing to revitalize municipalities through their transnational activities. As the scholars who have contributed to this collection attest, newcomers to the United States have greatly benefited the well-being of entire metropolitan areas, and as I have argued in particular, this revitalization has depended on the establishment and strengthening of transnational connections. When governments have placed excessive restrictions on cross-border mobility, the result has been to criminalize millions of people, forcing them to participate in shadow economies characterized by constant anxiety, grinding labor exploitation, and colossally wasteful inefficiencies. When governments have offered migrants opportunities to regularize their legal status and found ways to facilitate transnational mobility and exchange, they have generated tremendous economic growth and fostered neighborhood vitality. It would make sense for the U.S. government to follow the lead of Mexican officials by passing the kinds of laws that have allowed *migrantes* to broaden already-existing transnational connections that have become the lifeblood of communities on both sides of the border.

The second broad policy recommendation is to change the way we think about attracting people to U.S. cities. Too often, policy makers and public officials emphasize the desirability of elite professionals: influential formulations include talk of "highly skilled immigrants," the "creative class," or "high-tech workers" who are thought to be the most desirable city residents. What I think the past and present of Little Village and many similar neighborhoods has shown, however, is that urban revitalization has been as much or more the creation of working- and middle-class migrants and immigrants than it has been the province of executives, yuppies, technology wizards, or hipsters.[39] As I have sought to demonstrate, it was *migrantes* who initiated processes of neighborhood renewal that began almost as soon as the urban crisis itself, at a time when most white-collar professionals were still fleeing the city.[40] Even without the benefit of the kinds of cash subsidies, special incentives, tax breaks, and assorted wealth transfers that have been showered upon already-wealthy developers, investors, and employers, Latinos—some migrants, others immigrants, still others naturalized or native-born citizens—have brought neighborhoods and entire cities back from the brink of ruin. If our politics and policy making were driven less by the demonization, harassment, and hunting of migrants and their families and more by a consensus about the kinds of path-to-citizenship immigration reform favored by Democratic and Republican administrations, chambers of commerce and labor unions, and immigrant advocates and the general public alike, millions of people who have come to the United States from Latin America could continue to rejuvenate the neighborhoods where they live now, work to improve the pueblos and villas whence they came, and extend the benefit of their labors to still more places in need of revitalization.

CHAPTER 9

Liberian Reconstruction,
Transnational Development,
and Pan-African Community Revitalization

Domenic Vitiello and Rachel Van Tosh

Black immigrants and refugees have played major roles in recent metropolitan and neighborhood revitalization in cities such as New York, Minneapolis, Philadelphia, and Atlanta. At the same time, many African and Caribbean immigrants are working to rebuild their home regions and nations, often in collaboration with their African American neighbors. Both the black urban neighborhoods of the United States and the cities, towns, and villages of Liberia, Nigeria, Haiti, and other countries have been devastated in recent decades, though by distinct experiences of discrimination, uneven investment, wars, and epidemics. Confronting these challenges, black immigrants and African Americans have forged politics and institutions promoting shared opportunity. They engage in diverse forms of social and economic development in migrant sending and receiving communities, investing as much in repairing people's lives and rebuilding civil society and nation states as in infrastructure, enterprises, housing, or other place-based aspects of revitalization.

This chapter examines transnational development among Liberians in Philadelphia, who offer a window into the broader work of black immigrants and Americans mobilizing to rebuild places, institutions, and communities. It draws on twenty-six in-depth semistructured interviews conducted between 2006 and 2013 with twenty-two leaders of African organizations in Philadelphia, including fifteen Liberians, some who participated in more than one interview.[1] The Liberian community's experiences highlight the diversity of transnational development between and within different immigrant groups in U.S. cities and suburbs. They also illuminate the importance as well as some of the challenges and opportunities that transnational development holds for revitalizing sending and receiving communities.

Liberian and Pan-African civil society in U.S. cities contests and complicates the assumptions behind two of the most prominent critiques of migrant-led transnational development. First and popularly, critics of immigration—from Washington think tanks to conservative talk radio—deride immigrants and their hometown associations for sending money earned in the United States to other nations as opposed to investing it in local banks and communities.[2] Second, although migrant-led development has drawn considerable interest from urban and international development organizations, development economists and international organizations have often dismissed it as "sporadic and relatively small."[3] Most damning for development scholars and institutions is its general failure to produce what economists traditionally define as the goals of development, namely real economic growth measured largely in terms of jobs, income, and gross domestic product.[4] Social science research on migrant-led transnational activities has focused largely on economic activity. Scholars have paid the greatest attention to the projects of hometown associations, the promotion of entrepreneurship and business development,[5] and the sending of remittances.[6] Some have examined the variations of hometown and other associations, which range from small informal groups to large registered nonprofits that are part of regional confederations or national associations.[7]

To make sense of the wide variety of transnational activities that migrants and their allies pursue, scholars and development professionals must look beyond hometown associations, business ventures, and remittances to a wider field of community and economic development institutions that collaborate, complement, and sometimes compete with one another.[8] Understanding transnational development not just as a series of projects, but as an ecosystem of institutions and the overlapping networks of people who lead them, illuminates the processes and geographies of urban and community revitalization. Viewing transnational development in terms of not just economic growth and productivity but also family welfare, education, and other crucial aspects of social stability and mobility, urban scholars and professionals may find more inclusive and useful ways to theorize and support transnational and local community development.

It is equally important for social scientists, policy makers, and development professionals to understand how the diversity of immigration to the metropolitan United States has produced varied patterns of local and transnational development. Transnational projects in Liberia, investing in infrastructure and enterprise development (especially import-export and specialty products), generally resemble those of transnational organizations led by Mexican, Salvadoran, and Dominican immigrants in the United States. Similar to activities by immigrants from Latin America and the Caribbean, India, China, and other places, transnational initiatives in West Africa promote human capital development, often through support of schools and scholarships, as well as the conditions for revitalization, including government transparency and public health. However, African and Liberian immigrants' institutional, investment, and migration patterns differ in important ways. Unlike in most Latin American or Asian communities, transnational development among Africans in the United States involves and invests in African American and black immigrant communities in U.S. inner cities and suburbs. While Latin American and Asian immigrants' transnational projects often spend money in U.S. cities, they rarely work closely with receiving communities in the ways that African immigrants have since the 1990s. The Liberian community's mix of immigration statuses also differs from the status profiles of Mexicans, Dominicans, and even most West Africans. Most Liberians in the United States, like Sierra Leoneans until 2004 and Haitians since the 2010 earthquake, had temporary protected status (TPS), not permanent refugee status or asylum. (Many Liberians have also attained permanent residency, and some have naturalized in the United States). The U.S. government allowed Liberians' TPS to expire in 2007, shifting Liberians previously on TPS to the status of deferred enforced departure, renewable every eighteen months; however, in 2014 the Ebola crisis in West Africa prompted the United States to grant Liberians TPS again. As a result, most Liberians are expected to return to their homeland someday, which is one reason why many civil society organizations focus on migrants' dispersed families and home regions.

The groups that make up Liberian and Pan-African civil society discussed in this chapter show that (1) many transnational initiatives invest in U.S. communities and (2) revitalizing both sending and receiving communities necessarily entails much more than traditional measures of economic development. Liberian migrants' understandings of "home" are fluid, and the ties between sending and receiving communities are dynamic—a clear departure from old notions about immigrants' ties to their homelands diminishing over time. Their investments in social and economic development in both Africa and the United States are part of a larger process of community revitalization in which the fortunes of people and places in different parts of the world are increasingly interlaced.

African Migration in Philadelphia

Africans represent a small but growing portion of immigrants in the United States, and Philadelphia is one of the largest centers of African settlement. It has the nation's largest Liberian population and has been an important destination for West African immigrants since the 1960s, initially mostly university students and professionals from Nigeria, Ghana, and, since the 1980s, Liberia. Ethiopian and Eritrean refugees arrived in the 1980s, followed in subsequent decades by refugees and immigrants from Liberia, Sierra Leone, Guinea, Ivory Coast, Mali, Senegal, Sudan, and other parts of mainly sub-Saharan Africa. Since the 1980s, newcomers from Jamaica, Haiti, Trinidad, and other parts of the Caribbean have settled in most of the same neighborhoods.[9]

Black immigrants figured largely in the Philadelphia region becoming a "re-emerging gateway" at the end of the twentieth century, helping to reverse fifty-five years of population loss in 2007.[10] By 2000 Jamaicans were the fifth-largest foreign-born group in the city, and by 2006 Liberians were the tenth largest (numbering 4,000 in the city according to the census, though community leaders estimate that there could be as many as 15,000 in the region). The largest numbers of African immigrants have settled in the African American neighborhoods of West and Southwest Philadelphia and adjacent working-class suburbs, with some in upper North Philadelphia. Most of these places remain poor neighborhoods in fiscally stressed municipalities, experiencing only mixed or partial revitalization compared to more stable middle-class or gentrifying areas. However, black immigrants have played major roles in buoying the neighborhoods' and municipalities' populations, housing markets, and commercial corridors.

Africans have also transformed civil society in the region's black communities. Liberian community leaders and their constituents cite robust supports offered by migrant- and native-led workforce development, social service, and other institutions in Philadelphia—some of which are discussed below—for many Liberians' secondary migration to Philadelphia from New

York, New England, and other regions.[11] In addition to these local supports, African communities and their civil society organizations have introduced new and diverse transnational challenges and opportunities.

The Liberian Diaspora and the Diversity
of Transnational Development

The nation of Liberia itself was a project of transnational development by black Americans and Africans in the nineteenth century, but the civil war of the 1990s has largely defined Liberian transnational development in recent years. This inspired a dramatic shift in Liberian civil society, particularly among migrants in the United States. For example, the Lofa County Association of Liberia began as a student association in the 1970s, organized primarily for social purposes, but according to Reverend John Jallah, a Liberian community leader in Philadelphia, it "took on new meaning and new roles as a result of the crisis and the war." People in the United States "wanted to get in touch with family members, with the village, and everyone who had been uprooted from the village wanted to get in touch with each other." The association "sent delegates once the war started to end . . . [and we] sent people to see what had happened, and see how the village was." Ultimately, "the crisis really caused the county associations to take a little more [of a] role in keeping track of what was going on and the rebuilding effort."[12] But, like Latin American hometown associations, the county associations are part of a larger civil society engaged in this work.[13]

The long list of transnational activities in which Reverend Jallah participates reveals a diverse ecosystem of organizations that work between Philadelphia, other U.S. cities, and West Africa, embracing a broad range of community and economic development roles and concerns. A widely respected community leader, he has served on the Pennsylvania and national boards of the Union of Liberian Associations in the Americas (ULAA), the most influential institution in the political and social affairs of the diaspora. He has helped lead the state and national boards of the Lofa County Association, the diaspora's chief vehicle for promoting infrastructure, education, and health in his home region. He is a member of the Loma University Alumni Association, one of many African college and private school alumni groups active in American cities. Jallah serves as minister to at least two churches and helps lead church associations in Philadelphia and Liberia (other professional associations for Liberians in the United States exist for journalists and performing artists). His church in Liberia runs a school, for which he raises funds in Philadelphia. He is also the coordinator of a local farm collective in Lofa County.

In his day job, Jallah runs the Agape Senior Center out of the Lutheran refugee program office in West Philadelphia, offering English classes and other basic supports and orientation to mainly West African refugees and immigrants. This has drawn him into working with the Philadelphia Corporation for the Aging, the city's largest service agency for seniors. In his night job, he runs a cleaning service for offices and other commercial clients in the city and suburbs, part of a larger transnational labor market that has fueled migration to Philadelphia. In two of his many evening and weekend commitments, Jallah serves on the boards of the region's most prominent Pan-African institutions, the Coalition of African Communities in Philadelphia (AFRICOM), for which he has led the Conflict Resolution Committee, and the Philadelphia Mayor's Commission for African and Caribbean Immigrant Affairs.[14]

The variety of local and transnational work in which Jallah has engaged reflects an effort to "do everything I can to help my people." He has even joined African American churches in an effort to understand African Americans better, to put himself in a position to more effectively help African immigrants and African Americans live together in peace and promote mutual opportunity.[15] In his sentiment, and in his variety of organizational affiliations, Jallah is representative of a large group of Liberian and other black immigrant and native-born community leaders in Philadelphia and other U.S. cities. African associations in Philadelphia take roughly the same forms as and are often part of or networked with the larger range of African diaspora organizations in the United States. Similar patterns of involvement in multiple local, national, and transnational organizations are also prevalent among many other immigrant communities' leadership.

Like the Lofa County Association, many African migrant associations began as social groups. With increased migration and improvements in communication, transnational projects became more common since the 1990s, and for Liberians and some other immigrants, civil war and changing migration patterns dramatically transformed migrant civil society. For example, the ULAA mostly helped families cover funeral expenses and organized birthday parties and other social events in its early years in the 1980s. But by the mid-1990s as people fled Liberia during and after the civil war, the Liberian population of U.S. cities and suburbs was no longer mainly "college kids," according to ULAA past president Samuel Togba Slewion, a journalist, publisher, social worker, and, like Jallah, a leader of many organizations.[16] The ULAA also included people with limited education and people of all ages and backgrounds suffering severe problems resulting from the civil crisis and war.

This prompted the ULAA to focus on social services, policy, and advocacy. The ULAA deploys its chapters in Pennsylvania, Maryland, Ohio, and other states to work with local organizations, led by migrant and receiving communities, to coordinate and provide social and health services to families, seniors, and youths. Positioning themselves as advocates for the Liberian diaspora, the mainly professional class leaders of the ULAA have promoted and supported democratic elections and reforms in Liberia. A greater proportion of Liberian and other African immigrant community and organizational leaders are from the professional class, compared to Mexicans, Salvadorans, and Dominicans. At the national, county or state, and local levels in both Liberia and the United States, according to Sam Slewion, these leaders "stay involved in the government to make sure that government is treating people fairly."[17]

Similarly, Liberian county associations and their leaders engage in a mix of political, social, and—more than the ULAA—economic development pursuits in Liberia. Each of Liberia's fifteen counties has a corresponding nonprofit county association in the United States. Like Latin American hometown associations, they help to finance, plan, and build schools, health clinics, and road, water, and communications infrastructure, typically in collaboration with county governments, and they commonly launch agricultural enterprises and send medical and educational supplies. Unlike most Latin American hometown associations, they regularly provide scholarships for school and university students in Liberia. These acts of building and rebuilding came partly from the diaspora's recognition that the postwar interim government was not focused on local reconstruction but instead on immediate national goals such as security.

Like other diasporas and their hometown associations, they also push county governments to perform and help boost their capacity for development.[18] During the course of a large project in the county, the Liberian government may call and send meeting minutes to the Lofa association's leaders in Philadelphia, Providence, and other U.S. regions every week. Jallah and other community leaders provide oversight that helps lend further legitimacy, among Liberians in Africa and the United States, to reconstruction and development projects.[19] County associations and their leaders also back political candidates, sometimes provoking tensions in Liberia and the United States.[20]

The national boards of Liberian county associations usually determine and oversee the larger development projects in Africa, while their state chapters typically focus on the more immediate needs of their members in the United States and their families in Africa. State chapters support the national organization's projects with their dues and also engage in some smaller transnational projects themselves. The Maryland County Association of Pennsylvania, for example, funds scholarships for students in four schools in Liberia and gathers books and medical supplies to send annually. The national boards commonly send representatives to Africa on a monthly basis, and some associations maintain partner groups or employees in Liberia to assist with projects and communication—a pattern shared with other African transnational associations in Philadelphia and other U.S. and European cities.[21]

In their scale, complexity, and variety, Liberian county associations' development projects rival those of the most active Latin American hometown associations and regional confederations in the United States and of other African associations in the United States and Europe.[22] The Sinoe County Association of the Americas built and owns the $150,000 Center for Global Engagement in one of the county's largest cities, with offices and conference rooms and a library and media center. Development partners included the county and national governments along with Ohio-based Taylor University, an early tenant in the center. Liberian nonprofits also send representatives to the United States to seek the association's assistance, for example, a builder of low-cost housing for teachers in rural areas that gained the association's financial and political support. The Nema County association negotiated a community benefits agreement with a multinational firm that established a mine in the county, and the mining company has underwritten a development fund for the county government. In recent years the leaders of county associations, who are also often active in the ULAA, have begun to collaborate on larger regional projects such as roads, telecommunications, airports and seaports, and agricultural infrastructure.[23]

Also like Latin American hometown associations, county associations work to keep the diaspora connected to and invested in the counties. After Western Union declined to open an office in Sinoe County, in 2011 the county association raised funds to buy the necessary equipment and hire a clerk to work for Western Union, establishing the first money-wiring service in a region of 100,000 residents.[24] The Grand Gedeh Association built an Internet café in the county seat to expand computer access and improve transnational communication, a common practice among Latin American associations.[25]

Similar to but generally more than Mexican, Dominican, and Salvadoran hometown associations, Liberian county associations invest in the welfare of the diaspora as well as their sending communities. The Sinoe County Association is fairly representative in its mission to "assist with specific development projects and programs through planning, finance and manpower . . . [and] to seek the social welfare and well-being of all Sinoeans residing in the United States and the Republic of Liberia."[26] Association (national and Pennsylvania) past president Sam Slewion explained transnational organizations' diverse and dispersed interests in terms of community leaders' responsibility to help rebuild the country so people can return home:

> If [the organizations] can help to create a peaceful and stable environment in Liberia, the better it will be for them and their families. . . . [I]f Liberia is not stable, and has to resort to violence, they will feel the brunt also, because they have to worry about how to move [their families] to a new country, maintain, them, etc., . . . [E]ven though you are not in the country, [you] have to be engaged in the county . . . [and] remain engaged with the government and policy issues . . . because if the environment is better, then people will be able to go home.[27]

The county association's scholarships for students in the sciences, health care, agriculture, and teaching target sectors of particular need in the county. They seek to build its professional class, requiring recipients to work in the county for the ensuing two or three years.[28]

In addition to county associations, many Liberians have more recently established hometown associations that serve smaller communities in Liberia and the United States, usually first with mutual aid to members and their families and later via place-based and larger economic development projects. The Tallah Families Association, for example, began in 1998 as an effort of the roughly two hundred migrants in the United States from the township of Tallah to help fund extended family members' schooling and other personal and family needs in Liberia and America and to remain connected with one another. In 2009 leaders renamed it the Tallah Development Corporation, reflecting its increased focus on infrastructure and building projects, including wells that brought drinking water to six of the township's ten boroughs as well as a

$10,000 investment to repair and upgrade Tallah High School, raised in collaboration with the school's alumni association. This shift in orientation toward development, however, did not end the association's attention to the immediate needs of its members and their families in Philadelphia and Africa.[29]

Beyond county and hometown associations, social service and mutual aid organizations in Philadelphia and other cities have developed ambitious programs in Liberia and the neighboring nations to which Liberians fled. In the mid-2000s the Philadelphia region's largest Liberian-led social service agency, the African Cultural Alliance of North America (ACANA), formalized what heretofore had been informal assistance for people with transnational problems ranging from immigration services to support of families in Liberia. ACANA opened a satellite office in Monrovia, Liberia, and has collaborated with partners in Freetown, Sierra Leone, and Accra, Ghana. Though the Accra office later closed, these small offices have served refugees and internally displaced people with reintegration services, largely education, mental health, and access to jobs for people choosing to return to Liberia or stay in other countries. The Liberia and Sierra Leone offices worked to get computers in classrooms across the two countries and supported small business development.[30] Other Liberian-led social service organizations, such as the Multicultural Community Family Services (MCFS) in the working-class suburbs just beyond Southwest Philadelphia, help constituents with transnational family problems but have not launched formal transnational programs.[31]

Smaller and often (in American terms) less formalized mutual aid organizations rarely capture the attention of scholars and policy makers interested in transnational development. However, like mutual aid societies of European immigrants a century ago and like the Liberian social organizations that became development institutions, migrants' smaller ethnic and national associations in African, Latin American, and Southeast Asian communities in U.S. cities play active roles in transnational social and material support.[32] They sometimes also make place-based investments. In Philadelphia, Liberian and other West African associations commonly help new immigrants find jobs and housing, children enroll in school, and community members navigate trouble with the police (as do the staff of ACANA and the MCFS). Smaller ethnic and nationality associations also raise funds for weddings, births, and cultural festivals and to repatriate members' bodies (which can cost $8,000 to $10,000) and support their families in the United States and Liberia, again resembling the mutual aid societies of earlier immigrants.[33]

These activities help enable transnational community revitalization. In the view of many association leaders, economic and social stability in Philadelphia is a precondition for collective transnational development. This mirrors findings from the United Kingdom, where Mercer, Page, and Evans note that African associations "are concerned first and foremost with the welfare of their members."[34] In Philadelphia, the stability and welfare of constituents in the United States is typically the first priority of local migrant associations that *do* engage in transnational projects and programs, sometimes in collaboration with Pan-African intermediary organizations discussed below. In many cases, leaders of smaller associations aspire to transnational projects and programs, but meager resources and constituents' immediate needs limit their ability to work overseas.[35]

Transnational civil society in Liberian Philadelphia, Providence, Baltimore, and other regions pursues a diverse range of reconstruction and revitalization initiatives. Liberian organizations' mix of social, political, and economic development roles is familiar to scholars who have studied hometown associations in Latin America and elsewhere, as is their evolution from organizing the diaspora to partnering in development with government.[36] However, transnational community development projects and programs among African immigrants arguably take even more diverse forms than among Latin American immigrants and focus more on the welfare of the diaspora. This may be partially explained by Africans' greater diversity of class, educational attainment, and labor market experiences and by the need of some groups to rebuild communities and nations after civil war. Furthermore, Africans' engagement with receiving communities, especially with their African American neighbors, makes for more marked differences.

Pan-African Community Development

Liberians' community development initiatives, including much of their transnational work and especially their engagement in U.S. cities, grow not only out of the needs of the diaspora but also from the history of relationships among black immigrants and African Americans. Many black immigrant and African American organizations have embraced Pan-African missions and constituencies. This is partly in response to tensions and violence between African Americans and black immigrants, most famously in Philadelphia the brutal beating of a thirteen-year-old boy from Liberia on his way home from school in 2005. A variety of specifically Pan-African organizations have also evolved to support collaboration among diverse community leaders organizing social services, trade missions, and business and social enterprise development in and between Philadelphia and other cities in the United States, Africa, and the Caribbean. This work has created new opportunities for African Americans as well as immigrants, including investment in local neighborhood development in the United States and also access to international markets, helping to counter the disinvestment and isolation long experienced by American blacks.

Since the mid-2000s, Liberian social service organizations in Philadelphia, including ACANA and the MCFS, have broadened their constituencies and their missions from helping West African refugees to assisting a wider range of newcomer and receiving communities. African Americans and other immigrants came to them seeking help with many of the same health, education, child care, and other services.[37] ACANA's initial programs focused on arts and culture as a way to integrate mainly Liberians and Sierra Leoneans, many of whom were wary of the state and civil society, into human service programs. By 2010, the health and mental health, education, antiviolence, workforce development, entrepreneurship, and other programs run by or at ACANA served almost as many African Americans as Africans. While some of its social services operate transnationally, ACANA's housing counseling, commercial corridor planning, and neighborhood arts and educational facilities development concentrate its place-based investments in Southwest Philadelphia.[38]

Many immigrant- and native-led community organizations in West and Southwest Philadelphia have focused on improving relationships among and between African Americans and black immigrants, especially after the prominent beating in 2005. African American-led community and economic development and service organizations have hired African immigrant staff and actively incorporated black immigrants into their housing counseling, financial literacy, and other programs focused on community revitalization.[39] The region's leading workforce integration organization, the Welcoming Center for New Pennsylvanians, and several local merchants associations launched projects to improve relationships among immigrant and native shopkeepers and their neighbors and customers.[40]

Liberians collaborated with other black immigrants and African Americans in founding Philadelphia's two most prominent Pan-African organizations, AFRICOM (in 2000) and the Mayor's Commission for African and

Caribbean Immigrant Affairs (in 2008, on the occasion of the Live 8 concert in the city). Through monthly meetings and regular events focused on health, immigration, or culture, these organizations help structure the dense networks of relationships between African, Caribbean, and African American community and political leaders. Both have supported Liberian community leaders in connecting their constituents to health, education, employment, and other services and opportunities. AFRICOM and the Mayor's Commission also offer venues in which to raise concerns of their constituents to a wider audience; host official guests from overseas and from Washington, D.C.; and seek support for local and transnational projects.

The Mayor's Commission for African and Caribbean Immigrant Affairs has partnered on regular trade missions with the African and Caribbean Business Council (ACBC), a Pan-African membership organization. The ACBC's mission, resembling its partners in AFRICOM and the Mayor's Commission, is "promoting & preserving the business interests of African and Caribbean entrepreneurs in the Greater Philadelphia area while bridging the cultural divide between member countries and the larger community through education and the encouragement of mutual tolerance."[41] ACBC trade missions promote import-export and other transnational business ventures for companies large and small. Often planned with Liberians and other blacks in Baltimore and other cities, they have included trips to various African nations (including Liberia) and reciprocal visits from delegations of business and government representatives. The ACBC has also attempted to develop a credit union to help underwrite black-owned businesses in the United States. Still, like AFRICOM and the Mayor's Commission, much of the ACBC's meetings, listserv discussions, and work concentrate on building relations of tolerance and a politics of mutually supportive entrepreneurship among its Pan-African constituency.[42]

The ACBC is one of three Philadelphia-based organizations led by African immigrants that formally position themselves as transnational enterprise development intermediary and support organizations. These groups provide formal training, mentoring, technical assistance, and local and transnational networking opportunities for black entrepreneurs—all of which also focus on social and U.S.-based concerns as well as business operations and opportunities. The Afri-Caribe Microenterprise Network (AMEN), led by a woman from Sierra Leone and based in Philadelphia and Georgia, also organizes trade missions between the United States and African nations. Sharing the ACBC's politics of Pan-African prosperity but with a commitment to faith-based business and community development, AMEN aims to "empower women, youth, informal sector operators, immigrants and the poor throughout Africa, South America, the Caribbean and the USA."[43] AMEN mainly works with existing and aspiring transnational entrepreneurs, including Liberians, but also supports them in U.S.-based ventures and in learning about local issues in Philadelphia, Wilmington, Delaware, and Atlanta such as permits and zoning.[44] The ACBC similarly offers its technical assistance to transnational and local Philadelphia businesses alike.[45]

The third Pan-African transnational development intermediary is Palms Solutions, which supports mostly social entrepreneurship and community projects in the United States and Africa. Established in 2009 by a man from Ivory Coast who, like the founder and director of AMEN, formerly worked with the World Bank and other international development institutions, the Palms mission was initially one of networking and development with a narrower constituency to "enhance the social and economic status of the poor rural communities in the West African Francophone countries through new paradigms of sustainable social enterprises and productive interactions between the diaspora, U.S.-based organizations, academic institutions and the African Homeland's stakeholders."[46] Palms has since broadened its work to include Liberians, African Americans, and other Anglophones, maintaining a network of chapters in twelve U.S. states. Its projects include promoting women's education in Africa with the African Union's first ladies, funded by the Rockefeller Foundation; organizing volunteers from U.S. universities to conduct small development projects in Africa; and supporting microcredit circles for migrants to support members' businesses and families in Philadelphia and Africa.[47]

The broad social as well as economic development focus of AMEN and Palms grows partly from their founders' critiques of mainstream international development. The problems they cite include limited scale and types of assistance to diaspora-led enterprises, inadequate inclusion of diaspora community members in planning and decision making, and insufficient attention to social and community needs that must be met for economic development to succeed.[48] Indeed, African immigrant leaders' attention to local issues in black immigrant and receiving communities results partly from the dynamic in community revitalization in which civic leaders and organizations must often address people's most immediate problems before they can succeed in more ambitious or complex projects.[49]

While much of their work focuses squarely on helping their countrymen and women rebuild their lives and homelands, Liberian and other African leaders' transnational commitments cannot be understood in isolation from the context of Pan-African networks. As Mercer, Page, and Evans note about West African associations in the United Kingdom, "it is possible to overstate the distinction between 'development at home' and 'welfare in the diaspora.'"[50] As noted above, even organizations most focused on businesses rather than places and those least embedded in particular migrant sending regions, such as the ACBC, AMEN, and Palms, extend their activities to address social and place-based issues of conflict resolution and community building in U.S. cities and suburbs, Africa, and the Caribbean.

The work of Pan-African civil society grows out of concerted efforts to define and pursue common interests among newcomer and receiving communities in Philadelphia and other centers of black immigration. Efforts to address inter- and intragroup tensions have produced enduring networks of people and institutions working locally and transnationally for a broadly defined Pan-African community revitalization. Pan-African civil society has both rhetorically and practically tied the work of community revitalization in the United States to that of reconstruction and revitalization in Liberia, Nigeria, Haiti, and other parts of Africa and the Caribbean. Liberians in Philadelphia, Atlanta, New York, and other cities have thus drawn other black immigrants and African Americans into the work of rebuilding Liberia's economy, society, and communities. And conversely, transnational development initiatives among Liberians and other black immigrants afford new local and international opportunities for black Americans.

From Transnational Development to Urban and Community Revitalization

The structure, investments, and politics of community and economic development in Liberian and Pan-African Philadelphia challenge many social scientists' and development institutions' ideas about the value and purpose of migrant-led transnational development. Transnational organizations, and the individuals who comprise them, have complex goals of assisting individuals both in the United States and abroad and do so through methods ranging from social to economic. Liberian and Pan-African transnational civil society also invites scholars and development professionals to rethink traditional conceptions of the geographies and constituencies of transnational development. The transnational and local work of black immigrants and Americans can be best understood as a broad project of repairing and rebuilding communities focused on people and the relationships between them as much as on reconstructing places—in the United States as well as Africa.

These practices exist in tension with other visions and projects of revitalization. For instance, the administration of Philadelphia mayor Michael Nutter, an African American, made airport expansion its principal investment in immigrant attraction and associated economic development, to the consternation of many African community leaders and their allies. This contrasted with the greater focus on neighborhood redevelopment and social services under the previous mayor, John Street, an African American who treated black immigrants and their organizations as important parts of his constituency.

Some critics have argued that remittances and transnational development should be viewed as poverty alleviation and should not be forced to conform to the expectations of development agencies and economics.[51] Other social scientists have advocated broader metrics for evaluating transnational development projects than those of traditional economics, including attention to their ownership and sustainability.[52] Still others argue that diaspora-led associations are more closely connected to on-the-ground needs, can better leverage community donations and labor, and can engage communities in more participatory projects. They assert that in many cases, larger transnational associations have the capacity to expand their work with formal assistance from development intermediaries and the state.[53] And some development economists have tempered their critiques, seeking to value these various contributions of migrant associations.[54]

These terms of debate encourage an appreciation of the indirect economic impacts of social, health, and educational investments. Among them, the stability provided by mutual aid helps enable people in the United States and Africa to participate in more capital-intensive, collective projects such as those of Liberian county associations. Yet this frame of analysis is limiting, too. The leaders and institutions profiled above seek forms of shared prosperity and opportunity that transcend poverty alleviation, though at the same time they recognize the basic needs of communities that remain to a great extent poor and disadvantaged.

The work of transnational civil society may be better understood as a process of urban and community revitalization, including but beyond the more limited terms of infrastructure and economic development or poverty alleviation. From the perspective of most Liberian migrants engaged in transnational initiatives, as for other Africans and Latin Americans, transnational development is a broad project of diverse social, economic, political, and family stabilization and reconstruction. It involves investments in people and their interrelationships as much as physical development of places. Understanding transnational development in this more holistic sense can help policy and development professionals grasp the needs and leverage the assets of migrant and receiving communities to address both their distinct and shared challenges and opportunities, local and transnational.

NOTES

Introduction

1. Henri Lefebvre, *The Production of Space*, trans. Donald Nicholson-Smith (Malden, Mass.: Blackwell, 1991).

2. Prominent celebrations of urban revitalization in recent social science and policy literature include Edward Glaeser, *Triumph of the City: How Our Greatest Invention Makes Us Richer, Smarter, Greener, Healthier, and Happier* (New York: Penguin, 2011); Richard Florida, *The Rise of the Creative Class—Revisited* (New York: Basic, 2012); Bruce Katz and Jennifer Bradley, *The Metropolitan Revolution: How Cities and Metros Are Fixing Our Broken Politics and Fragile Economy* (Washington, D.C.: Brookings Institution Press, 2013).

3. Robert Fishman, "The American Metropolis at Century's End: Past and Future Influences," *Housing Facts & Findings* 1, 4 (Winter 1999). See also Robert Fishman, "The American Metropolis at Century's End: Past and Future Influences," *Housing Policy Debate* 11, 1 (2000): 199–213.

4. Dowell Myers, "Immigration: Fundamental Force in the American City," *Housing Facts & Findings* 1, 4 (Winter 1999); Myers, "Demographic Dynamism and Metropolitan Change: Comparison of Los Angeles, New York, Chicago, and Washington, D.C.," *Housing Policy Debate* 10, 4 (1999): 919–54; Myers, *Immigrants and Boomers: Forging a New Social Contract for the Future of America* (New York: Russell Sage, 2007); Dowell Myers and John Pitkin, "Demographic Forces and Turning Points in the American City, 1950 to 2040," *ANNALS of the American Academy of Political and Social Sciences* 626 (November 2009): 91–111; Domenic Vitiello, "The Migrant Metropolis and American Planning," *Journal of the American Planning Association* 75, 2 (2009): 245–55.

5. Robert Fishman, "The Fifth Migration," *Journal of the American Planning Association* 71, 4 (2005): 357–66.

6. Robert J. Sampson, "Open Doors Don't Invite Criminals: Is Increased Immigration Behind the Drop in Crime?" *New York Times*, March 11, 2006. See also Robert J. Sampson, "Rethinking Crime and Immigration," *Contexts* 7 (2008): 28–33; Robert J. Sampson, *Great American City: Chicago and the Enduring Neighborhood Effect* (Chicago: University of Chicago Press, 2012).

7. Associated Press, "Without Immigrants, Metro Areas Would Shrink," April 5, 2007.

8. Jessica Michele Herring, "Immigration Reform 2013: More Cities Pass Measures Welcoming Immigrants," *Latino Post*, December 3, 2013; Keystone Crossroads, "Pittsburgh Looks to Immigrants as Economic Development Tool," *Keystone Crossroads*, December 15, 2014.

9. See Michael Jones-Correa, *All Immigration Is Local: Receiving Communities and Their Role in Successful Immigrant Integration* (Washington, D.C.: Center for American Progress, 2011); *Practice to Policy: Lessons from Local Leadership on Immigrant Integration* (Toronto: Cities of Migration, 2012); *Welcoming Cities: Framing the Conversation* (Decatur, Ga.: Welcoming America, 2013).

10. Tarry Hum, *Making a Global Immigrant Neighborhood: Brooklyn's Sunset Park* (Philadelphia: Temple University Press, 2014); Devashree Saha and Audrey Singer, "EB-5 Visas: A Smarter, Cleaner Plan," *Brookings Institution* (2014); Julie Shaw, "State Announces Grant to Help Build High-Rise Near Chinatown," *Philadelphia Daily News*, October 30, 2014; Paul Nussbaum, "Chinese Investors Sign Up to Fund I-95-Pa. Turnpike Link," *Philadelphia Inquirer*, December 1, 2014.

11. Monica Varsany, ed., *Taking Local Control: Immigration Policy Activism in U.S. Cities and States* (Stanford, Calif.: Stanford University Press and Center for Comparative Immigration Studies, 2010); Domenic Vitiello, "The Politics of Immigration and Suburban Revitalization: Divergent Responses in Adjacent Pennsylvania Towns," *Journal of Urban Affairs* 36, 3 (August 2014): 519–33; Maria-Teresa Vazquez-Castillo, "Anti-Immigrant, Sanctuary, and Repentance Cities," *Progressive Planning* (Winter 2009); Patrick J. Carr, Daniel T. Lichter, and Maria J. Kefalas, "Can Immigration Save Small-Town America? Hispanic Boomtowns and the Uneasy Path to Renewal," *ANNALS of the American Academy of Political and Social Science* 641 (May 2012): 38–57; Justin P. Steil and Ion B. Vasi, "The New Immigration Contestation: Social Movements and Local Immigration Policy Making in the United States, 2000–2011," *American Journal of Sociology* 119, 4 (January 2014): 1104–55; Michael Matza, "Ten Years after Immigration Disputes, Hazleton Is a Different Place," *Philadelphia Inquirer* (April 4, 2016).

12. James Smith and Barry Edmonston, eds., *The New Americans: Economic, Demographic, and Fiscal Effects of Immigration* (Washington, D.C.: National Academy Press, 1997); Myers, *Immigrants and Boomers*.

13. Richard Alba and Victor Nee, *Remaking the American Mainstream: Assimilation and Contemporary Immigration* (Cambridge, Mass.: Harvard University Press, 2003); Nancy Foner and George Frederickson, eds., *Not Just Black and White: Historical and Contemporary Perspectives on Immigration, Race, and Ethnicity in the United States* (New York: Russell Sage, 2004); Mary Waters and Reed Ueda, eds., *The New Americans: A Guide to Immigration since 1965* (Cambridge, Mass.: Harvard University Press, 2007); Marilyn Halter, Marilynn S. Johnson, Katheryn P. Viens, and Conrad Edick Wright, eds., *What's New About the "New" Immigration? Traditions and Transformations in the United States Since 1965* (New York: Palgrave, 2014).

14. William Frey, *Diversity Spreads Out: Metropolitan Shifts in Hispanic, Asian, and Black Populations Since 2000* (Washington, D.C.: Brookings Institution, 2006);

Heather A. Smith and Owen J. Furuseth, eds., *Latinos in the New South: Transformations of Place* (Burlington, Vt.: Ashgate, 2006); Mary Odem and Elaine Lacy, eds., *Latino Immigration and the Transformation of the U.S. South* (Athens: University of Georgia Press, 2009); Audrey Singer, Susan Hardwick, and Caroline Brettell, eds., *Twenty-First Century Gateways: Immigrant Incorporation in Suburban America* (Washington, D.C.: Brookings Institution Press, 2008); Douglas Massey, *New Faces in New Places: The Changing Geography of American Immigration* (New York: Russell Sage, 2008).

15. Wei Li and Emily Skop, "Enclaves, Ethnoburbs, and New Patterns of Settlement Among Asian Immigrants," in *Contemporary Asian America: A Multi-Disciplinary Reader*, 2nd ed., ed. Min Zhou and James V. Gatewood (New York: New York University Press, 2007), 222–36; Singer et al., *Twenty-First Century Gateways*; Massey, *New Faces in New Places*.

16. Douglas S. Massey, "International Migration at the Dawn of the Twenty-First Century: The Role of the State," *Population and Development Review* 25, 2 (1999), 303–22; Roger Waldinger and Michael Lichter, *How the Other Half Works: Immigration and the Social Organization of Labor* (Berkeley: University of California Press, 2003); Robin Cohen, *Migration and Its Enemies: Global Capital, Migrant Labour and the Nation-State* (Burlington, Vt.: Ashgate, 2006).

17. U.S. Citizenship and Immigration Services, "Executive Actions on Immigration," November 20, 2014.

18. Dowell Myers and Julie Park, "The Role of Occupational Achievement in the Attainment of Homeownership by Immigrants and Native-Borns in Five Metropolitan Areas," *Journal of Housing Research* 10, 1 (1999): 61–93; Dowell Myers, Gary Painter, Zhou Yu, SungHo Ryu, and Liang Wei, "Regional Disparities in Homeownership Trajectories: Impacts of Affordability, New Construction, and Immigration," *Housing Policy Debate* 16, 1 (2005): 53–83; Thomas Carter and Domenic Vitiello, "Immigrants, Refugees, and Housing," in *Immigrant Geographies of North American Cities*, ed. Carlos Teixeira, Wei Li, and Audrey Kobayashi (Toronto: Oxford University Press, 2011).

19. John R. Logan and Charles Zhang, "Global Neighborhoods: New Pathways to Diversity and Separation," *American Journal of Sociology* 115 (2010): 1069–1109.

20. Michael B. Katz, Mathew J. Creighton, Daniel Amsterdam, and Merlin Chowkwanyun, "Immigration and the New Metropolitan Geography," *Journal of Urban Affairs* 32, 5 (2010): 523–47; Audrey Singer, Domenic Vitiello, Michael B. Katz, and David Park, *Recent Immigration to Philadelphia: Regional Change in a Re-Emerging Gateway* (Washington, D.C.: Brookings Institution, 2008).

21. Sharon Zukin, "Gentrification: Culture and Capital in the Urban Core," *Annual Review of Sociology* 13 (1987): 129–47; Neil Smith, *The New Urban Frontier: Gentrification and the Revanchist City* (New York: Routledge, 1996); Japonica Brown-Saracino, *The Gentrification Debates: A Reader* (New York: Routledge, 2013).

22. Michael B. Katz, "Immigration as Urban Revitalization," *Urban Link: Penn Institute for Urban Research* 9 (2013); Bernard Frieden and Lynne Sagalyn, *Downtown, Inc.:*

How America Rebuilds Cities (Cambridge, Mass.: MIT Press, 1989); David Ley, *The New Middle Class and the Remaking of the Central City* (Oxford: Oxford University Press, 1996); Michael E. Porter, "The Competitive Advantage of the Inner City," *Harvard Business Review* (May–June 1995): 55–71; Richard Florida, *The Rise of the Creative Class: And How It's Transforming Work, Life, Community and Everyday Life* (New York: Basic Books, 2002); Alexander Garvin, *The American City: What Works, What Doesn't?* (New York: McGraw-Hill, 2002); Bruce Katz, *Transformative Investments: Unleashing the Potential of American Cities* (Washington, D.C.: Brookings Institution, 2006).

Chapter 1

1. Michael B. Katz, *Why Don't American Cities Burn?* (Philadelphia: University of Pennsylvania Press, 2012).

2. Thomas J. Sugrue, *The Origins of the Urban Crisis: Race and Inequality in Post-War Detroit* (Princeton, N.J.: Princeton University Press, 1996).

3. Frank Van Riper, "Ford to City: Drop Dead," *New York Daily News*, October 30, 1975.

4. James Q. Wilson and George Kelling, "Broken Windows: The Police and Neighborhood Safety," *Atlantic* 127 (1982): 29–38.

5. William Julius Wilson, *The Truly Disadvantaged: The Inner City, the Underclass, and Public Policy* (Chicago: University of Chicago Press, 2012 [1987]).

6. Mike Davis, *City of Quartz: Excavating the Future in Los Angeles* (New York: Verso, 1990).

7. Spike Lee's *Summer of Sam* captures well the fear of New Yorkers in the 1970s, in this case because a serial murderer was on the prowl in 1977. A deeply disturbing movie series in the 1970s, *Death Wish*, fulfilled the apparent wishes of would-be vigilantes in the form of actor Charles Bronson. It was Bernhard Goetz, however, who became a real folk hero to many New Yorkers after shooting four black males on a subway in 1984 during what he described as an attempted robbery. Both the Son of Sam and Goetz cases received tremendous media coverage, stoking debate both locally and nationally.

8. "Chicago Homicide Rates per 100,000 residents, 1870–2000," *Encyclopedia of Chicago*, http://www.encyclopedia.chicagohistory.org/pages/2156.html.

9. In New York in the early 1980s, I was the victim of two daytime car burglaries in addition to vandalism, and I witnessed a knife-wielding junkie try to rob a bodega on Broadway near 125th Street and a man waving a machete late at night on the #1 subway. Initially, Chicago promised to be no different. When I arrived at the University of Chicago, the first advice I got was to carry loose $20 bills for holdups—"robbing money." Personal anecdotes are not determinative, of course, but in my experience these were widespread. Indeed, such incidents were commonly discussed and openly acknowledged. Crime was such a concern at the University of Chicago that I was asked to chair a campus-wide committee on safety.

10. J. David Goodman and Al Baker, "Murders in New York Drop to a Record Low, But Officers Aren't Celebrating," *New York Times*, December 31, 2014.

11. William J. Bennett, John J. Dilulio Jr., and John P. Walters, *Body Count: Moral Poverty . . . and How to Win America's War Against Crime and Drugs* (New York: Simon and Schuster, 1996).

12. Robert J. Sampson, "Open Doors Don't Invite Criminals: Is Increased Immigration Behind the Drop in Crime?," *New York Times*, March 11, 2006.

13. Alfred Blumstein and Joel Wallman, *The Crime Drop in America* (New York: Cambridge University Press, 2000).

14. Lead reduction is arguably the other factor that was largely ignored. Jessica Wolpaw Reyes, "Environmental Policy as Social Policy? The Impact of Childhood Lead Exposure on Crime," NBER Working Paper 13097 (2007).

15. Robert J. Sampson, "Rethinking Crime and Immigration," *Contexts* 7 (2008): 28–33. For comments on the essay, see http://contexts.org/articles/winter-2008/sampson/.

16. S. Markides and J. Coreil, "The Health of Hispanics in the Southwestern United States: An Epidemiologic Paradox." *Public Health Reports* 101 (1986): 253–65.

17. Robert Hummer, Daniel A. Powers, Starling G. Pullum, Ginger L. Gossman, and W. Parker Frisbie, "Paradox Found (Again): Infant Mortality Among the Mexican-Origin Population in the United States," *Demography* 44 (2007): 441–57; Samuel H. Preston and Irma T. Elo, "Anatomy of a Municipal Triumph: New York City's Upsurge in Life Expectancy," *Population and Development Review* 40, 1 (2014): 1–29.

18. Robert J. Sampson, Jeffrey D. Morenoff, and Stephen W. Raudenbush, "Social Anatomy of Racial and Ethnic Disparities in Violence," *American Journal of Public Health* 95 (2005): 224–32.

19. Ramiro Martinez Jr., *Latino Homicide: Immigration, Violence, and Community* (New York: Routledge, 2002); John MacDonald and Robert J. Sampson, "The World in a City: Immigration and America's Changing Social Fabric," *ANNALS of the American Academy of Political and Social Science* 624 (2012): 6–15; Daniel P. Mears, "The Immigrant-Crime Nexus: Toward and Analytic Framework for Assessing and Guiding Theory, Research, and Policy," *Sociological Perspectives* 44 (2001): 1–19; Bianca E. Bersani, Thomas A. Loughran, and Alex R. Piquero, "Comparing Patterns and Predictors of Immigrant Offending Among a Sample of Adjudicated Youth," *Journal of Youth and Adolescence* 42, 10 (2013): 1–20.

20. Robert J. Sampson, *Great American City: Chicago and the Enduring Neighborhood Effect* (Chicago: University of Chicago Press, 2012).

21. MacDonald and Sampson, "The World in a City."

22. I wish to be clear that I am neither positing nor denying that immigration was a factor in the remarkable crime increases of the 1960s and 1970s. The crime increase of that era is beyond my scope here, although I would note that there is no consensus in the criminological community on an explanation. It is also worth noting that one can have asymmetric explanations: what causes something to rise is not necessarily the same thing as what leads to its descent.

23. Jacob L. Vigdor, *Immigration and New York City: The Contributions of Foreign-Born Americans to New York's Renaissance, 1975–2013* (New York: Americas Society/Council of the Americas, 2014).

24. Sampson, *Great American City*, 254–55. I focused on language diversity because it taps diffusion and cultural contact among different groups more directly than the foreign-born proportion.

25. Jacob I. Stowell, Steven F. Messner, Kelly F. Mcgeever, and Lawrence E. Raffalovich, "Immigration and the Recent Violent Crime Drop in the United States: A Pooled, Cross-Sectional Timeseries Analysis of Metropolitan Areas," *Criminology* 47 (2009): 601–40.

26. See also Graham C. Ousey and Charis E. Kubrin, "Exploring the Connection Between Immigration and Violent Crime Rates in U.S. Cities, 1980–2000," *Social Problems* 56 (2009): 447–73; Elizabeth Kneebone and Steven Raphael, *City and Suburban Crime Trends in Metropolitan America* (Washington, D.C.: Brookings Institution, 2011); Ruben G. Rumbaut and Walter A. Ewing, *The Myth of Immigrant Criminality and the Paradox of Assimilation: Incarceration Rates Among Native and Foreign-Born Men* (Washington, D.C.: American Immigration Law Foundation, 2007).

27. John M. MacDonald, John R. Hipp, and Charlotte Gill, "The Effects of Immigrant Concentration on Changes in Neighborhood Crime Rates," *Journal of Quantitative Criminolology* 29 (2013): 191–215.

28. Vigdor, *Immigration and New York City*.

29. MacDonald and Sampson, "The World in a City."

30. Aaron Chalfin, "What Is the Contribution of Mexican Immigration to U.S. Crime Rates? Evidence from Rainfall Shocks in Mexico," *American Law and Economic Review* 16, 1 (Spring 2014), 220–68.

31. Sampson, *Great American City*, 251–59.

32. Wilson and Kelling, "Broken Windows."

33. Vigdor, *Immigration and New York City*.

34. Katz, *Why Don't American Cities Burn?*, 100.

35. Sampson, *Great American City*, chap. 6.

36. Robert Putnam, "E Pluribus Unum: Diversity and Community in the 21st Century: The 2006 Johan Skytte Prize Lecture," *Scandinavian Political Studies* 30 (2007): 137–74.

37. For further discussion on the complexities induced by migration, see Paul Collier, *Exodus: How Migration Is Changing Our World* (New York: Oxford University Press, 2013).

38. Alan Ehrenhalt, *The Great Inversion and the Future of the American City* (New York: Knopf, 2012).

39. David S. Kirk and John H. Laub, "Neighborhood Change and Crime in the Modern Metropolis," in *Crime and Justice*, ed. Michael Tonry (Chicago: University of Chicago Press, 2010), 441–501.

40. John R. Logan and Charles Zhang, "Global Neighborhoods: New Pathways to Diversity and Separation," *American Journal of Sociology* 115 (2010): 1069–1109.

Chapter 2

1. The author is grateful to Mayuri Valvekhar for outstanding research assistance and to participants at the Penn Social Science and Policy Forum and the Federal Reserve Bank of Atlanta for helpful feedback on this work. The analysis described in this chapter underlies a policy brief issued by the Partnership for a New American Economy and the Americas Society/Council of the Americas: Jacob L. Vigdor, *Immigration and the Revival of American Cities: From Preserving Manufacturing Jobs to Strengthening the Housing Market* (New York: Partnership for a New American Economy and Americas Society/Council of the Americas, 2013).

2. William J. Carrington, Enrica Detragiache, and Tara Vishwanath, "Migration with Endogenous Moving Costs," *American Economic Review* 86, 4 (1996): 909–30.

3. Joseph G. Altonji and David Card, "The Effects of Immigration on the Labor Market Outcomes of Less-Skilled Natives," in *Immigration, Trade and the Labor Market*, ed. John Abowd and Richard Freeman (Chicago: University of Chicago Press, 1991), 201–34. Altonji and Card, in turn, credit the initial insight to Ann P. Bartel, "Where Do the New U.S. Immigrants Live?," *Journal of Labor Economics* 7 (1989): 371–91.

4. Gianmarco Ottaviano and Giovanni Peri, "The Effects of Immigration on U.S. Wages and Rents: A General Equilibrium Approach," in *Migration Impact Assessment: New Horizons*, ed. Peter Nijkamp, Jacques Poot, and Mediha Sahin (London: Edward Elgar, 2012), 107–46; Albert Saiz, "Immigration and Housing Rents in American Cities," *Journal of Urban Economics* 61 (2007): 345–71.

5. A common rule of thumb in IV analysis is that the instruments should have an F-statistic above 10 in the first-stage regression. See Douglas O. Staiger and James H. Stock, "Instrumental Variables Regression with Weak Instruments," *Econometrica* 65 (1997): 557–86. That standard is easily met here.

6. Matteo Iacoviello, "Housing Wealth and Consumption," Board of Governors of the Federal Reserve System International Finance Discussion Paper #1027 (2011).

7. Vigdor, *Immigration and New York City*.

8. Jacob L. Vigdor, "Is Urban Decay Bad? Is Urban Revitalization Bad Too?," *Journal of Urban Economics* 68 (2010): 277–89.

Chapter 3

1. For example, Gary Painter and Zhou Yu, "Immigrants and Housing Markets in Mid-Size Metropolitan Areas," *International Migration Review* 44, 2 (2010): 442–76; Gary Painter and Zhou Yu, "Caught in the Housing Bubble: Immigrants' Housing Outcomes in Traditional Gateways and Newly Emerging Destinations," *Urban Studies* 51, 4 (2014): 782–810.

2. Gary Painter, Stuart Gabriel, and Dowell Myers, "Race, Immigrant Status, and Housing Tenure Choice," *Journal of Urban Economics* 49 (2001): 150–67.

3. The author gratefully acknowledges support from the University of Southern California Lusk Center for Real Estate. The author thanks Julia Wolfson, Ray Calnan, Jung Hyun Choi, and Arthur Acolin for terrific research assistance.

4. For example, Painter and Yu, "Immigrants and Housing Markets in Mid-Size Metropolitan Areas"; Painter and Yu, "Caught in the Housing Bubble"; Audrey Singer, *The Rise of New Immigrant Gateways* (Washington, D.C.: Brookings Institution, 2004).

5. For example, Cathy Y. Liu, Gary Painter, and Qingfang Wang, "Immigrant Entrepreneurship and Agglomeration in High-Tech Industries in the U.S.," in *Innovation and Entrepreneurship in the Global Economy: Knowledge, Technology and Internationalization*, ed. Charlie Karlsson, Urban Gråsjö, and Sofia Wixe (Northampton, MA: Edward Elgar, 2014).

6. Albert Saiz, "Room in the Kitchen for the Melting Pot: Immigration and Rental Prices," *Review of Economics and Statistics* 85, 3 (2003): 502–21; Saiz, "Immigration and Housing Rents in American Cities," *Journal of Urban Economics* 61, 2 (2007): 345–71.

7. For example, William Frey, *The Great American Migration Slowdown: Regional and Metropolitan Dimensions* (Washington, D.C.: Brookings Institution, 2009); Singer, *The Rise of New Immigrant Gateways*.

8. For example, Painter and Yu, "Immigrants and Housing Markets in Mid-size Metropolitan Areas" and "Caught in the Housing Bubble."

9. Ibid.

10. Axel Borsch-Supan, "Household Formation, Housing Prices, and Public Policy Impacts," *Journal of Public Economics* 25 (1986): 145–64; Donald R. Haurin, Patric H. Hendershott, and Dongwook Kim, "The Impact of Real Rents and Wages on Household Formation," *Review of Economics and Statistics* 75 (1993): 284–93; J. Ermisch and P. Di Salvo, "The Economic Determinants of Young People's Household Formation," *Economica* 64 (1997): 627–44.

11. Donald R. Haurin and Stuart Rosenthal, "The Influence of Household Formation on Homeownership Rates Across Time and Race," *Real Estate Economics* 35, 4 (2008): 411–50; Dowell Myers and Zhou Yu, "Misleading Comparisons of Homeownership Rates Between Groups and Over Time? The Effects of Variable Household Formation," *Urban Studies* 47 (2010): 2615–40.

12. Andrew Paciorek, "The Long and the Short of Household Formation," *Real Estate Economics* 44, 1 (Spring 2016): 7–40.

13. Kwan Ok Lee and Gary Painter, "What Happens to Household Formation in a Recession?," *Journal of Urban Economics* 76 (2013): 93–109.

14. J. H. Choi and Gary Painter, "Household Formation and Unemployment Rate: A Vector Autoregressive Approach," USC Price School of Public Policy, Working Paper (2014).

15. Painter and Yu, "Caught in the Housing Bubble."

16. Ibid.

17. Painter, Gabriel, and Myers, "Race, Immigrant Status, and Housing Tenure Choice"; Gary Painter and Zhou Yu, "Leaving Gateway Metropolitan Areas: Immigrants and the Housing Market," *Urban Studies* 45, 5–6 (2008): 1163–91.

18. Saiz, "Room in the Kitchen for the Melting Pot"; Saiz, "Immigration and Housing Rents in American Cities."

19. Painter and Yu, "Immigrants and Housing Markets in Mid-Size Metropolitan Areas" and "Caught in the Housing Bubble."

20. Painter and Yu, "Caught in the Housing Bubble."

21. Ibid.

22. Justin Wolfers, "Did Unilateral Divorce Laws Raise Divorce Rates? A Reconciliation and New Results," NBER Working Paper 10014 (2003).

23. Painter and Yu, "Immigrants and Housing Markets in Mid-Size Metropolitan Areas."

24. Painter and Yu, "Caught in the Housing Bubble."

25. F. C. Billari and A. C. Liefbroer, "Should I Stay or Should I Go? The Impact of Age Norms on Leaving Home," *Demography* 44, 1 (2007): 181–98; F. C. Billari, D. Philipov, and P. Baizán, "Leaving Home in Europe: The Experience of Cohorts Born Around 1960," *International Journal of Population Geography* 7 (2001): 339–56.

26. Painter and Yu, "Caught in the Housing Bubble."

27. Ibid.

28. Lee and Painter, "What Happens to Household Formation in a Recession?"

29. Ibid.

30. Larry Ford, Florinda Klevisser, and Francesca Carli, "Ethnic Neighborhoods and Urban Revitalization: Can Europe Use the American Model?," *Geographical Review* 98, 1 (2008): 82–102.

31. Painter and Yu, "Caught in the Housing Bubble."

32. Saiz, "Room in the Kitchen for the Melting Pot"; Saiz, "Immigration and Housing Rents in American Cities."

Chapter 4

1. See, for example, Joel Millman, *The Other Americans: How Immigrants Renew Our Country, Our Economy, and Our Values* (New York: Viking Penguin, 1997); Thomas Muller, *Immigrants and the American City* (New York: New York University Press, 1993); Jacob L. Vigdor, *Immigration and the Revival of American Cities* (New York: American Society/Council of the Americas, 2013); Robert Sampson, "Open Doors Don't Invite Criminals," *New York Times*, March 11, 2006.

2. Audrey Singer, Susan W. Hardwick, and Caroline Brettell, eds., *Twenty-First Century Gateways: Immigrant Incorporation in Suburban America* (Washington, D.C.: Brookings Institution, 2008).

3. My definition of greater Boston generally follows what the 2000 census defined as the Boston Primary Metropolitan Statistical Area in Massachusetts (which excludes the old mill cities of Lawrence, Lowell, and Brockton and their adjoining suburbs). For more on definitions of suburbia that de-emphasize class distinctions, see the introduction to Kevin M. Kruse and Thomas J. Sugrue, eds., *The New Suburban History* (Chicago: University of Chicago Press, 2006), 1–10.

4. On one-step-up communities, see Tom L. Chung, "Asian Americans in Enclaves— They Are Not One Community: New Modes of Asian-American Settlement," *Asian American Policy Review*, 5 (1995): 78–94.

5. Barry Bluestone and Mary Huff Stevenson, *The Boston Renaissance: Race, Space, and Economic Change in an American Metropolis* (New York: Russell Sage Foundation, 2000), 75–77.

6. Triple-deckers are three-story apartment buildings—built mainly around the turn of the twentieth century—that were popular with earlier generations of immigrant families in the region. "Escalating Rents Drive Immigrants out of Boston, City Officials Say," *Boston Globe*, March 25, 1989; Leslie Bauman, *Hispanics in Chelsea: Who Are They? A Demographic Portrait*, (Boston: Center for Community Planning and Collaborative for Community Service and Development, College of Public and Community Service, University of Massachusetts at Boston, 1990), 16.

7. Beth Siegel et al., "Small Cities, Big Problems: Urban Economic Development Is Tougher Outside the Metropolis," *Commonwealth Magazine*, Spring 2001; Ramon Borges-Mendez and Miren Uriarte, "Tales of Latinos in Three Small Cities," Paper presented at Harvard University, September 1, 2003, 2; Lake Coreth, "Chelsea Under Fire: Urban Industrial Life, Crisis, and the Trajectory of Jewish and Latino Chelsea," Senior honors thesis, Boston College, 2011. For an insightful account of the postwar evolution of a Massachusetts mill town, see Llana Barber, *Latino City: Immigration and Urban Crisis in Lawrence, Massachusetts, 1945–2000* (Chapel Hill: University of North Carolina Press, forthcoming 2017).

8. Bluestone, *The Boston Renaissance*, 93.

9. Institute for Asian American Studies, *Chinese Americans in Massachusetts* (Boston: University of Massachusetts Boston, 2006), 7–8; James P. Allen and Eugene Turner, "Boston's Emerging Ethnic Quilt: A Geographic Perspective," Paper presented at the Population Association Annual Meeting, Boston, 2004, 5, http://www.csun.edu/~hfgeg005 /eturner/pubs/pubs.htm; "International Influx of Students Hits Some Schools," *Boston Globe*, March 25, 1990; "Moving Out and Moving Up: Asian Americans Establish Growing Presence in Suburbs," *Boston Globe*, May 19, 1991 (Ho quote); "Vibrant New Look of Western Suburbs: Immigrants Alter Region Culturally and Economically," *Boston Globe*, November 28, 1999 (Indians quote); "A High-Tech Home for Indians," *Boston Globe*, July 22, 2000; "An Educated Move," *Boston Globe*, May 7, 2001; "Driven to Prosper: A Growing Immigrant Enclave Makes it Mark on the City," *Boston Globe*, September 23, 2006.

10. Bluestone, *The Boston Renaissance*, 93, 99; Massachusetts Commission Against Discrimination, *Route 128: Boston's Road to Segregation*, 1975, 37–39, 42, 44–46.

11. Chung, "Asian Americans in Enclaves," 78–94.

12. Chi-kan Richard Hung, "Separate But Connected: Challenges Amid Progress for Chinese American Enclaves in Boston," paper presented at New Immigrants in Urban New England Conference, Brown University, April 16, 2004, 5–6, http://www.brown .edu/Departments/Sociology/faculty/hsilver/immigneng_04/papers/martes.pdf; "Asian Influx Forging a New Community in Historic Quincy," *Boston Globe*, March 8, 1998; "City's Growing Asian Population Keeps a Low Profile," *Patriot Ledger*, March 18, 1988; Paula Bock and Ken Brusic, *The Asians: Quincy's Newest Immigrants* (Quincy, Mass.: [Patriot Ledger], 1989), 7–8, 17, 19.

13. "Lutheran Church to Help Asians," *Patriot Ledger*, February 27, 1988; "Ministering to Newcomers," *Patriot Ledger*, May 12, 1988; Bock and Brusic, *The Asians*, 7–8; Hung, "Separate But Connected," 7; Institute for Asian American Studies, *Chinese Americans in Massachusetts*, 5.

14. Paul Watanabe, Michael Liu, and Shauna Lo, "Asian Americans in Metro Boston," paper prepared for the Boston Equity Initiative of the Harvard Civil Rights Project, 3; "Immigrants from India in a Growing Community in Quincy," *Patriot Ledger*, July 2, 2003; "Arab Americans: A Family Tree of Immigrants with Deep Community Roots," *Patriot Ledger*, September 29–30, 2001.

15. "Chinatown South: Many Anticipate Quincy Is Becoming THE NEXT CHINATOWN," *Patriot Leger*, June 28, 2003; "Flushing: A Model for Quincy? NYC's Other Chinatown Could Be a Pattern for Quincy," *Patriot Leger*, June 29, 2003.

16. *The Changing Face of Framingham* (reprints from Middlesex News Diversity Series, April 1995), 7, 12, 13, 19.

17. Teresa Sales, *Brazilians Away from Home* (New York: Center for Migration Studies, 2003), 133; Joel Millman, *The Other Americans* (New York: Viking, 1997), 229–30; Stephen W. Herring, *Framingham: An American Town* (Framingham, Mass.: Framingham Historical Society, 2000), 359–60; Teresa Sales and Márcia Loureiro, "Between Dream and Reality: Adolescent and Second Generation Brazilian Immigrants in Massachusetts," in *Becoming Brazuca: Brazilian Immigration to the United States*, ed. Clémence Jouet-Pastré and Leticia J. Braga (Cambridge, Mass.: Harvard University Press, 2008), 296.

18. Carlos Eduardo Siqueira and Tiago Jansen, "Updating Demographic, Geographic, and Occupational Data on Brazilians in Massachusetts," in Jouet-Pastré and Braga, *Becoming Brazuca*, 114–15. It should be noted that the Boston area Brazilian population likely declined after 2008, as many undocumented immigrants returned to Brazil amid high U.S. unemployment and a rebounding economy in Brazil. Although there is no reliable data available for Framingham, anecdotal evidence from local service providers suggests that many have left. Nevertheless, Brazilians remain the town's largest immigrant community and will continue to be an important part of its social and economic life in the future. See "Illegal Immigrant Couple Going Back to Brazil after 6 Years," *MetroWest Daily News*, March 28, 2009; "MetroWest Seeing Fewer Immigrants," *MetroWest Daily News*, February 3, 2010; "ESL Students Reflect Changing Face of Immigration in MetroWest," *MetroWest Daily News*, September 30, 2010.

19. Sales, *Brazilians Away from Home*, 54; Herring, *Framingham*, 360; "North of the Border," *Boston Globe*, April 14, 2005; "Like Long-Lost Friends: Brazilian City Mayor Tours Framingham as Part of Partnership," *Metrowest Daily News*, December 3, 2004. A 2007 study of Brazilians in Metro Boston said that about 70 percent of migrants surveyed were undocumented and estimated the total migrant population at 64,000, a percentage that is 29 percent higher than the 2000 Census figures. Enrico Marcelli et al., *(In)Visible (Im)Migrants: The Health and Socioeconomic Integration of Brazilians in Metropolitan Boston* (San Diego: Center for Behavioral and Community Health Studies, San Diego State University, 2009), 42.

20. Watanabe et al., "Asian Americans in Metro Boston," 5; Hung, "Separate But Connected," 6; Sheryl Dong, "The Lines of Migration," typescript copy in Quincy Public Library files, 2, 4, 7.

21. Watanabe et al., "Asian Americans in Metro Boston," 5; Daniel Brasil Becker, "The Brazilian Immigrant Experience: A Study on the Evolution of a Brazilian Community in Somerville and the Greater Boston Area," paper for Urban Borderlands course, Tufts University, 2006, 49, http://dca.lib.tufts.edu/features/urban/MS083.005.024.00003.pdf; 2000 and 2008 Malden population data from American Factfinder; "A Place Where All Belong; Immigrants Transforming Malden Anew," *Boston Globe*, December 23, 2009.

22. Domenic Vitiello, "The Politics of Immigration and Metropolitan Revitalization: Divergent Response in Adjacent Pennsylvania Towns," *Journal of Urban Affairs* 36 (2014), 519–33. For a similar but more quantitative approach to immigrant suburbanization in the Philadelphia area, see Michael B. Katz, Matthew Creighton, Daniel Amsterdam, and Merlin Chowkwanyun, "Immigration and the New Metropolitan Geography," *Journal of Urban Affairs*, 32 (2010): 523–47; Audrey Singer, Domenic Vitiello, Michael Katz, and David Park, "Recent Immigration to Philadelphia: Regional Change in a Re-emerging Gateway," (Washington, D.C.: Brookings Institution, Metropolitan Policy Program, November 13, 2008), http://www.brookings.edu/research/reports /2008/11/13-immigration-singer.

23. For more on Passaic, Patterson, and Bridgeport, see the chapter by Michael Katz and Kenneth Ginsburg in this volume. On Chicago suburbs, see Rob Paral, "Chicago's Immigrants Break Old Patterns," Migration Policy Institute, 2003, http://www.migration policy.org/article/chicagos-immigrants-break-old-patterns; Natalie P. Voorhees Center for Neighborhood and Community Improvement, "Open to All: Different Cultures and Communities, a Look at Immigrants and Housing in Chicago's Northern Suburbs," prepared for the Interfaith Housing Center of the Northern Suburbs, 2011, http://www .voorheescenter.com/#!publications/cvk7.

Chapter 5

1. Audrey Singer, Susan Wiley Hardwick, and Caroline Brettell, *Twenty-First Century Gateways: Immigrant Incorporation in Suburban America* (Washington, D.C.: Brookings Institution, 2008).

2. "Honoring Paterson's History," *New York Times*, July 30, 2006; Richard Alba and Victor Nee, *Remaking the American Mainstream: Assimilation and Contemporary Immigration* (Cambridge, Mass.: Harvard University Press, 2005).

3. Nate Schweber, "Shuttered Oasis Lives On," *New York Times*, February 3, 2012; Antoinette Martin, "A Gritty Area With Awesome Views," *New York Times*, April 2 2006.

4. "Museum in Jersey Celebrates Life of the American Worker," *New York Times*, December 2, 1984; Julia Lawlor, "Cities: A Glorious Past," *New York Times*, December 21, 2003.

5. Edward Jay Pershey, " 'Life and Times in Silk City': An Exhibit in Paterson, New Jersey, at the American Labor Museum, the Paterson Museum, and the Lambert Castle Museum," *Technology and Culture* 26, 3 (1985).

6. James Callahan et al., "Bridgeport, CT," in *The Encyclopedia Americana: A Library of Universal Knowledge* (New York: Encyclopedia Americana Corporation, 1918).

7. Committee on Budget and Appropriations, *General Fund Budget* (Bridgeport: City of Bridgeport, 2010).

8. Ibid.

9. Mary K. Witkowski et al., "Bridgeport Working: Voices from the 20th Century," Bridgeport Public Library Historical Collections Department.

10. Laura Anker, "Women, Work & Family: Polish, Italian and Eastern European Immigrants in Industrial Connecticut, 1890–1940," *Polish American Studies* 45, 2 (1988).

11. John F. Snyder, *The Story of New Jersey's Civil Boundaries, 1606–1968* (Trenton: Bureau of Geology and Topography, 1969); "Virtual Jewish World: New Jersey, United States," Gale Group, http://www.jewishvirtuallibrary.org/jsource/vjw/New Jersey.html.

12. Stephanie W. Greenberg, "Industrial Location and Ethnic Residential Patterns in an Industrializing City: Philadelphia, 1880," in *Philadelphia: Work, Space, Family, and Group Experience in the Nineteenth Century*, ed. Theodore Hershberg (New York: Oxford University Press, 1981).

13. Reuben G. Rumbaut, "Exceptional Outcomes: Achievement in Education and Employment among Children of Immigrants," ANNALS of the *American Academy of Political and Social Science* 620 (2008).

14. Robert J. Sampson, "Rethinking Crime and Immigration," *Contexts* 7 (2008): 28–33. John M. MacDonald and Robert J. Sampson, "Don't Shut the Golden Door," *New York Times*, June 19, 2012; Corina Graif and Robert J. Sampson, "Spatial Heterogeneity in the Effects of Immigration and Diversity on Neighborhood Homicide Rates," *Homicide Studies* 13 (2009): 242–60.

15. Dolores Hayden, *Building Suburbia: Green Fields and Urban Growth, 1820–2000* (New York: Pantheon, 2003); Kevin M. Kruse and Thomas J. Sugrue, eds., *New Suburban History* (Chicago: University of Chicago Press, 2006).

16. David L. Kirp, *Improbable Scholars: The Rebirth of a Great American School System and a Strategy for America's Schools* (New York: Oxford University Press, 2013), 128–29.

Chapter 6

1. Sharon Zukin, Robert Baskerville, Miriam Greenberg, Courtney Guthreau, Jean Halley, Mark Halling, Kristin Lawler, Ron Nerio, Rebecca Stack, Alex Vitale, and Betsy Wissinger, "From Coney Island to Las Vegas in the Urban Imaginary: Discursive Practices of Growth and Decline," *Urban Affairs Review* 33, 5 (1998): 628. Portions of this chapter are drawn from Jamie Winders, "Chapter 8," in *Nashville in the New Millenium: Immigrant Settlement, Urban Transformation, and Social Belonging* (New York: Russell Sage Foundation, 2013). © Russell Sage Foundation, 112 East 64th Street, New York, NY 10065. Reprinted with permission.

2. Ash Amin, "Ethnicity and the Multicultural City: Living with Diversity," *Environment and Planning A* 34 (2002): 959–80; Richard Wright, Mark Ellis, and Virginia Parks, "Re-Placing Whiteness in Spatial Assimilation Research," *City and Community* 4, 2 (2005): 111–35; Raymond Rocco, "Citizenship, Culture, and Community: Restructuring in Southeast Los Angeles," in *Latino Cultural Citizenship: Claiming Identity, Space, and Rights*, ed. William Flores and Rina Benmayor (Boston: Beacon, 1997), 97–123.

3. Nancy Foner, "How Exceptional Is New York: Migration and Multiculturalism in the Empire City," *Ethnic and Racial Studies* 30, 6 (2007): 999–1023; Wendy Cheng, "'Diversity' on Main Street? Branding Race and Place in the New 'Majority-Minority' Suburbs," *Identities: Global Studies in Culture and Power* 17 (2010): 458–86; Mike Davis, *Magical Urbanism: Latinos Reinvent the US City* (London: Verso, 2000).

4. For example, Gabriela Arrendondo, "Navigating Ethno-Racial Currents: Mexicans in Chicago, 1919–1939," *Journal of Urban History* 30, 3 (2004): 399–427.

5. Davis, *Magical Urbanism*; Michael Mendez, "Latino New Urbanism: Building on Cultural Preferences," *Opolis: An International Journal of Suburban and Metropolitan Studies* 1, 1 (2005): 33–48.

6. David Ley, "Between Europe and Asia: The Case of the Missing Sequoias," *Ecumene* 2, 2 (1995): 185–210.

7. See Cheng, "'Diversity' on Main Street?"; Davis, *Magical Urbanism*.

8. Alfred Eckes, "The South and Economic Globalization, 1950 to the Future," in *Globalization and the American South*, ed. James Cobb and William Stueck (Athens: University of Georgia Press, 2005), 36–65.

9. Leon Fink, "New People of the Newest South: Prospects for the Post-1980 Immigrants," *Journal of Southern History* 75, 3 (2009): 739–50.

10. Davis, *Magical Urbanism*, 9.

11. Winders, *Nashville in the New Millennium*.

12. Jamie Winders, "'New Americans' in a 'New South' City? Immigrant and Refugee Politics in the Music City," *Social and Cultural Geography* 7, 3 (2006): 421–35.

13. Amin, "Ethnicity and the Multicultural City"; Caroline Brettell and Faith Nibbs, "Immigrant Suburban Settlement and the 'Threat' to Middle Class Status and Identity: The Case of Farmers Branch, Texas," *International Migration* 49, 1 (2011): 1–30; Ley, "Between Europe and Asia"; Rocco, "Citizenship, Culture, and Community."

14. Lise Nelson and Nancy Hiemstra, "Latino Immigrants and the Renegotiation of Place and Belonging in Small Town America," *Social and Cultural Geography* 9, 3 (2008): 319–42 (quote on 337); Mary Odem, "Our Lady of Guadalupe in the New South: Latino Immigrants and the Politics of Integration in the Catholic Church," *Journal of American Ethnic History* 24, 1 (2004): 26–57; Mark Ellis, "Unsettling Immigrant Geographies: US Immigration and the Politics of Scale," *Tijdschrift voor Economische en Sociale Geografie* 97, 1 (2006): 49–58; Arrendondo, "Navigating Ethno-Racial Currents."

15. Portions of these arguments were first presented in Winders, *Nashville in the New Millennium.*

16. Wilbur Zelinsky and Lee Barrett, "Heterolocalism: An Alternative Model of the Sociospatial Behaviour of Immigrant Ethnic Communities," *International Journal of Population Geography* 4 (1998): 281–98.

17. Odem, "Our Lady of Guadalupe in the New South," 123.

18. Monica Whitaker, "Melting Pot Worries," *Tennessean*, November 7, 2001, 1A.

19. Lee Ann O'Neal, "Residents Object to Workers' Gathering Spot," *Tennessean*, August 11, 2005, 1B.

20. Andy Humbles, "El Protector Comes to East Davidson to Help the Hispanic Community," *Tennessean*, January 11, 2006.

21. Interview with long-term residents who grew up in the Tennessee Industrial School, 2007, in possession of author.

22. Matthew Lassiter and Kevin M. Kruse, "The Bulldozer Revolution: Suburbs and Southern History Since World War II," *Journal of Southern History* 75, 3 (2009): 691–706; Elizabeth Henry and Katherine Hankins, "Halting White Flight: Parent Activism and the (Re)shaping of Atlanta's 'Circuits of Schooling,' 1973–2009," *Journal of Urban History* 38, 3 (2012): 532–52.

23. Interview with long-term residents who grew up in the Tennessee Industrial School, 2007.

24. Kevin M. Kruse, "The Politics of Race and Public Space: Desegregation, Privatization, and the Tax Revolt in Atlanta," *Journal of Urban History* 31, 5 (2005): 610–33.

25. Cheng, " 'Diversity' on Main Street?"

26. Ellis, "Unsettling Immigrant Geographies," 54.

27. Woodbine file at Nashville Public Library, accessed June 29, 2007.

28. Zukin et al., "From Coney Island to Las Vegas in the Urban Imaginary," 629.

29. Suzanne Normand Blackwood, "Area Can Officially Call Itself Cane Ridge," *Tennessean*, December 15, 2006.

30. Lillian Brown Johnson, *Historic Cane Ridge and It's [sic] Families* (Nashville: Blue and Grey, 1973).

31. Jannell Ross, "Post Office Puts Stamp on Cane Ridge Area," *Tennessean*, October 19, 2007.

32. The relationship between demographic change and Cane Ridge's borders was not always clear. In 2007, the most recent census figures showed that Cane Ridge was approximately 69 percent white, 14 percent African American, and 9 percent Hispanic,

making it slightly whiter than Antioch (62 percent white, 27 percent black, 5 percent Hispanic). An early newspaper article suggested that Cane Ridge's emergence "high-light[ed] the power of perception and class divisions" vis-à-vis neighborhoods and was driven by a desire to raise property values by identifying the area as something other than Antioch (Ross, "Post Office Puts Stamp on Cane Ridge Area"). Cane Ridge's orga-nizers, however, framed it as not only an economic solution to declining property values but also a political space and "to rally around" and "help our image" within the broader Nashville community.

33. Cheng, "'Diversity' on Main Street?," 460. See also Brettel and Nibbs, "Immi-grant Suburban Settlement and the 'Threat' to Middle Class Status and Identity"; Odem, "Our Lady of Guadalupe in the New South."

Chapter 7

1. David Diaz, *Barrio Urbanism: Chicanos, Planning, and American Cities* (New York: Routledge, 2005); Martin Anderson, *The Federal Bulldozer: A Critical Analysis of Urban Renewal, 1942–1962* (New York: McGraw-Hill, 1964); Herbert Gans, *The Urban Villagers: Group and Class in the Life of Italian-Americans* (New York: Free Press, 1962).

2. Raymond A. Mohl, "The Interstates and the Cities: The U.S. Department of Transportation and the Freeway Revolt, 1966–1973," *Journal of Planning History* 20, 2 (2008): 193–226; Marc Weiss, "The Origins and Legacy of Urban Renewal," in *Urban and Regional Planning in an Age of Austerity*, ed. Pierre Clavel, John Forester, and Wil-liam W. Goldsmith (New York: Pergamon, 1980), 53–80; Jon Teaford, "Urban Renewal and Its Aftermath," *Housing Policy Debate* 11, 2 (2000): 443–65.

3. Eric Avila, "The Folklore of the Freeway: Space, Culture, and Identity in Postwar Los Angeles," *Aztlan* 23, 1 (1998), 15–31; Eric Avila and Mark Rose, "Race, Culture, Politics, and Urban Renewal: An Introduction," *Journal of Urban History* 35, 3 (2009): 335–47; Clavel, Forester, and Goldsmith, eds., *Urban and Regional Planning in an Age of Austerity*.

4. David Diaz and Rodolfo D. Torres, *Latino Urbanism: The Politics of Planning, Policy, and Redevelopment* (New York: New York University Press, 2014), 8.

5. Tara Yosso and David Garcia, "'This Is No Slum!': A Critical Race Theory Anal-ysis of Community Cultural Wealth in Culture Clash's Chavez Ravine," *Aztlan* 32, 1 (2007): 145–79.

6. Avila and Rose, "Race, Culture, Politics, and Urban Renewal."

7. Quoted in Avila, "The Folklore of the Freeway," 15.

8. John Powell and Kathleen Graham, "Chapter 7: Urban Fragmentation as a Barrier to Equal Opportunity," in *Report of the Citizens' Commission on Civil Rights: Rights at Risk, Equality in an Age of Terrorism* (2002), 85–103; Mohl, "The Interstates and the Cities."

9. Anderson, *The Federal Bulldozer*; June M. Thomas, *Redevelopment and Race: Plan-ning a Finer City in Postwar Detroit* (Baltimore: Johns Hopkins University Press, 1997).

10. Mohl, "The Interstates and the Cities."

11. Robert D. Bullard, Glenn S. Johnson, and Beverly H. Wright, "Confronting Environmental Injustice: It's the Right Thing to Do," *Race, Gender and Class* 5, 1 (1997): 63–79.

12. Eva Cockcroft, "The Story of Chicano Park," *Aztlan* 15, 1 (1984): 79–103.

13. Hank Dittmar and Gloria Ohland, *The New Transit Town: Best Practices in Transit-Oriented Development* (Washington, D.C.: Island Press, 2004).

14. Ian Cartlon, "Histories of Transit-Oriented Development: Perspectives on the Development of the TOD Concept," Institute of Urban and Regional Development University of California Berkeley, Working Paper 2009-02 (2007); Owen Kirkpatrick, "The Two 'Logics' of Community Development: Neighborhoods, Markets, and Community Development Corporations," *Politics & Society* 35, 2 (2007): 329–59.

15. Maureen Kennedy and Paul Leonard, "Dealing with Neighborhood Change: A Primer on Gentrification and Policy Choices" (Washington, D.C.: Brookings Institution, 2001).

16. Gerardo Sandoval, *Immigrants and the Revitalization of Los Angeles: Development and Change in MacArthur Park* (Amherst, N.Y.: Cambria, 2010).

17. Kennedy and Leonard, "Dealing with Neighborhood Change."

18. Angela Blackwell, "Promoting Equitable Development," *Indiana Law Review* 34 (2000): 1273–90.

19. Jason Kandel, "New LAPD Chief Shows Off Stars: Bratton Takes Tour of Streets," *Daily News of Los Angeles*, October 30, 2002, N3.

20. Adam Cohen, "Los Angeles: Gangsta Cops," *Time* 155, 9, March 6, 2000.

21. Héctor Tobar, *The Tattooed Soldier* (Harrison, N.Y.: Delphiniums/HarperCollins, 1998).

22. Sandoval, *Immigrants and the Revitalization of Los Angeles.*

23. Paul Gonzales, "Housing Secretary Tours Metro's Westlake/MacArthur Park Transit Oriented Development," *The Source*, July 29, 2013, http://thesource.metro .net/2013/07/29/housing-secretary-tours-metros-westlakemacarthur-park-transit -oriented-development/.

24. Gerardo Francisco Sandoval and Roanel Herrera, *Transit-Oriented Development and Equity in Latino Neighborhoods: A Comparative Case Study of MacArthur Park (Los Angeles) and Fruitvale (Oakland), NITC-RR-544* (Portland, Ore.: Transportation Research and Education Center, 2015), http://dx.doi.org/10.15760/trec.58.

25. Sandoval, *Immigrants and the Revitalization of Los Angeles.*

26. Sandoval and Herrera, *Transit-Oriented Development and Equity in Latino Neighborhoods.*

27. Sandoval, *Immigrants and the Revitalization of Los Angeles*, Interview with the author (2014).

28. Sandoval, *Immigrants and the Revitalization of Los Angeles*, 69.

29. Ibid, 69.

30. Ibid, 69–70.

31. Sandoval and Herrera, *Transit-Oriented Development and Equity in Latino Neighborhoods.*

32. Sandoval, *Immigrants and the Revitalization of Los Angeles*; Kelly Main and Gerardo Francisco Sandoval, "Placemaking in a Translocal Receiving Community: The Relevance of Place to Identity and Agency," *Urban Studies* 52, 1 (2014): 71–86.

33. Sandoval, *Immigrants and the Revitalization of Los Angeles*, Interview with the author (2014).

34. Ibid., Interview with the author (2014).

35. Cornelia B. Flora and J. L. Flora, *Rural Communities: Legacy and Change* (Boulder, Colo.: Westview, 2013).

36. Sandoval and Herrera, *Transit-Oriented Development and Equity in Latino Neighborhoods.*

37. Main and Sandoval, "Placemaking in a Translocal Receiving Community."

38. Ibid.

Chapter 8

1. Extensive literature on the urban crisis includes Arnold R. Hirsch, *Making the Second Ghetto: Race and Housing in Chicago, 1940–1960* (New York: Cambridge University Press, 1983); Kenneth T. Jackson, *Crabgrass Frontier: The Suburbanization of the United States* (New York: Oxford University Press, 1985); Thomas J. Sugrue, *Origins of the Urban Crisis* (Princeton, N.J.: Princeton University Press, 1996); Becky M. Nicolaides, *My Blue Heaven: Life and Politics in the Working-Class Suburbs of Los Angeles, 1920–1965* (Chicago: University of Chicago Press, 2002); Robert O. Self, *American Babylon: Race and the Struggle for Postwar Oakland* (Princeton, N.J.: Princeton University Press, 2003); Alison Isenberg, *Downtown America: A History of the Place and the People Who Made It* (Chicago: University of Chicago Press, 2005); Kevin M. Kruse, *White Flight: Atlanta and the Making of Modern Conservatism* (Princeton, N.J.: Princeton University Press, 2005); Matthew D. Lassiter, *The Silent Majority: Suburban Politics in the Sunbelt South* (Princeton, N.J.: Princeton University Press, 2006). On the problems of the twenty-first-century city, see Sharon Zukin, *Naked City: The Death and Life of Authentic Urban Places* (New York: Oxford University Press, 2010); Michael B. Katz, *Why Don't American Cities Burn?* (Philadelphia: University of Pennsylvania Press, 2011); Arlene Dávila, *Culture Works: Space, Value, and Mobility Across the Neoliberal Americas* (New York: New York University Press, 2012).

2. A. K. Sandoval-Strausz, "Latino Landscapes: Postwar Cities and the Transnational Origins of a New Urban America," *Journal of American History* 101 (December 2014): 804–31.

3. See, for example, David Harvey, *The Urbanization of Capital* (Baltimore: Johns Hopkins University Press, 1985); Saskia Sassen, *Cities in a World Economy*, 4th ed. (New York: Sage, 2013). For a detailed survey of this literature, see Michael Peter Smith, *Transnational Urbanism: Locating Globalization* (London: Wiley-Blackwell, 2000).

4. See, for example, Michael Peter Smith and Luis Guarnizo, eds., *Transnationalism from Below* (New Brunswick, N.J.: Transaction Publishers, 1998); Arturo Escobar, "Culture Sits in Places: Reflections on Globalism and Subaltern Strategies of Localization," *Political Geography* 20, 2 (2001): 139–74; Jim Glassman, "From Seattle (and Ubon) to Bangkok: The Scales of Resistance to Corporate Globalization," *Environment and Planning D: Society and Space* 20, 5 (2002): 513–33; Smith, *Transnational Urbanism*.

5. "Dick Dolejs, the Man behind the Name 'Little Village,'" *Lawndale News*, May 30, 1991. On South Lawndale, see Louis Wirth and Margaret Furez, eds., *Local Community Fact Book 1938* (Chicago: Chicago Recreation Commission, 1938), Area 30: South Lawndale; Philip M. Hauser and Evelyn M. Kitagawa, eds., *Local Community Fact Book for Chicago 1950* (Chicago: University of Chicago Press, 1951), 126–29; Christopher R. Reed, "South Lawndale," in James R. Grossman et al., *The Encyclopedia of Chicago* (Chicago: University of Chicago Press, 2004). Population figures were calculated using 2010 Census Tracts 3005, 3006, 3007, 3008, 3009, 3011, 3012, 3016, 3017.1, 3017.2, 3018.1, 3018.2, 3018.3, 8305, 8407, 8408, and 8417 (or earlier equivalent tracts). Tract 8435 was excluded because its occupants are almost exclusively inmates of the Cook County Jail (see note 16 below).

6. Gabriela Arredondo, *Mexican Chicago: Race, Identity, and Nation, 1916–1939* (Urbana: University of Illinois Press, 2008); Lilia Fernández, *Brown in the Windy City: Mexicans and Puerto Ricans in Postwar Chicago* (Chicago: University of Chicago Press, 2012); Michael Innis-Jiménez, *Steel Barrio: The Great Mexican Migration to South Chicago, 1915–1940* (New York: New York University Press, 2013).

7. U.S. Censuses of Population and Housing, *1960, PHC(1)-25*, Table P-1; *1970 Census of Population and Housing, PHC(1)-38*, Table P-2; *1980 Census of Population and Housing, PHC80-2-131*, Table P-7; *1990 Census of Population and Housing, CPH-3-125A*, Table 8; "Census 2000 Summary File 1 (sf 1), QT-P3: Race and Hispanic or Latino," table created from data at U.S. Census Bureau, *American Fact Finder*, http://factfinder2.census.gov.

8. Chicago Police Department, *Chicago Police Statistical Report* or *Statistical Summary*, issued yearly; Chicago Police Department, *Chicago Murder Analysis 2011*. Note that the peak rate was influenced by the city's gradually declining population. Note also the questions raised about crime reporting in the city in David Bernstein and Noah Isackson, "The Truth About Chicago's Crime Rate," *Chicago Magazine*, April 7, 2014.

9. Ruth D. Peterson and Lauren J. Krivo, "The National Neighborhood Crime Study, 2000," *Inter-University Consortium for Political and Social Research, University of Michigan* (2010); *Chicago Tribune* crime statistics, http://crime.chicagotribune.com/chicago/community.

10. D. Bradford Hunt and Jon B. DeVries, *Planning Chicago* (Chicago: American Planning Association, 2013), 139. See also "Views on Development Were Distorted," *Chicago Tribune*, March 3, 1998, 12; Little Village Community Development Corporation,

Little Village: Capital of the Mexican Midwest, Quality-of-Life Plan 2005 (Chicago: LISC, 2005), 7; "Little Village, Big Business," *Crain's Chicago Business*, http://www.chicago business.com/section/little-village.

11. Eric Klinenberg, *Heat Wave* (Chicago: University of Chicago Press, 2002); William Julius Wilson and Richard P. Taub, *There Goes the Neighborhood* (New York: Knopf, 2006); Robert J. Sampson, *Great American City: Chicago and the Enduring Neighborhood Effect* (Chicago: University of Chicago Press, 2012); Robert J. Sampson, "Rethinking Crime and Immigration," *Contexts* 7, 1 (2008): 28–33.

12. Alejandro Escalona, "Pride in 26th Street Marred by Reality of Little Village Violence," *Chicago Sun-Times*, March 21, 2012, 8. See also Joseph M. Boyce, "All Politics Is Local," *Wall Street Journal*, May 7, 1997, A1; U.S. Representative Luis Gutiérrez, testimony in the House of Representatives on May 17, 2007, reported in the *Political Transcript Wire* (Lanham, Md.: CQ Roll Call, 2007), May 21, 2007; Enlace Chicago, *Little Village*, pamphlet, May 12, 2011; Frank S. Magallon, *Chicago's Little Village* (Charleston, SC: Arcadia, 2010), 109–13.

13. Sassen, *Cities in a Global Economy*, 2.

14. Luis Eduardo Guarnizo, "The Economics of Transnational Living," *International Migration Review* 37, 3 (2003), 666–99.

15. Nancy Foner, "What's New About Transnationalism? New York Immigrants Today and at the Turn of the Century," *Diaspora: A Journal of Transnational Studies* 6, 3 (1997): 355–75; Sanjeev Khagram and Peggy Levitt, eds., *The Transnational Studies Reader* (New York: Routledge, 2007), esp. Section 3.

16. For prison population information on this facility, see "Block 1023, Tract 843500, Cook County, Illinois," Prison Policy Initiative, http://www.prisonersofthecensus.org/data /2010blocks/170318435001023/. On the importance of incarceration for urban history, see Heather Ann Thompson, "Why Mass Incarceration Matters: Rethinking Crisis, Decline, and Transformation in Postwar American History," *Journal of American History* 97 (2010): 708–33.

17. Census data are taken from the sources listed in note 7 above. On Pilsen, see Fernández, *Brown in the Windy City*, 213.

18. *Chicago Criss-Cross Directory* (Schaumburg, Ill.: Haines, 1980), 26th W.

19. Marta Tienda and Rebeca Raijman, "Forging Mobility in a Low-Wage Environment: Mexican Immigrants in Chicago's Little Village Neighborhood," *Focus* 18, 2 (1996), 36.

20. City of Chicago, *Chicago's Spanish-Speaking Population: Selected Statistics* (1973), 19; Melaniphy & Associates for the City of Chicago, *Chicago Comprehensive Neighborhood Needs Analysis: South Lawndale Community Area*, Vol. 2 (1982), 18, 23, 28.

21. "An Oasis of Harmony in the Inner City," *Chicago Tribune*, January 16, 1977; "Old Mexico Is a Hit in Old Chicago," *Chicago Tribune*, September 6, 1987; "Enterprising Immigrants Converge on Little Village," *Chicago Tribune*, September 6, 1987.

22. Louise Año Nuevo Kerr Papers, Special Collections, University Library, University of Illinois at Chicago.

23. Louise Año Nuevo Kerr Papers, Jesus Serrato transcript, 1, 3, 9–11; Rosalio Torres transcript, 4; Agustín Delgado transcript, 6, 13; Bertha Martínez transcript, 1.

24. Louise Año Nuevo Kerr Papers, Miguel Ramírez biographical data form, 1, and transcript, 2–4; Eustolia Martínez transcript, 6–8; José Pérez transcript, 3–5; Jesús Serrato transcript, 5–7; Margarita Arredondo transcript, 18–20.

25. Louise Año Nuevo Kerr Papers, Rosalio Torres transcript, 22; Jesús Serrato transcript, 17; Gustavo Mellado transcript, 11; Rosina Magaña transcript, 26; Margarita Arredondo transcript, 20, 24.

26. Louise Año Nuevo Kerr Papers, Rosa María Silva transcript, 24–28, 32, 51; "Dad Thwarts Gangs, Sends Son to Mexico," *Chicago Tribune*, December 11, 1984; Robert Courtney Smith, *Mexican New York: Transnational Lives of New Immigrants* (Berkeley: University of California Press, 2006), chap. 7.

27. Louise Año Nuevo Kerr Papers, Margarita Arredondo transcript, 26–27; Gustavo Gómez transcript, 17–18; Rosa Nungaray transcript, 11–12.

28. David A. Badillo, "Religion and Transnational Migration in Chicago: The Case of the Potosinos," *Journal of the Illinois State Historical Society* 94, 4 (2001): 420–40, and Juan J. Pescador, "¡Vamos Taximaroa! Mexican/Chicano Soccer Associations and Transnational/Translocal Committees, 1967–2002," *Latino Studies* 2, 3 (2004): 352–76, both cited in Xóchitl Bada, *Mexican Hometown Associations in Chicagoacán: From Local to Transnational Civic Engagement* (New Brunswick, N.J.: Rutgers University Press, 2014), 47. Bada's indispensable book includes a bibliography on hometown associations.

29. On Little Village and Latino Chicago, see John J. Betancur, "The Settlement Experience of Latinos in Chicago: Segregation, Speculation, and the Ecology Model," *Social Forces* 74 (June 1996): 1266–324; Ana Y. Rámos-Zayas, *National Performances: The Politics of Class, Race, and Space in Puerto Rican Chicago* (Chicago: University of Chicago Press, 2002); Arlene Dávila, *Barrio Dreams: Puerto Ricans, Latinos, and the Neoliberal City* (Berkeley: University of California Press, 2004); Nicholas De Genova, *Working the Boundaries: Race, Space, and 'Illegality' in Mexican Chicago* (Durham, N.C.: Duke University Press, 2005); Timothy Ready and Allen Brown-Gort, *This Is Home Now: The State of Latino Chicago* (South Bend, Ind.: University of Notre Dame Institute of Latino Studies, 2005); Xóchitl Bada et al., eds., *Latino Immigrants in the Windy City: New Trends in Civic Engagement*, Reports on Latino Immigrant Civic Engagement, 6 (Washington, D.C.: Woodrow Wilson International Center, 2010); Amalia Pallares and Nilda Flórez-González, eds., *¡Marcha! Latino Chicago and the Immigrant Rights Movement* (Urbana: University of Illinois Press, 2010); Leonard G. Ramírez et al., *Chicanas of 18th Street: Narratives of a Movement from Latino Chicago* (Urbana: University of Illinois Press, 2011); John J. Betancur, "Gentrification and Community Fabric in Chicago," *Urban Studies* 48 (2011): 383–406; Sarah Lynn Lopez, *The Remittance Landscape: Spaces of Migration in Rural Mexico and Urban U.S.A.* (Chicago: University of Chicago Press, 2015).

30. Bada, *Mexican Hometown Associations in Chicagoacán*, 44–46.

31. *Chicago Criss-Cross Directory* (Schaumburg, Ill.: Haines, 1990), 26th W; *Chicago Criss-Cross Directory* (Schaumburg, Ill.: Haines, 2000), 26th W; "Arch to Be Built on

26st. as 'Tourism Attraction," *Lawndale News*, June 22, 1986, 1; "Mexican President to Visit Little Village," *Lawndale News*, January 17, 1991, 5.

32. Bada, *Mexican Hometown Associations in Chicagoacán*, 48–50.

33. Natasha Iskander, *Creative State: Forty Years of Migration and Development Policy in Morocco and Mexico* (Ithaca, N.Y.: Cornell University Press, 2010), chaps. 7–9.

34. Secretaría de Desarrollo Social (SEDESOL) spreadsheets from 2004, received on January 9, 2013, from Roberto Joaquin Galíndez, the *secretaría*'s U.S. Eastern Zone representative.

35. Donna Gabaccia, *Italy's Many Diasporas* (New York: Routledge, 2000).

36. SEDESOL, "Directorio de Organizaciones," compiled October 18, 2012, and received on January 9, 2013, from Roberto Joaquin Galíndez, the *secretaría*'s U.S. Eastern Zone representative.

37. Michael Peter Smith and Luis Eduardo Guarnizo, "Global Mobility, Shifting Borders, and Urban Citizenship," *Tijdschrift voor Economische en Sociale Geografie* 100, 5 (2009): 614.

38. Dipesh Chakrabarty, "Introduction," in *Provincializing Europe: Postcolonial Thought and Historical Difference* (Princeton, N.J.: Princeton University Press, 2000).

39. The paradigmatic text is Richard Florida, *The Rise of the Creative Class* (New York: Basic, 2002). See also Elizabeth Currid, *The Warhol Economy: How Fashion, Art, and Music Drive New York City* (Princeton, N.J.: Princeton University Press, 2007); Ann Markusen and Anne Gadwa, *Creative Placemaking* (Washington, D.C.: National Endowment for the Arts, 2010); Barry R. Chiswick, ed., *High-Skilled Immigration in a Global Labor Market* (Lanham, Md.: Rowman & Littlefield, 2010); Jeh Charles Johnson, "Policies Supporting U.S. High-Skilled Businesses and Workers," Department of Homeland Security memorandum, November 20, 2014. For a study suggesting that neighborhoods with a broader spectrum of class backgrounds among residents enjoy higher economic growth rates, see D. D. Kalleck et al. for the Fiscal Policy Institute, *Across the Spectrum: The Wide Range of Jobs Immigrants Do* (New York: Fiscal Policy Institute, 2010).

40. For recent scholarship on other groups of people who were moving into the city during the urban crisis, see Suleiman Osman, *The Invention of Brownstone Brooklyn: Gentrification and the Search for Authenticity in Postwar New York* (New York: Oxford University Press, 2011); Pamela Karimi and Thomas Stubblefield, eds., *Reinventing the American Postindistrial City*, special issue of *Journal of Urban History* 41, 2 (2015); Aaron Shkuda, *The Lofts of Soho: Gentrification, Art, and Industry in New York, 1950–1980* (Chicago: University of Chicago Press, 2016).

Chapter 9

1. Together, they represent more than twenty-five Liberian and at least six Pan-African organizations in the Philadelphia area and nationally that operate transnationally (not including alumni associations). Vitiello also participated as a member, guest,

or board member in Liberian and Pan-African organizations during this period. This research is part of a larger book project comparing community and economic development organizations among immigrant groups in the city and region. The authors thank research assistant Hannah Wizman-Cartier for her collaboration in this work.

2. Victor Davis Hanson, "Addictive Remittances," *Washington Times*, May 12, 2006; William Kramer, "Shame on CNN: Remittances Become Political," *Next Billion*, October 20, 2006.

3. Claire Mercer, Ben Page, and Martin Evans, "Unsettling Connections: Transnational Networks, Development and African Home Associations," *Global Networks* 9, 2 (2009): 141–61.

4. Samuel M. Maimbo and Dilip Ratha, *Remittances: Development Impact and Future Prospects* (Washington, D.C.: World Bank, 2005); Bob Davis, "Migrants' Money Is Imperfect Cure for Poor Nations: Earnings Sent Home from U.S. Fuel Increased Spending But Not Much Investment," *Wall Street Journal*, November 1, 2006; Pablo Fajnzylber and J. Humberto Lopez, eds., *Close to Home: The Development Impact of Remittances in Latin America* (Washington, D.C.: World Bank, 2007); Dilip Ratha, *Leveraging Remittances for Development* (Washington, D.C.: World Bank working paper, 2007).

5. Peggy Levitt, *The Transnational Villagers* (Berkeley: University of California Press, 2001); Alison Paul and Sarah Gammage, "Hometown Associations and Development: The Case of El Salvador," Destination D.C. Working Paper 3, 2005; John Page and Sonia Plaza, "Migration Remittances and Development: A Review of Global Evidence," *Journal of African Economies* 15, 2 (2006): 245–336; Manuel Orozco and Kate Welle, "Hometown Associations and Development: Ownership, Correspondence, Sustainability and Replicability," in *New Patterns for Mexico: Observations on Remittances, Philanthropic Giving, and Equitable Development*, ed. Barbara J. Merz (Cambridge: Harvard University Press, 2005); Patricia Landolt, "Salvadoran Economic Transnationalism: Embedded Strategies for Household Maintenance, Immigrant Incorporation, and Entrepreneurial Expansion," *Global Networks* 1, 3 (2001): 217–42; Robert C. Smith, *Mexican New York: Transnational Lives of New Immigrants* (Berkeley: University of California Press, 2006); Kathleen Newland and Hiroyuki Tanaka, *Mobilizing Diaspora Entrepreneurship for Development* (Washington, D.C.: USAID and Migration Policy Institute, 2010).

6. Ratha, *Leveraging Remittances for Development*; Dean Yang, "International Migration, Remittances, and Household Investment: Evidence from Philippine Migrants' Exchange Rate Shocks," *Economic Journal* 118, 528 (2008): 591–630; Hein de Haas, "Remittances, Migration and Development: Policy Options and Policy Illusions," in *South-South Migration: Implications for Social Policy and Development*, ed. Katja Hujo and Shea McClanahan (New York: Palgrave, 2010), 158–90; Yaw Nyarko and Kwabena Gyimah-Brempong, "Social Safety Nets: the Role of Education, Remittances and Migration," *European Report on Development*, 2010.

7. Levitt, *The Transnational Villagers*; Rafael Alarcon, "The Development of the Hometown Associations in the United States and the Use of Social Remittances in Mexico," Departamento de Estudios Sociales El Colegio de la Frontera Norte, Mexico, 2002;

Giles Mohan, "Embedded Cosmopolitanism and the Politics of Obligation: the Ghanaian Diaspora and Development," *Environment and Planning A* 38, 5 (2006): 867–83; Alejandro Portes, Luis Guarnizo, and Patricia Landolt, eds., *La globalizacion desde abajo: Transnacionalismo inmigrante y desarrollo* (Mexico City: Facultad Latinoamericana de Ciencias Sociales, 2003); Manuel Orozco and Eugenia Garcia-Zanello, "Hometown Associations: Transnationalism, Philanthropy, and Development," *Brown Journal of World Affairs* 15, 2 (2009): 57–73; Valentina Mazzucato and Mirjam Kabki, "Small Is Beautiful: The Micro-Politics of Transnational Between Ghanaian Hometown Associations and Communities Back Home," *Global Networks* 9, 2 (2009): 227–51; Claire Mercer, Ben Page, and Martin Evans, "Unsettling Connections: Transnational Networks, Development and African Home Associations," *Global Networks* 9, 2 (2009): 141–61; Petra Mezzetti and Matteo Guglielmo, "Somali Diaspora Associations in Italy: Between Integration and Transnational Engagement," Working Paper 62/2009, Centro Studi di Politica Internazionale, 2009; Newland and Tanaka, *Mobilizing Diaspora Entrepreneurship for Development*.

8. Faranak Miraftab, "Faraway Intimate Development: Global Restructuring of Social Reproduction," *Journal of Planning Education and Research* 31, 4 (2011): 392–405; Anaya Roy, "Commentary: Placing Planning in the World—Transnationalism as Practice and Critique," *Journal of Planning Education and Research* 31, 4 (2011): 416–22.

9. Daniel Amsterdam and Domenic Vitiello, "Immigration to Philadelphia, c.1930–present," *Encyclopedia of Greater Philadelphia*, 2013; Audrey Singer, Domenic Vitiello, Michael Katz, and David Park, *Recent Immigration to Philadelphia: Regional Change in a Re-emerging Gateway* (Washington, D.C.: Brookings Institution, 2008); Leigh Swigart, "Extended Lives: The African Immigrant Experience in Philadelphia," Historical Society of Pennsylvania, 2001.

10. Singer et al., *Recent Immigration to Philadelphia*.

11. Voffee Jabateh, interview with author, November 28, 2008; Sam Slewion, interview with author, September 3, 2010.

12. Reverend John Jallah, interview with author, April 11, 2011.

13. Levitt, *The Transnational Villagers*; Smith, *Mexican New York*; Nik Theodore and Nina Martin, "Migrant Civil Society: New Voices in the Struggle over Community Development," *Journal of Urban Affairs* 29, 3 (2007): 269–87; Carolina S. Sarmiento and Victoria A. Beard, "Traversing the Border: Community-Based Planning and Transnational Migrants," *Journal of Planning Education and Research* 33, 3 (2013): 336–47.

14. Jallah interview, April 11, 2011.

15. Ibid.

16. Slewion interview.

17. Ibid.

18. Kla Brownell, interview with author, April 19, 2011; Fred Gwyan, interview with author, March 27, 2011; Slewion interview.

19. Jallah interview, April 11, 2011.

20. Slewion interview.

21. Brownell interview; John Etim, interview with author, March 25, 2011; Gwyan interview.

22. Ben Lampert, "Diaspora and Development? Nigerian Organizations in London and the Transnational Politics of Belonging," *Global Networks* 9, 2 (2009): 92–110; Mercer, Page, and Evans, "Unsettling Connections"; Carolyne Ndofor-Tah, "Diaspora and Development: Contributions by African Organisations in the UK to Africa's Development," African Foundation for Development, 2000; Awil Mohamoud, "African Diaspora and Development of Africa," Netherlands African Diaspora Summit, 2003; Mohan, "Embedded Cosmopolitanism and the Politics of Obligation"; Orozco and Welle, "Hometown Associations and Development."

23. Slewion interview.

24. Sinoe County Association in the Americas, http://www.scaainc.org; Slewion interview.

25. Gwyan interview.

26. "About Us: History," Sinoe County Association of the Americas, accessed September 11, 2016, www.scaainc.net/about-us/history/.

27. Slewion interview.

28. Ibid.

29. Portia Kamara, interview with author, November 30, 2011.

30. Voffee Jabateh, interviews with author, August 15 and October 30, 2006, and November 28, 2008.

31. Kamara interview.

32. Peggy Levitt, "Social Remittances: Migration Driven Local-Level Forms of Cultural Diffusion," *International Migration Review* 32, 4 (1998): 926–48.

33. Eric Edi, interviews with author, December 19 and 22, 2006; Jabateh interviews, August 15, 2006, and November 28, 2008; Tiguida Kaba, interview with author, April 20, 2011; Kamara interview; Siddiq Hadi, interview with Leigh Swigart, June 13, 2001; Tanko, interview with author, April 7, 2011.

34. Mercer, Page, and Evans, "Unsettling Connections," 150.

35. Edi interviews; Jabateh interview, November 28, 2008; Slewion interview; Kaba interview; Kamara interview.

36. Levitt, *The Transnational Villagers*; Luin Goldring, "Mexican State and Transmigrant Organizations: Negotiating the Boundaries of Membership and Participation," *Latin American Research Review* 37, 3 (2002): 55–99; Ayse Caglar, "Hometown Associations, the Rescaling of State Spatiality and Migrant Grassroots Transnationalism," *Global Networks* 6, 1 (2006): 1–22; Smith, *Mexican New York*.

37. Jabateh interviews, August 15 and October 30, 2006; Jallah, interview with author, February 27, 2008; Kamara interview.

38. Jabateh interview, November 28, 2008.

39. Alisa Orduna-Sneed, interview with author, November 10, 2006; Lansana Koroma, interview with author, November 10, 2006.

40. Anne O'Callaghan, interview with author, January 10, 2007; Jabateh interview, November 28, 2008.

41. African Caribbean Business Council, http://globalphiladelphia.org/organiza tions/african-caribbean-business-council.

42. Azuka Anyiam, interview with author, March 26, 2011.

43. Afri-Caribe Microenterprise Network brochure, in author's possession.

44. Agatha Johnson, interview with author, December 14, 2006.

45. Anyiam interview.

46. Palms Solutions, http://palmssolutions.org/.

47. Jean-Marie Kouassi, interview with author, March 29, 2011.

48. Johnson interview; Kouassi interview.

49. Nina Martin, "Toward a New Countermovement: A Framework for Interpreting the Contradictory Interventions of Migrant Civil Society Organizations in Urban Labor Markets," *Environment and Planning A* 43, 3 (2011): 389–416; Jallah interviews, February 27, 2008, and April 11, 2011.

50. Mercer, Page, and Evans, "Unsettling Connections," 150.

51. Ezra Rosser, "Immigrant Remittances," *Connecticut Law Review* 41, 1 (2008): 1–62.

52. Orozco and Garcia-Zanello, "Hometown Associations."

53. Ndofor-Tah, "Diaspora and Development"; Mohamoud, "African Diaspora and Development of africa"; Joel D. Barkan, Michael L. McNulty, and M. A. O. Ayeni, " 'Hometown' Voluntary Associations, Local Development, and the Emergence of Civil Society in Western Nigeria," *Journal of Modern African Studies* 29, 3 (1991): 457–80.

54. Ratha, *Leveraging Remittances for Development.*

LIST OF CONTRIBUTORS

Kenneth Ginsburg is a cost estimator at American Axle and Manufacturing.

Marilynn S. Johnson is a professor of history at Boston College.

Michael B. Katz was Annenberg Professor of History at the University of Pennsylvania.

Gary Painter is a professor of public policy at the University of Southern California.

Robert J. Sampson is Henry Ford II Professor of the Social Sciences at Harvard University.

Gerardo Francisco Sandoval is an associate professor of planning, public policy, and management at the University of Oregon.

A. K. Sandoval-Strausz is an associate professor of history at the University of New Mexico.

Thomas J. Sugrue is a professor of social and cultural analysis and history and director of the Global Urban Initiative at New York University.

Rachel Van Tosh is the assistant commissioner for financial and business services at the New York City Department of Small Business Services.

Jacob L. Vigdor is Daniel J. Evans Professor of Public Affairs at the University of Washington and a research associate with the National Bureau of Economic Research.

Domenic Vitiello is an associate professor of city planning and urban studies at the University of Pennsylvania.

Jamie Winders is a professor of geography at Syracuse University.

INDEX

ACKNOWLEDGMENTS

This book grew out of a lively conversation on immigration and urban revitalization sponsored by the Penn Social Science and Policy Forum (SSPF), then under the direction of coeditor Thomas J. Sugrue. We owe a special thanks to our late colleague and dear friend Michael B. Katz. Over a spirited lunch meeting, he suggested that we convene a group of urbanists to consider the impact of immigration on American metropolitan areas. The SSPF's executive committee and its advisory group on immigration and citizenship enthusiastically endorsed the idea. For their advice and support, we thank Professors Eugenie Birch, Charles Branas, Michael Delli Carpini, Sarah Barringer Gordon, Robert Inman, Roberta Iversen, Michael Katz, Julia Lynch, John McDonald, Emilio Parrado, Vincent Price, Rogers Smith, Deborah Thomas, Susan Wachter, and Stanton Wortham. We would like to acknowledge Amada Armenta, Erick Guerra, Philip Kasinitz, Laurencio Sanguino, Mark Stern, Lorrin Thomas, Susan Wachter, James Walsh, and Stanton Wortham for their valuable comments and challenging questions.

The conference—and this volume—would not have been possible without the brilliant stewardship of Matthew Roth. The Penn Institute for Urban Research provided indispensable financial assistance. Peter Agree and Robert Lockhart at Penn Press deserve high praise for supporting this project and shepherding it through the publication process.

Previously published material in this volume includes the following:

A shorter version of Chapter 2 was published as Robert J. Sampson, "Immigration and America's Urban Revival," *American Prospect* (Summer 2015).

Material in chapter 3 is drawn from Jacob L. Vigdor, *Immigration and New York City: The Contributions of Foreign-Born Americans to New York's Renaissance, 1975–2013*, Americas Society/Council of the Americas Policy Brief, 2014.

Material in chapter 5 is drawn from Marilynn Johnson, *The New Bostonians: How Immigrants Have Transformed the Metro Area Since the 1960s* (Amherst: University of Massachusetts Press, 2015).

A version of chapter 6 was published as Michael B. Katz and Kenneth Ginsburg, "Immigrant Cities as Reservations for Low Wage Labor," *Contexts* 14, 1 (Winter 2015): 26–31.

Material in chapter 7 is drawn from Jamie Winders, "Chapter 8," *Nashville in the New Millenium: Immigrant Settlement, Urban Transformation, and Social Belonging* (2013), © Russell Sage Foundation, 112 East 64th Street, New York, NY 10065. Reprinted with Permission.